To Will and To Do

To Will and To Do

An Introduction to Christian Ethics

Volume 1

Jacques Ellul

Translated by Jacob Marques Rollison

James Clarke & Co

James Clarke & Co
P.O. Box 60
Cambridge
CB1 2NT
United Kingdom

www.jamesclarke.co
publishing@jamesclarke.co

Paperback ISBN: 978 0 227 17934 5
PDF ISBN: 978 0 227 17935 2

British Library Cataloguing in Publication Data
A record is available from the British Library

First published by Cascade Books, 2020

This edition published by James Clarke & Co, 2023,
by arrangement with Wipf and Stock Publishers

Copyright © Editions Labor et Fides, 2020

All rights reserved. No part of this edition may be reproduced, stored electronically or in any retrieval system, or transmitted in any form or by any means, electronic, mechanical, photocopying, recording, or otherwise, without prior written permission from the Publisher (permissions@jamesclarke.co).

Contents

Acknowledgments | vii

Translator's Introduction: Rediscovering Ellul's Theological Ethics | 1
A Note on the Translation | 13

Part I: **Origins** | 17
1. Knowledge of the Good | 19
2. The Good | 34
3. Morality Is of the Order of the Fall | 49
4. Morality Is of the Order of Necessity | 67
5. The Double Morality | 79

Part II: **Morality of the World** | 113
1. Diversity of Moralities | 118
2. Theoretical Moralities | 126
3. Values | 137
4. Lived Moralities | 151
5. The Attitude of Man toward Morality: Moralism and Immoralism | 162
6. Technical Morality | 172

Part III: **The Impossibility and Necessity of a Christian Ethic** | 183
1. The Impossibility of a Christian Ethic | 185
2. Historical Creation of Christian Moralities | 208
3. The Necessity of a Christian Ethic | 224

Bibliography | 243
Name Index | 247
Scripture Index | 251

Acknowledgments

This new translation is a testament to the generosity and support of many. Thanks are due to The Issachar Fund for supporting this project and seeing it through to its completion; to David Gill and Ted Lewis at the International Jacques Ellul Society, whose support and guidance were invaluable throughout; and to Professor Frédéric Rognon in the Faculty of Protestant Theology at the University of Strasbourg for overseeing this project, for helpful feedback, and for aid in locating resources. Thanks to Professor Anne-Marie Andreasson-Hogg, Hervé Mousset, and Professor Philip Ziegler for their careful evaluations of the translations. Thanks to Professor Mike Mawson for his initial help in conceiving this project and to Professor Brian Brock for his encouragement. Special thanks are due to Declan Kelly for his help in locating citations and for our continual conversation. Thanks are also due to Kevin O'Farrell, Amy Erickson, Michael Morelli, Andrew Errington, Dan Patterson, and Taido Chino for dialogue, proofreading, and editorial feedback. Thanks to Zack Rollison for his comments on an early version of chapter 1. Thanks to Dr. Kate Kirkpatrick for help with citations of Jean-Paul Sartre. Thanks to Elisabetta Ribet, Jean-Sebastien Ingrand, and Guillaume Joseph, along with Professor Rognon, for their continued discussion of Ellul in our Club Ellulien. Thanks to Jérôme Ellul and the Ellul family for their support and encouragement of this project. Many thanks to my wife, Mélanie, for her continual love and support, as well as to our families for unending hospitality.

This work of translation is dedicated to Professor Read Mercer Schuchardt, who sparked and fanned the flames of my interest in Ellul, in gratitude for his many years of encouragement, support, guidance, and friendship.

Translator's Introduction
Rediscovering Ellul's Theological Ethics

In his book *Orthodoxy*, G. K. Chesterton describes the special kind of pleasure found only in a *re*discovery: the thrill of adventure and novelty dovetails with the beloved familiarity of a homecoming.[1] Creating this new translation of *To Will & To Do* offered this unique pleasure, uniting the adventure of uncovering a lost and unknown manuscript with the joy of revisiting a classic text from a singular writer.

While exploring Ellul's vast and multifaceted corpus for my doctoral research, I felt I had stumbled upon a forgotten gold mine. When I described this impression to Stanley Hauerwas, he replied, "I think you're right." When juxtaposed with giants such as Barth, Bonhoeffer, Hauerwas, etc., Jacques Ellul's relatively minor place in contemporary Protestant theological dialogue might lead one to believe that the light of his theological contribution is waning, its relevance now largely behind us. On the contrary, I suggest that a full understanding of Ellul's true importance is still to come. This new translation of *To Will & To Do* hopes to mark a key moment in this rediscovery among anglophone readers, who continue to show a strong (and growing) interest in his work.

But why should a new edition of *To Will & To Do* play such a central role? Should not this rediscovery belong to a new translation of one of his more celebrated texts—such as the book that first secured his North American notoriety, *The Technological Society*? Even in the theological domain, his *Meaning of the City* and *Humiliation of the Word* have had more sustained echoes than any of his theological-ethical volumes. Could it be that these ethical volumes were forgotten for a reason?

---

1. Chesterton, *Orthodoxy*, 2–5.

In fact, Ellul's volumes of ethics have yet to make their true mark on anglophone readers. In what follows, I will set out the case for why we need to revisit Ellul's theological-ethical works; offer a short overview of Ellul's plan for these works, and the place of *To Will & To Do* within them; concisely summarize the contents of *To Will & To Do*, volume 1; briefly situate *To Will & To Do* within twentieth-century theological-ethical discussion; and propose ways in which it might be relevant for us today.

The Need for a New Hearing

If we are to hear him seriously, we must recognize that despite its many merits, the anglophone reception of his work has not allowed Ellul's voice to come through loud and clear. Reading Ellul can be a challenge at times, even in French or in an excellent translation. His writing—which spanned specialist domains such as politics, communication, sociology, law, history, biblical commentary, and ethics—was intended as an address to the intellectual layperson. He tried to present a huge amount of specialized material in a relatively accessible way, challenging his reader to do the intellectual work necessary to understand their present age and formulate an ethical response. However, this meant that he sometimes eschewed academic conventions, which—when combined with his often polemical directness and his penchant for criticizing his friends and saying nothing to those he disagreed with—led him to be taken less seriously in the academy. And yet, his communicative style risks leading the lay reader to think they have understood him when in fact they have not. This means that the anglophone reader should be doubly on guard: this balance between accessibility and rigor can be tricky to negotiate.

Something is always lost in any translation, but the varying quality of existing English translations of Ellul's works means that even a careful reader of these translations would come out with the wrong impression. I am not referring to simple typographical errors, misspellings, or even misunderstandings, which are inevitable in any work of this kind (and will undoubtedly plague even the present translations). Beyond these errata, Ellul's English translations have been plagued by historical mistakes, strange editorial choices, and huge gaps. Some translators misread Ellul's references, failing to acknowledge the discussions in which Ellul took part. Some translators removed quotation marks where they should not have, leaving discerning readers to think that Ellul simply plagiarized Karl Barth or Karl Marx. Due to Ellul's popularity in North America, some of Ellul's books were published in English before he finished writing them in French, which means that the French editions are more polished, complete, and sometimes greatly expanded compared to the English translations. These problems have been flagrant in translations of Ellul's theological ethics, and most particularly *The Ethics of Freedom*: compared to the three-volume French edition, it lacks more than a full volume of Ellul's argument, leaving out important passages that show Ellul's detailed engagement with the intellectual currents of his time. Anglophone readers are left with a piecemeal account that cannot communicate the true nuance of Ellul's structured thought.

It is no wonder, then, that Ellul's largest and most careful works are overlooked and forgotten in anglophone discussions. Focusing on his studies of technology or politics veils the fact that on the sociological side, Ellul was a *legal historian* at heart. His largest sociological work is his as yet untranslated five-volume *Histoire des institutions* (History of Institutions). What drives his sociology is less a concern for technology (which is nevertheless important) than an interest in understanding social unity, the bond between the individual and the group. It is because of this interest that Ellul's *Technological Society* sees *technique* as a threat to societal development—not the other way around. Things are similar in his theology: focusing on his more accessible and provocative works veils the fact that theologically, Ellul was not a biblical scholar or a systematician but a *theological ethicist* at heart. His theological ethics comprise his most significant (and weighty) contributions; unless these are accounted for, we give Ellul only a partial hearing, ignoring some of his most serious work.

(Re)discovering Ellul's Theological-Ethical Project

These two parts of Ellul's corpus—the sociological and the theological—were meant to be taken together, confronting one another. Ellul's theology confronts the reality observed by his sociology with a truth of a different order. His sociology confronts his theology, ensuring that it does not cloister itself away in a hermetic discourse or try to ignore the problems of the world. If the church is willing to perform a serious self-critique, Ellul's sociology gives her an impressive set of diagnostic tools to do so. "Do not be conformed to this world, but be transformed by the renewing of your minds, so that you may discern what is the will of God—what is good and acceptable and perfect" (Rom 12:2 NRSV). For Ellul, sociology was an attempt to describe this "conforming" world. If sociology can describe the church in precisely the same way as any other sociological group, perhaps she ought to question if she is guided by the Holy Spirit or by some sociological force or pressure.[2] His ethics, then, attempts to offer the church ways to orient herself, to incarnate the presence of Jesus Christ in the modern world.

Ellul planned his theological ethics in four parts. After a substantial introduction (part one), parts two, three, and four would be an ethical outworking of Saint Paul's trio of faith, hope, and love. For faith, Ellul envisaged an ethics of holiness; for hope, an ethics of freedom; and for love, an ethics of relationship. This massive project was never completed. Ellul began with *To Will & To Do*, which constitutes his introduction (though, as we shall see below, it was never fully available until now). Convinced of its contemporary urgency, he then wrote *The Ethics of Freedom*, which includes three volumes in French (of which only two are partially rendered in the English translation). A full manuscript of *The Ethics of Holiness* exists; we are hopeful that it will be published in French in coming years, after which it may be translated into English. Ellul never managed to write *The Ethics of Relationship*. *To Will & To Do* thus introduces Ellul's ethics, laying the groundwork for all that follows. It was originally published in French in 1964 and translated into English in 1969, followed by a second French edition in 2013.

However, this is not the whole story. More than a decade after the 1964 publication of *To Will & To Do*, in his preface to *The Ethics of Freedom* (1976), Ellul remarked that though the full Introduction had not yet been published, he felt the need to move onto the next major portion of his ethics. This sign that there might be a further, still unpublished portion of *To Will & To Do* was happily confirmed when a lost manuscript of this second volume was recently rediscovered.[3] Published in French for the first time in 2018, volume 2 of *To Will & To Do* picks up where volume 1 left off, filling a major gap in our grasp of Ellul's ethical project. The present translation of (what we now know to be) volume 1—following its initial English translation by fifty years—complements a first English edition of volume 2. Anglophone readers are thus offered a quality presentation of Ellul's introduction to Christian ethics, putting part one of his ethical project on a timely par with the French editions.

To Will & To Do: Laying the Foundations

To Will & To Do is divided into five parts, with the first three parts comprising volume 1 and the last two parts comprising volume 2. The three parts in volume 1 include critiques of ethics as a discipline and of what the good is *not*, descriptions of different goods adopted by societies, and a discussion

---

2. This is especially visible in Ellul, *False Presence in the Modern World*.
3. See my introduction to volume 2 for more detail.

of the *impossibility* and *necessity* of a distinctively Christian ethic. The two parts in volume 2 approach the conditions, characteristics, and content of a Christian ethic. Ellul is clear at the outset that his ethics deals with biblical revelation; it is *Christian* ethics. However, he is also hopeful that non-Christians will not dismiss it on these grounds; the whole value of his work comes from confrontation in dialogue.

Part one discusses the origins of the ethical question of good and evil. In these chapters, Ellul clearly lays out his basic positions, which go hand in hand with his interpretation of the biblical narrative recounting the temptation of Adam and Eve in Genesis. For Ellul, human knowledge of good and evil already displays a broken communion with God. Ellul says his position is explicitly "nominalist": a thing is good *because* God says it is, and not the other way around. Anything humans call good is necessarily set up in opposition to what God calls good. All human morality, therefore, is made in separation from God, in the "order of the fall" and the "order of necessity." Ellul uses "necessity" to imply that human morality is a kind of social constraint on freedom. He notes that morality is crucial to the individual-society link. Because morality is something inevitably produced in social groups, an individual's decision to disobey morality may not harm them, but questions the group and their place in it. Part one concludes with a chapter on "the double morality." For Christians, morality is "double" because on the one hand, they cannot be conformed to the same morality as the rest of society. And yet, this other morality is nevertheless important and ought to be accounted for and respected when possible. The morality of our society is thus one part of the double; the ethic that results from the community gathered around scriptural revelation marks the other part.

Part two offers a brief sociological examination of the various "moralities of the world." Ellul notes, first, that there is indeed a diversity of moralities. As it is lived out in different societies throughout world history, morality is not absolute but relative and changing. Since morality is a human phenomenon, "We must approach it from the relative point of view of human understanding, not the absolute point of view of metaphysics" (122). If one refuses this approach and adopts a metaphysical standpoint, one treats morality only theoretically, as many thinkers have done. Without claiming to address all such theories, and in dialogue with sociologists of his era, Ellul treats the ensemble of theoretical moralities as a phenomenon. He notes that theoretical morality springs primarily from Mediterranean, "Judeo-Greek" civilization (126). Offering strong critiques of existentialism and of the philosophy of values popular at the time, Ellul notes that these moralities offer idealized images of their own society; they remain theoretical and are never actually applied. In practice, morality is neither absolute nor unimportant: it is inevitably produced by human groups, linked to their individual and social life. However, the behavior of individuals never fully aligns with their group's morality. Either individuals assume their group's morality, in which case it becomes a destructive moral*ism*, or they reject it, in which case it is an equally isolating *im*moralism. Part two finishes with a chapter on "technical morality," a morality adapted to the world of techniques. Ellul sees this morality progressively replacing the old bourgeois morality derived from Christendom, which still characterizes much of Western society.

Part three describes the *impossibility* and the *necessity* of a Christian ethic. For all the reasons laid out in part one and more, a Christian morality is impossible. Like any other morality, it is set up in the order of the fall, of necessity, and in opposition to God. The New Testament does not give us a complete ethical system; it discusses human action with a different vocabulary. Christian ethics is a function of God's free gift of grace, which cannot be made into a law. Christian ethics cannot be a casuistic system—that is, a description of possible situations and the right or wrong action to perform in each case. Christian ethics implies following the Holy Spirit, whose action cannot be reduced to a law. The freedom of God and the freedom of the Christian liberated in Christ and living in God's presence problematize any theoretical ethical construction. Ellul continues with a schematic of the formulation of Christian moralities in the history of the Western church. From the very beginning, the church posed ethical questions to Paul, to elders and bishops, to which they cautiously responded. But in later centuries, less caution, Greek philosophical influence, and the rise of Christendom led to a transformation: ethics became more collective and objective, less personal and relative. Ellul finishes his historical schematic with a provocative charge: "While the Reformers reaffirmed the authentic content of the Revelation, despite appearances, they did not elaborate an Ethic corresponding to their Theology" (223). Nevertheless, Christian ethics is *necessary*, because as a human group, the church will spontaneously produce a morality, whether consciously or not. It is thus better that it be conscious and willed, purposely articulated as something relative. Otherwise, Christian ethics might collapse into a naïve use of Scripture to create an absolute moral law—and thus remain too transcendent and unrelated to this world; or contemporary problems may be seen as having no relation to biblical revelation, since times have changed. For Ellul, the difficult task of Christian ethics is to maintain the importance of human life and works while acknowledging their relativity. This relativity ought to be appropriate to their situation in time: neither untainted works of a past creation nor works in the fullness of the eschatological kingdom of God, the Christian's works are works of the in-between, the already-but-not-yet; we ought to treat them commensurate with their transitional and fleeting character.

A Moment in Dialogue

To Will & To Do is perhaps the finest example of Ellul's dialogue with major voices in twentieth-century theological ethics. Throughout both volumes, we find Ellul engaged in extended appreciative dialogue with Karl Barth, Dietrich Bonhoeffer, Paul Ricoeur, Reinhold Niebuhr, Oscar Cullmann, Gunner Hillerdal, Niels Søe, Hans Reiner, and Gerhard von Rad, as well as more interdisciplinary voices such as Émile Durkheim, Georges Gurvitch, and Henri Bergson. His dialogue with Bernard Häring, Jean-Paul Sartre, Simone de Beauvoir, and the philosophers of "value" is more critical than appreciative, but it importantly demonstrates the range and depth of his awareness and engagement in the broader conversations of his time. Briefly reviewing a few elements of these dialogues can help us see how Ellul positions himself therein.

Barth and Bonhoeffer are unquestionably Ellul's two most prominent interlocutors in *To Will & To Do*. Almost without exception, Ellul's citations and interactions with both (primarily from Barth's *Church Dogmatics* II.2 and Bonhoeffer's *Ethics*) display agreement with and support for their positions. I will address Barth below; concerning Bonhoeffer, *To Will & To Do* marks Ellul as a very early and careful reader of the German theologian's *Ethik*.[4] This latter work was not translated into French until 1965, a year after *To Will & To Do*'s initial publication. Even upon its translation, it received little attention, for "[*Ethics*] was no sooner eclipsed . . . by [Bonhoeffer's] *Letters and Papers from Prison*."[5] Ellul's attention to *Ethics* thus distinguishes his reading of Bonhoeffer from the lesser importance accorded to this volume among the majority of his contemporaries. In their introduction to the 2013 French edition, Müller and Rognon note that Ellul particularly drew out Bonhoeffer's "dialectic of the ultimate and the penultimate."[6] Only later (in his treatise on secularity, *The New Demons*) does Ellul concentrate on his sole serious criticism of Bonhoeffer, concerning the latter's statements on "man come of age"—which, first, come not from Bonhoeffer's *Ethics* but from *Letters and Papers from Prison*, and second, were the subject of varying interpretations in the French discussion.[7]

---

4. Müller and Rognon, "Introduction," 9; see also 11.
5. Müller and Rognon, "Introduction," 9.
6. Müller and Rognon, "Introduction," 12.
7. See Ellul, *The New Demons*, 19–20, 45, and especially 215–18; Ellul, *Hope in Time*

Ever since his discovery of Barth through his friendship with the French Barthian Jean Bosc, the Swiss theologian remained one of Ellul's most significant lifelong dialogue partners (alongside Søren Kierkegaard and Karl Marx). In the 1930s, Ellul found that Barth's thought "unblocked" an impasse in the French Reformed church, split between "conservative" Calvinists and a "liberal" approach that applied science to interpretation.[8] Barth caused Ellul to rethink his earlier Calvinist stance on human freedom and the question of salvation, eventually pushing him toward his distinct theological emphases on freedom and universal salvation, yet still opposed to a thoroughgoing theological liberalism. Still, Ellul wrote,

> . . . [I] had the impression that the ethical consequences of Barth's theology had never been elicited. I was not satisfied with his volumes of ethics and politics, which seemed to be based on an insufficient knowledge of the world and politics. However, there was everything there necessary to formulate an ethic without losing any of the rediscovered truth, being totally faithful to the Scriptures, but without legalism or literalism. But this work seemed possible to me only if one conserved the groundwork laid by Barth . . .[9]

Much the same as his approach to Marx—in which Ellul much preferred Marx's own writings to Marxists and their application thereof—Ellul highly esteemed Barth's work but thought that his ethics were insufficiently developed, a situation that led Barthian Christians into conformism. He thus set out to construct an ethic on Barthian foundations to remedy this problem. Additionally, Ellul specifies that it was to be primarily an Old Testament ethic:

> After Luther's and Barth's commentaries on the Epistle to the Romans, it was not worth the trouble to do another one, and at that time I thought the Gospels were clear and easily understood. So I was especially attracted by the Old Testament . . . That is why I wrote biblical commentaries on the books of Kings, Jonah, and Job . . . I also searched the Old Testament for the foundations of an ethic, and this led me progressively to construct one.[10]

Alongside the Old Testament books mentioned, Ellul drew significantly on the prophets, the legal texts, and above all on the book of Ecclesiastes,

---

of Abandonment, 98n4; and indirectly, Ellul, *Prayer and Modern Man*, 85–90.

8. Ellul, "Karl Barth and Us," 22.
9. Ellul, "Karl Barth and Us," 24.
10. Ellul, *In Season, Out of Season*, 175.

which informed his thought more than any other biblical book.[11] As his theology changed throughout his life, Ellul took more critical distance from Barth, moving more resolutely toward his Kierkegaardian roots. *To Will & To Do* thus sees Ellul simultaneously in as close a dialogue with Barth's writings as he will ever be, and, as a function of this same careful dialogue, critically appropriating Barth's theology for his own Old Testament–based ethical project.

With this combination of dominant emphases—Kierkegaard (whom Ellul read as an ironic anti-philosopher par excellence) and Ecclesiastes (which Ellul read as a Hebrew crusade to ironically undermine Greek philosophical thinking)—it should come as no surprise that Ellul remains hostile toward any explicit philosophical influence in his theology. This is at the heart of his criticisms of Paul Ricoeur's Protestant philosophy. While Ellul is appreciative of Ricoeur's work, he primarily criticizes the philosopher on two accounts. First, Ellul sees sin as more of a negative, radical break than Ricoeur. This means that Ellul is closed off to any mediating notion of human goodness that would enter into competition with the grace shown in Jesus Christ. Second, Ellul is critical of Ricoeur's concept of love-at-a-distance, described as "long relations" (as opposed to the physical proximity implied in "short relations"); for Ellul, physical proximity is a crucial part of what makes a neighbor a neighbor. Likewise, Ellul's critiques of Reinhold Niebuhr cut along the same lines. For Ellul, Niebuhr extracts "love" from its christological context, making it into a principle of ethical reasoning. Ellul sees this as problematic, allowing Christians to fill the abstract concept of love with whatever content they please.

While the reader will have to continue with volume 2 to see more fully how Ellul orients himself with respect to Luther and Calvin (whose presence in this volume is restricted mostly to critical dialogue in lengthy footnotes), we can still safely say that *To Will & To Do* is a robustly Protestant ethical treatise. Renewing classical Reformation emphases such as justification by faith alone, in Christ alone, and in a spirit of fidelity to Scripture alone, Ellul aims to place the reader in the presence of God, allowing them no other justification or mediation than that provided in God's gracious gift of himself in Jesus Christ.

---

11. For the prophets, see especially Ellul, *On Being Rich and Poor: Christianity in a Time of Economic Globalization*; for the legal texts, see *To Will & To Do*, volume 2; for Ecclesiastes, see Ellul, *Reason for Being*, 1.

To Will & To Do, Today

If Ellul's full relevance has yet to be fully uncovered, what suggestions might we make about what his ethics has to say to us today? To conclude, I will name a few contributions that I think the text might make to contemporary issues and debates.

First, I suggest that his description of the morality of the West as in mid-transition from a bourgeois morality with elements derived from Christianity to a new technical morality still aptly characterizes much of contemporary morality in North America and Europe. The trajectories identified in Ellul's technological studies have only intensified since the advent of the Internet and the smartphone. I have suggested that as a historian of law, Ellul is interested in law as the link between society and the individual; he sees technique as altering this link. In this context, what is the world of *social media* if not explicitly an alternative way of linking the individual to the society around them? If Ellul views morality as a uniting force for social groups, what are the ramifications of this alternative mediation for social morality? Ellul's work robustly suggests that a society whose everyday life is affected as much by its Internet and app use as by its laws has been significantly transformed; it is indeed less of a traditional society and more of a technological society, or perhaps—reflecting the shift in language between two of Ellul's books on technique—a technological *system*.

Second, I suggest that Ellul was sensitive to the use of words in a way that we often are not. In his contribution to *The Ellul Forum* upon Ellul's death, Hauerwas noted his reaction upon reading Ellul's *Presence in the Modern World*: "I am sure I did not understand it then and I am not sure I 'get it' now, but I understood enough to see here Christian language was working."[12] If we expand our scope to include his works on propaganda and language, it becomes clear that Ellul took words very seriously and thought that their denigration or misuse was destructive of our individual and collective life.[13] His work suggests that careful attention to our use of words (whether in sociology or theology) is crucial to our communal well-being. For example, in *To Will & To Do*, Ellul insists that the practice of deriving "values" or "Christian principles" from the biblical text is ethically dangerous, for we ultimately attribute whatever content we please to these concepts. What might be the difference between "love" as used by the writers of the New Testament and "love" used as a principle of Christian thought? As the language of "Christian principles," values, and virtues continues to

---

12. Hauerwas, "Jacques Ellul, Courage and the Christian Imagination," 4.

13. See especially Ellul, *Propaganda*; *A Critique of the New Commonplaces*; and *The Humiliation of the Word*.

be widely used in Christian ethics today, Ellul calls the church to interrogate whether (and how) these ways of conceiving of Christian ethics might be helpful or harmful. Or again, some denominations might ask themselves what changes when traditional words for roles in the church, such as "elder," are replaced with titles such as "leader." If Ellul is right, the nuance matters greatly.

Finally, I suggest that because of his awareness of the communal stakes of morality, Ellul has something to say to our increasingly polarized political climate. Ellul lived and suffered through the harrowing Second World War. Like many other postwar continental thinkers, Ellul yearned for true community and was understandably sensitive to the risks involved with any idea, politics, or image that claimed to offer this community. Hitler, Mussolini, and Stalin certainly had their own visions of a certain kind of group unity. Constantly refusing belief in any sort of historical-moral "progress," Ellul calls us to recognize our vulnerabilities: we may resemble the German, Italian, and Russian citizens of that time more than we would like to think. The chilling final lines of part II, chapter 3 of this volume highlight the price of our desire for any completely unified social entity: "Let us never forget that a communion which creates itself demands the excommunication of outsiders; and that in the fallen world whose Prince we know, this affirmation of being is always paid for by the sacrifice of this being itself, or the annihilation of the other." Ellul calls us to ask ourselves, If we *do* establish a community on this or that ground, who is left out? This should not be read as a call to reject our belonging to a nation, tribe, or people group but as an attempt to give these group identities a properly relative status. Ellul's proposed "double morality" attempts to strike the balance of "in the world, but not of it"[14] for the Christian community, to become conscious of the church as a different kind of social unity, linked not by its morality but by the sacrificial death of its Lord, whose body it constitutes—yet without hostility to groups that are linked by their morality. At a time when the remnants of Western Christendom are in decline and institutional churches see their ranks decreasing, Ellul reminds readers that at its heart, the church is not a sociological institution; right now, forgoing or limiting its institutional character might be the most loving way to rediscover its neighbors. Ellul offers a way for churches faithfully to commit to be the people of God, to hear and be transformed by the word of God in Jesus Christ, rather than to be primarily defined by a law or morality. This approach recasts ideas of community, inclusion, and exclusion, reminding the church where her true unity lies.

14. See John 17:14–18.

Among many of his readers—whether they profess the Christian faith or not—Ellul's voice is often recognized as ahead of his time, or even as prophetic. If this is indeed the case, we ought to perk up our ears and listen; we may hear him today more clearly than ever before. And as was always his intention, I can only hope that by confronting him in this translation of his text, we will be provoked and inspired—not to agreement, but to a lived response, and to a renewed freedom in continual dialogue.

Jacob Marques Rollison
Strasbourg, France
August 2019

A Note on the Translation

This translation was produced under the supervision of Frédéric Rognon, Professor of Philosophy of Religions in the Faculty of Protestant Theology at the University of Strasbourg. In the hopes of ensuring an accurate and quality edition, the translation went through several checks: it was examined by Professor Rognon, two professional translators, and a professor of theology at an anglophone institution.

The translation is based on the 2013 French edition published by Labor et Fides, which reproduced the 1964 edition with several small corrections and additions. In the 2013 edition, Ellul's idiosyncratic capitalization was left untouched; punctuation was occasionally modified; several passages or citations were altered (these are indicated in footnotes); Ellul's citations of Karl Barth were verified, and ellipses were added to indicate Ellul's omission of passages. Bibliographical footnotes were verified, corrected, and expanded where necessary, and the bibliography at the end of the book was newly added. The 2013 edition cross-referenced Ellul's citations of the German edition of Bonhoeffer's *Ethics* with the French edition and the most recent German edition.

I have retained the idiosyncratic capitalization in my translation. I have reproduced nearly all the footnotes in the 2013 edition, including Rognon and Müller's editorial footnotes. In editorial footnotes, I have eliminated references to French texts and replaced them with English texts where possible. Concerning Ellul's references, I have provided citations from English editions where possible, especially for citations of Barth, Bonhoeffer, Ricoeur, and Bergson. The 1969 edition adhered to the original French subtitle, translating it as *An Ethical Research for Christians*; the 2013 edition changed the subtitle to *Une critique théologique de la morale* (*A Theological Critique of Morality*). I have used the subtitle *An Introduction to Christian Ethics* to include the content of both the original subtitle and its designation as introduction, and to denote this translation as different from the first English edition.

I have attempted to preserve Ellul's communicative style as much as possible. I made frequent comparative use of Hopkin's 1969 translation. Hopkin seems to have been a fine reader of Ellul's French; I cannot say I have improved his style, but I do believe my translation pays closer attention to Ellul's specific vocabulary and sources. Naturally, I have been able to correct some errors in his translation (as the careful reader will hopefully correct my own). With some exceptions, I have tried to retain Ellul's paragraph breaks and style, which sometimes results in long sentences; I have nevertheless tried to make these as clear as possible. I am very grateful to those who have edited and reviewed my work for the many improvements they have made.

J. M. R.

To Yvette

PART I

Origins

> For it is God who works in you both to will and to do for His good pleasure.
>
> —Phil 2:13 (NKJV)

Lay the cards on the table. When writing about morality, one must adopt an attitude of intellectual and personal humility from the outset. Any fakery would disqualify the work; for there can be no question of a merely intellectual construction when the search for the meaning[1] of life is itself the search for how to live. Pretending to pursue a moral inquiry without presuppositions would be useless. Such an inquiry does not exist; we will have to demonstrate this. It is better to have clear presuppositions that one openly admits than to pretend to have none, which would only be ignorance or deceit. "Here, I wish I could wear a mask," said Stendhal.[2] And undoubtedly, anyone who writes about the conduct of life—that is, of that which constitutes the most secret fabric of their life, in its truth and its reality—will also say this. But this must remain only a wish; they may not wear a mask. They must give their account with an uncovered face. I confess,

---

1. Translator's note (henceforth TN): Fr. *sens*, implying both signification and orientation. Cf. Ellul, *L'Homme et L'argent*, in *Le défi et le nouveau*, 258.

2. TN: pen name of the nineteenth-century French writer Marie-Henri Beyle (1783–1842).

therefore, that in this study and this search, the criterion of my thought is biblical revelation; the content of my thought is biblical revelation; my point of departure is provided by biblical revelation; the method is the dialectic according to which biblical revelation is addressed to us; and the goal is the search for the significance of biblical revelation as it bears on Ethics. This rigor in no way implies that this book is addressed to Christians; on the contrary, I believe that its true value would come from a confrontation. Nor does it concern preoccupations exclusive to Christians—everybody in our decadent Western civilization is questioning the norms of their life—or at any rate, no more than biblical revelation is limited to the narrow circle of the elect: it speaks firstly of others. We will have to speak of the life and morality of the men and women of the world. Having thus affirmed my starting biases, having stated my position sharply enough that there can be no misunderstanding, I must say that I have no competence to write this book. I am neither a theologian nor a philosopher by profession. I possess none of the qualifications of the specialist, since in our time philosophy has become a technique and one is disqualified for not having climbed the steps of this edifice in an academic career. I am only trying to be human. I am trying to live fully in this time. I experience the anguish of the men and women who surround me. I know our common laxity in a society without structures and without norms. My occupation is to reflect, and I have undertaken to do so as a man, nothing more. It will happen that I will encounter numerous problems studied hundreds of times by specialists. I approach them with the innocence and the fresh eyes of the incompetent. I will refrain from giving a definition of Ethics. The reader may adopt any of the several thousand definitions that exist; all of them are partially correct, but only partially. The specialists will shrug their shoulders. Perhaps a man will hear . . .

I

Knowledge of the Good

The serpent said to Eve, "You will be like gods, knowing good and evil." Such is the point of the departure. Before this decision of man, Adam never posed the problem of good and evil. He did not know them. He did not know that there was a good and an evil. He found himself in communion with the will of God, which he recognized directly in his relation of love with the Creator. His heart beat to the rhythm of the heart of God and his face was constantly turned toward the face of the Father, which he reflected for the world and for creation. He was free before God—which is to say that he could love him, as well as cease to love him. He was free before God—but this freedom in no way referred to some choice between doing and not-doing, between a yes and a no, the fruit of a laborious deliberation; by conceiving freedom in this manner, we demonstrate that we obviously no longer know anything about it; we disfigure and mutilate it, we mummify it. Precisely because it is freedom, freedom cannot be defined by the indeterminacy of choice in this way. It is neither the fruit of correct reasoning, nor of an autonomous will. Likewise, there is no test of freedom, since for Adam the free man, his freedom (of which he was ignorant) was a continual test unto itself, and its own proof—the offering of a joyous life in response to the gift of life that had been given beforehand. And here, by the intermediary of Satan, the awareness of an absence is produced, of a lacuna, of the missing link[1] of this suddenly perceived chain that attached Adam to God, that—when unknown, was only play—once known, becomes a question. The awareness of a forbidden domain, which was joyful and obvious, now becomes a tragic

---

1. TN: *missing link* in English in the original.

absence. Before this moment, there was no moral conscience, no ethic. What is proposed therefore is not the grasping of good and evil, as if good and evil were objects, things within reach of Eve's hand. They do not grasp good and evil. They only receive knowledge, comparable to that of Elohim. They will know that there is a good and an evil, that there is disobedience and obedience, that there is love and hate. They will know, too, that there is a yes and a no that they can say, and that can be said about them. But does this knowledge concern the content of good and of evil? The entirety of biblical revelation attests to the impossibility of such an interpretation. In the Bible, the Good does not precede God, the good is not God; the Good is the will of God. All that God wills is good, not because God is subordinate to the good, obedient to this good, but simply because He wills it.[2] It is not the Good in itself that determines the will of God; it is the will of God that determines what is the Good. And there is no good outside of this decision. We will develop this in chapter 2.[3]

Let us not say that this is simple divine "voluntarism." But affirming that the good is nothing other than what God decides (i.e., his commandment) means for man that the good is not *his* decision, nor a simple possibility. For this good has its own independent reality. The good is given, laid down by God ("*he has told you*, O mortal, what is Good" [Mic 6:8]),[4]

---

2. We thus clearly adopt what might be called a nominalist position. The commandment is not based on the divine essence but on the sovereign will of God. The commandment taken in itself has no meaning: it only takes on a meaning because God says it and gives it. But we must take care to avoid the errors that traditional theological nominalism eventually fell into—for example, that ultimately the only virtue required is that of pure obedience (how could this be if the Word of God awakens us to freedom?); that it is a question of a simple moral perfectionism (which is impossible, if precisely there is no pre-established morality) and of legalism (which goes against the idea of a commandment *hic et nunc*). These errors are not necessarily contained in Nominalism—quite the contrary! However, the main error to guard against is the absurd: "The more the commandment of God is absurd, the more certainly it expresses the pure will of God." But here, we are in the presence of a systematic deviation: it is unacceptable to say that the Good is a mere external label that God sticks onto whatever he wants. His word is creative, and when he speaks the Good exists, as Good. God is neither arbitrary nor tyrannical: he is Love, and when he expresses his will, it is a will of Love. Thus, the good given by God is good for us. These two revealed truths keep nominalism in its rightful place. All other attitudes, even as nuanced as that of Häring, lead to making the good into an independent value with an intrinsic foundation, corresponding to a natural order of "authentic" things, to positing norms of eternal wisdom that delimit the will of God. Now, it seems to us that Scripture gives us a different vision of the Majesty and freedom of God (Häring, *The Law of Christ*).

3. Bonhoeffer, *Ethics*, 47 [TN: see especially note 3 on the cited page].

4. TN: Ellul's italics. The NRSV emphasizes that this good is *told*, as in Ellul's *dit*, contrary to many English translations that use the word *shown*.

and man is forbidden from discovering it by himself. Man cannot act well except when he listens to the Word of God. For "what is said to man is the Word and work of divine election which has taken place and been revealed in Jesus Christ . . . What right conduct is for man is determined absolutely in the right conduct of God. It is determined in Jesus Christ . . . 'to realize the good' never means anything other than to become obedient to the revelation of the grace of God."[5] In all this there is neither a metaphysic nor an indication of the transcendence of the good, but the affirmation of the gospel, of the very movement of the Word of God. *Only* this Word allows us to say that "no one is good but God alone" (Mark 10:18), for "He is the God who . . . has spoken of the good *by doing it*; He has spoken of Himself by delivering Himself up for us." "What God wills of us is the same as He wills and has done for us." Thus, only the "Name of Jesus Christ" legitimates that the good is the will of God. "We must seek the command of God only where it has itself *torn off the veil of all human opinions and theories about the will of God* and manifested itself unequivocally. We must seek it only where He has revealed Himself as grace . . ."

This also allows us to understand (and this is another difference from the theory of voluntarism) that there is never an abstract, general, divine command in itself, but only very concrete divine commands. Now, precisely, Adam cannot have any knowledge of this good in the situation where he is placed; first, because this would mean that the will of God is fixed, immobilized in an objectively perceptible content, permanent, without evolution; and that for man (who lives in time) God is definitively *relegated to the past*: God *has willed*. I know this will, which is the Good. I know the Good, and now God is limited to always wanting the same thing (this good) like a broken record, playing the same part over and over. In other words, if man could know the content of the good by himself, this would mean that God is not free. The result of the disobedience of man interpreted as knowledge of the good would thus be to give man an outstanding power, and to take away God's freedom. But we must go further: if this were really the meaning of these words, it would mean that before his disobedience, Adam was unaware of the will of God; he accomplished it in the spontaneity of love, but he never penetrated its permanent content nor the secret of deliberation. And then, after the fall, Adam would be invested with this wonderful power of penetrating the mystery of the decision of God, he would know how God determines what is good. That which he never knew in love and communion, he now knows in disobedience and rupture.

5. This and the following citations in this paragraph come from Barth, *Church Dogmatics*, vol. II.2, 538–39, 565, 568, 559. Henceforth *CD* II.2. [Italics in the final citation are Ellul's.]

Now that he has turned away from God's face, he knows the mystery of God's will! And he knows it by nature, of himself, autonomously, since it is a capability that he claims for himself! We can see the absurdity of this approach.

Finally, let us recall that this will of God is qualified throughout the Bible as "holy": that is, definitively separate, intimate, autonomous, now radically separated from man who is not Holy. To say that this will is holy is thus to say that Adam cannot know it at all. Only the Holy One can be in conjunction with this will, but Adam is not this Holy One. It will take Jesus Christ to teach us who alone is conformed to the holiness of God, and that the only way—by grace, and when man has lost all his pretensions—is to be made to conform to God's will and holiness concurrently. Man cannot know this will except when he is conformed to it because it is a holy will.[6]

And numerous biblical texts tell us that this is not the situation of man after the fall. He knows absolutely nothing of this will of God. He is totally unaware of the mystery of the decision of God's love—the mystery that Paul tells us the angels themselves would have liked to contemplate. And we only discern it in Jesus Christ. How, then, would Adam have this power

---

6. Claiming to find another origin than the fall for natural moral phenomena is to go against everything that the Bible can say to us. Non-Christians are obviously free to give a completely different explanation, but it is astonishing that Christians would be so seduced by the good accomplished in the world that they try either to find a reason for it in God or to formulate conciliations between the natural and revealed good. Natural Morality (which is good anterior to God) leads to a constant confusion (for example, between the law of life and the law of love: Nichols, [*Primer for Protestants*], 107; cooperation and love: Peabody, *Jesus Christ and the Social Question*; the Ideal and Nature, etc., with the Good: Bois, *Le problème de la morale chrétienne*), or we place these moralities in a constant prolongation of one another (more recently: de Vos, "Zur Frage der natürlichen Sittlichkeit," *Zeitschrift für Evangelische Ethik* [henceforth ZEE] 6,) and Reiner tries to show that anthropology is the bridge between the two (Reiner, "Ethik und Menschenbild," ZEE 5, 1958). It seems to us that nothing in the Bible authorizes this conception of an autonomous morality observing a good *according to God*. Regarding the well-known texts of Calvin in which it is a question of natural morality and of natural law [*droit naturel*] (though they should be understood carefully), it is certain that Calvin does not want to justify a Good that man could boast about before God, nor an autonomous morality. But he was subject to the influence of his time on this point. Insofar as he still lived under Christendom and depended on the philosophical ideas of his time, particularly concerning the nature of man, he was prevented from drawing the conclusions that his theology implied for natural morality and natural law. But today, Christians who rely on the existence of a permanent human nature—from which they have elaborated the doctrine of a partial fall, of the possibility of natural knowledge of the good by man, etc., and who have imposed this interpretation on the biblical texts—must be in an awkward position, since scientific observations tend to deny the existence of this "Nature," except sociologically. We are obliged to look at the biblical text while disregarding "natural" premises, which, in the current state of affairs, no longer appear certain.

that the angels lack? Because he ate the fruit from the tree? What magical operation would have opened his eyes to see the invisible, would essentially have allowed Adam to lay hold of Revelation? But there was no magic in Eden. Because he disobeyed and departed from this will? But precisely, we know that this will is only known by the one who perfectly accomplished it: Jesus Christ alone has known it; where does this leave Adam? Nothing remains of the all-too-obvious, overly simplistic interpretation according to which Adam would have known what was good and evil, would have received—before Moses—a sort of graven Tablet of stone, inscribed with all he had to do.

This knowledge of good and evil places man in this astonishing situation where he ultimately lives in ignorance of the truth. Of course, this ignorance is not in the domain of intellectual knowledge; it concerns the truth of the mystery of God. Now, the mystery of God is not knowledge; the mystery of God concerns the entire existence of man. The knowledge taken by Adam hides this mystery of God from him, all while giving him remarkable means to act in the world. But, as Crespy says perfectly, "Ignorance is not a deficit in knowing, it is a deficit in living," and it is because it concerns the totality of human activity that this ignorance is ultimately presented as confusedly voluntary.[7]

We must link this very precise affirmation that the good is nothing other than the will of God to the commandment found throughout Scripture to not judge one another. Man cannot judge his brother because he cannot know the good; he cannot decide what is good by himself. God alone can judge, precisely because there is an identity between the will of God and the good. Every time that man pretends to judge his brother, he renews the error of Adam by again trying to be the one who speaks the good (and in this case, his brother would be the one who does not know the good). Judgment, in fact, is the division between the one who has grasped a good in itself, a good detached from the person of God, and the one who would be stripped of this good. But precisely, Scripture continually tells us: the one who is judged and rejected by others, God accepts, God loves and God saves; on the contrary, the one who purports to judge others is rejected by God.

The text of Genesis clarifies Adam's true situation for us: "You will be like gods." Once again, if there were a good outside of the will of God—to which,

---

7. Crespy, "Une morale pour les Chrétiens II," 830.

we would have to admit, the will of God must submit—we could imagine that Adam, knowing[8] this good, would indeed find himself in the situation of God, who also knows and does the good. But this would mean that God is not God, that he is not sovereign since he is determined by a value superior to himself. If God is God, it is he who determines the good. If Adam in his fallen state were limited to *knowing* a good determined by God, if God remains the master of the Good, of which Adam is only the scrutineer (which we have already recognized to be impossible), then the other part of Satan's promise would not be accomplished. Yet the two remain. This discernment of good and evil is precisely the qualification given to God. And the entirety

---

8. It seems impossible for us to accept the interpretation of Humbert, who takes the "knowing" as the object of the problem rather than the good, thus excluding a strictly moral meaning. In the traditional sense of Morality, yes; but the problem of the good is precisely not a moral problem from the biblical point of view. We must recall that the good relates to life, and evil relates to death. We can thus say that this knowledge bears on that which gives life and that which brings death, but recalling that it is God who gives life! Consequently this "good and evil" is still the most important element, more than the understanding itself, for it ultimately concerns an understanding that bears on everything! How could we maintain that it is a question of discernment, of knowledge, of all that makes one experienced, capable, wise, when nothing permits us (if we do not carve up the biblical text) to say that before disobeying, Adam had no knowledge? (Quite the contrary!) How could we maintain that the problem is not that of the Good, when all throughout Scripture the question concerns this Good that God speaks? The interpretation of Humbert does not stand up to examination, except in *opposing* the biblical accounts referring to Yahweh to those referring to Elohim. And certainly one of Ricoeur's weaknesses is to have adopted this interpretation because it corresponds to his reconstruction. But we must at least ask ourselves the two following questions: 1. How is it that these two accounts came to be put alongside one another? How is it that these rabbis, who were not idiots, did not seek to harmonize them? How can it be that they were delivered to us as such as the Word of God through Israel and Jesus? 2. What if, by chance, their confrontation, their relation, contains *one* teaching, *one* truth that is illuminated by both accounts? Subsequently, instead of dissociating and opposing them (as Humbert does), they should be heard in their diversity as teaching complementary aspects of a single revelation.

We note here that this is the danger of the Notion of Myth: from the moment that this text is qualified as Myth, we believe ourselves capable of manipulating it—retaining whatever we please, rejecting what does not seem to be the meaning of the myth, etc. And Ricoeur performs this operation when he selects the elements from this account that diminish the importance of Adam's act, those that could show that this myth is only a construction from the prophetic accusation directed against man, and those that eliminate the relation between the works of human civilization and sin. In particular, when he labels the destruction of Babel, the condemnation of Cain, and the expulsion of Adam from Eden, as "recessive forms of the 'jealousy' of the tragic god," and explains this latter by a "clerical resentment against the heroic greatness of the man of action," we are sorry to see such an unjustified discrimination, and the ease with which any elements that would put in question the entire rest of the construction are set aside in a footnote. (Ricoeur, *Symbolism of Evil*, part II, chapter 3.) [TN: Ellul is citing note 3 in Ricoeur, *Symbolism of Evil*, 240.]

of Satan's promise is fulfilled: God himself attests, "the man has become like one of us . . ." What does this mean? Exactly that, like God, Adam now has the power to *determine* what is good and evil.[9] Until this point, we have reasoned as if the knowledge in question were of an intellectual order, as the Westerner understands it. To know means to understand by the intelligence what is good, what is evil. And in this way, we could suppose that there is a good in itself. But in Hebrew, "to know" does not have this meaning; it has a living and active meaning. Knowledge is a participation of the whole being, a commitment, an intervention. It supposes a sort of creation in the very act of knowing. And the origin of knowledge is a decision. When Genesis tells us of this knowledge, it thus means that from now on, Adam possesses the decision of good and evil; in some way, he creates good and evil in acting. It is in this that his knowledge consists, which simultaneously makes him similar to God. Henceforth his will fixes the content of the good, just like the will of God does. But it is not the same content. It is not the same good. What Adam will call good from now on is not what *God* calls good. In this the promise of the Serpent is accomplished—yet not accomplished in truth, but only in lie; the Serpent is the father of Lies. It is indeed correct to say that from now on Adam will know that the good exists, and he will seek to define it by his own will. But the lie resides in the fact that there is no more communion with God, and consequently, this good is not God's good. And when God decides to prevent Adam from laying his hand on the tree of life, it is an act of grace—for if this situation were eternal for Adam, there would be no solution; he would be in the same situation as the demons. He is like god, but separated from God; he is far from God's face, he has no more communion with his will. He is alone—and alone, too, in affirming what is good and evil. Indeed, the biblical text illuminates the meaning of this knowledge for us when it describes what happens next: as a result of this knowledge, what do Adam and Eve now know? What flows from this experiment, what elevation proceeds from this fruit that is good to eat, pleasing to the eye, useful for awakening understanding? First of all, they learned that they were naked . . . They knew shame[10] before one another,

9. For Adam, this is a matter of defining himself as an autonomous person, in the etymological sense: having, in himself and by himself, his own law. This would mean that his conduct is no longer a matter of relating to God. He would know the good in himself, without God telling him. While the whole ethical vision of the Revelation is founded on relationship (love), an ethics founded on man out of his knowledge (that is, his intrinsic definition) of the good will be necessarily an ethic of non-relation, of isolation. And Genesis shows us this straightaway: man's establishment of distance with God, the rupture between the man and his wife. But to see things in this way is to refuse traditional moral categories!

10. Bonhoeffer—on the meaning of shame, *Ethics*, beginning on 304.

which is to say that true love ceased between them at the same time as their love toward God ceased—shame . . . of a distinctly moral character, at once positive and negative. It is positive, as a rebuke of what is no longer permitted; negative, as a reminder of original and lost innocence. Certainly, shame is a preservation that is not useless in the world of lust and disorder. But just as much a despicable sign of the evil that has entered into the heart of man.

Then, hearing the footsteps of God, they hid themselves far from the face of the Eternal One. "I was afraid." Here is the second thing they know: the fear that springs from remorse. And here too we are plunged into morality and remorse: now we know disobedience. What was the law of love has become a law of constraint. This remorse, too, is positive and negative: a legitimate warning, a debate with oneself in a rebellious nature—but at the same time a gnawing cancer that attacks the heart of man, sapping it, eating and destroying it, rendering it incapable of ever receiving sufficient forgiveness. And Fear! This moral knowledge is a spontaneously acquired science of punishment. From where did Adam get this fear—he who formerly knew only domination over creation and mutual trust with his Creator? Now he has learned that God is a terrible and vengeful God. And the question that God poses to him derisively manifests the lofty science produced by the fruit of knowledge: "Who told you that you were naked? Have you eaten of the fruit?" Such, then, was the Knowledge gained—to know oneself naked, to know one's shame, but also one's solitude (for it is true that the man who is no longer in communion with his creator is completely alone), and even more one's weakness and destitution. The royal robe that covered him, the robe of the love of God, is torn—oh, how naked you are, Adam!

And why is this weakness so tragic? Precisely because from now on, Adam will have to decide on his own what is Good and what is Evil.[11] And

---

11. It is obvious that we absolutely cannot accept the interpretation that we find in Ricoeur (253–54) that, by the fact of disobedience, "man has effectively realized his likeness to God, which remained dormant, as it were, in his innocence . . . Sin represents a certain advance in self-consciousness . . ." "This likeness to gods by means of transgression is something very profound: when the limit ceases to be creative . . . man seeks his freedom in the unlimitedness of the Principle of existence . . . the era opened up to freedom by fault is a certain experience of infinity . . ." This interpretation, which ultimately sees the rupture with God as a progress for man, who realizes his similarity with God, contradicts the entirety of Revelation. Man wants to be God and in this finds himself *annihilated*, man wants to be free from God and by this fact is submitted to death and evil: there is no advancement, no development of the human. And it does not suffice to nuance this position, as Ricoeur does, by saying that it concerns a "bad infinity," because what is dubious here is pretending that there is an accession to something more than what was before in communion with God. Neither is it sufficient to purport to include this adventure in the "how much more . . ." of grace, and to consider sin on the basis that "there where sin abounded, grace abounded even more," because

here, at this moment, his weakness takes on a terrifying dimension! God's sovereign power of discernment is now in his hands. But alas, his hands are not God's hands. Now, in this creation that goes completely adrift along with him, it is he who will say what is Just and Unjust, but he is not the Just One. At the start, the essential element of all the knowledge promised to him thus boils down to the discovery of his nudity. And when his eyes are opened, what does he see? Not the unattainable absolute of a complete Good that he would possess but the staggering ridicule of his nudity. And the discovery of morality concludes this Genesis account in accusation: the man accuses the woman, and she the serpent; the law of love is truly broken. But moral law emerges, one aspect of which is this blame shifting, this capacity to discern who is guilty and to what degree, this façade that we put up before the accusation: I am just, Lord, it is not me, it is the other. This is the last result spoken of by this first text of this discovery by man, in the fall, of Good and Evil.[12]

From this moment onward, we are engaged in a very strange adventure! For the very act by which man wants to decide on what is good, to know the good by himself—this act is sin. Sin, therefore, is not disobeying a morality; it is precisely the will to determine this morality independently of God, a will that is simultaneously lust, a will to power. Thus, the most virtuous man who, at the end of a long and intense asceticism, cries out, "Here is the good!"—this very man reproduces for everyone and in everyone the sin of Adam.[13]

Ricoeur's explanation, in contrast with that of Karl Barth, leads to justifying not the sinner but the sin. When he writes that thanks to Adam's disobedience, thanks to the sin described by the Myth, "there begins an irreversible adventure, a crisis in the becoming of man, which will not reach its dénouement until the final process of justification," we are obliged to wonder at the idea that the man created by God was not truly man, that it is only through disobedience, forgiveness and resurrection, at the end of human history, that man will finally be man. If the second creation is superior to the first (about which we know nothing), this will be by a free act of God, and not by the accumulated work of human history. And on the other hand, we absolutely cannot know if the man created by God did not have, in his submissiveness, a knowledge of the love of God as complete as we can have in Jesus Christ. In any case, from any angle, the work of God is neither necessitated nor even conditioned by the disobedience and the condition of man. This would be precisely to follow the path of the first-century heretics who adored Adam—the sinner—since it is thanks to his disobedience that we have had the incredible fortune of being saved by Jesus Christ. One must have a truly extreme love for history and a very high estimation of human works to consider it good fortune that God had to sacrifice his Son.

12. Cf. Bonhoeffer, *Ethics,* starting on 299.

13. It is this *exact* and *true* view of the origin of human morality in its mythical aspect that best explains the indissoluble and ambiguous relationship of Morality and Religion. Even those who pretend to deny this relation always obliquely refer to it when

Without trying to force the text, perhaps the last verse of Ecclesiastes targets this good and evil established by man, which God calls into judgment. In effect, if we take Neher's translation (which seems to us the most faithful), this verse says, "Every work, it is God who will bring it into Judgment, upon all that is eternalized, whether good or evil." It seems that we could say that the work is not good or evil, but that the work of man here is the Good and the Evil. And this is confirmed by Isaiah (41:23): "Do, therefore, whatever Good or Evil so that we can know if you are gods."[14] Here it is truly a question of the divine attribute of doing the good. And man claims to bring this Good and this Evil to the level of Eternity, to eternalize it. And God calls this creation of man into judgment. The judgment of God is not actually a discrimination of Good and Evil according to the criteria that man has laid down, that he has chosen. This judgment bears just as much on the Good as on the Evil, on what man calls the Good—which the judgment will confront and measure according to the Good of God expressed in his will.

Such is the situation. Man knows that a good exists. He knows that from now on a choice must be made. Finding himself in disobedience, in ruptured relation to God, he perceives the existence of this good in the form of an accusation. He aspires to this good because in attaining it, he will be delivered from the accusation. But he does not know this good, since he does not know the Counsel of God. He is ignorant of the eternal decision of God, just as he is ignorant of God's will for him *hic et nunc*. He cannot depend on any absolute to discern the good. But he has received the gift, the terrible and ridiculous gift of declaring by himself, and for himself, what is good. And so he is armed for this combat, in which he will both deliver himself from his anguish and overburden himself with futile demands. In recalling this biblical account, we can see how far we are from the interpretation of old theologians according to which after the fall, man would have kept his knowledge of good and evil intact, and the whole domain

---

morality must be applied. In this way, applying morality often leads to the development of beliefs and myths of a religious character in a system or a society that views itself as areligious (as in the USSR). An autonomous ethic always disguises a masked religion, as is shown in Søe, *Christliche Ethik,* §6. But it seems to us that according to biblical interpretation, this "religious" that inspires, creates, or is hidden in morality is in no way an expression of the will of God. It is "religious" in the human sense of the general undertaking of man to ascend to heaven, to seize God and subjugate him, or even to divinize himself; and in any case, to substitute something else for the will of God.

14. TN: Many English translations separate these two items joined in the translation given by Ellul: for example, the NRSV reads, "Tell us what is to come hereafter, that we may know that you are gods; do good, or do harm, that we may be afraid and terrified."

of the conscience and intelligence would have been maintained; only the will would be fallen. According to these theologians, man would know the true good but would no longer be capable of doing it. Of course, this explanation can be justified on the basis of philosophical premises; indeed, Thomas Aquinas constructs his system from philosophical givens. We can give all kinds of possible explanations, from different metaphysical viewpoints—but all of this has nothing biblical about it.[15] What the Bible tells us is much more radical: before the separation, Adam had no *knowledge* of the good. It is precisely to have this knowledge that he eats the fruit, which is good for opening the eyes. Adam had an existential communion with the Good, which is something entirely different. Now he will have a duplicating knowledge—knowledge in separation from this something that itself becomes an object, and that at the same time is completely foreign to him. Through disobedience, Adam thus does not *retain* something that he would have had beforehand. Moreover, we have seen that he has no knowledge of the true good, the only good, the intimate will of God. This would lead to absurdities that theologians have avoided by veiling the reality of the problem. The error surely derives from having treated the good like any other object, just one thing to know among others. And since man was capable of knowing the stars and of knowing himself, since this science was exact, and led to an appropriate action, it became certain that man had kept his capacity for knowing intact. And among all the various objects to which he applies his reason, why shouldn't he *also* know the good? The Socratic experience clearly demonstrated that man was capable of discerning a good, precisely in appealing to this reason. Each one's experience allowed them to see that they could sense a call toward something that they called Good, lacking only the will to accomplish it. But this is all founded on ignorance of biblical revelation, or rather on the primacy given to philosophy or to experience, through which divine revelation was interpreted. This is easily refuted biblically. In innumerable texts, after having *revealed* his will to *his* people (and to them alone), God concludes, "See, I place before you today Good and Evil, do the good so that you may live" (Deut 30).[16] If all men and women had knowledge of the good, how could God call his revealed will the good? How could he give his people (and to them alone) the knowledge of the good, if everybody had it spontaneously? What need would there be

---

15. We do not think that when Calvin treats reason as an exception to total depravity, he means that man is capable of discerning the true and good by his reason, nor even that reason would be the privileged point of insertion for receiving revelation.

16. TN: Ellul's citation corresponds most closely to Deut 30:19. The NRSV reads, "I call heaven and earth to witness against you today that I have set before you life and death, blessings and curses. Choose life so that you and your descendants may live."

for a revelation if the good was inscribed in nature? What does this "today" signify, if, since the fall and even beforehand, men had been faced with this choice?

The debate over the possibility of natural human knowledge of the good according to God is obviously open-ended. Everything depends on the point of departure. If we adopt a strictly biblical frame of reference, it seems we cannot do otherwise than follow K. Barth on the subject of the impossibility of natural knowledge of God by man, which leads to the same impossibility of human knowledge of the good.[17] If we adopt another, all interpretations become possible. We might feel the need for an intermediary by which man could grasp the good (e.g, Conscience, Reason, as for Thomas Aquinas or even Augustine); we could refer to the recognition of a human reality which points us back to the good, which implies that this good is known;[18] we could lay an anthropological foundation, even a "Christian" anthropology, from which we derive the potentiality of man to know the good by himself;[19] the good could appear as a counterpart of clear effects of evil for man.[20] Or again, as with Brunner, the fact of the law of natural "orders" which constrain us to a common life with men causes us to discover the Christian truth of love for one's neighbour, for it is the God of love who makes us live in these orders. In any case, what man recognizes as just according to his nature, in these orders, is conformed to the will of God. All these investigations ultimately originate in man's impossibility to accept his incapacity to define the good by himself, to grasp it on his own, and his injustice in nevertheless wanting to wield the discernment of good and evil.

In Scripture, no possible knowledge of the good exists outside of a living and personal relation with Jesus Christ.[21]

But in truth, man does not know true evil any more than he knows the Good. Only at the moment of the Revelation of this Good as the Will of God—a revelation given, not as condemning justice, but justice of Love—does man learn what is evil, that is, discover himself to be a sinner. This occurs exclusively at this moment. He cannot discover this by any true natural experience, for every natural experience of evil will be necessarily

---

17. Cf. Søe, *Christliche Ethik*, §2; Prunet, *La morale chrétienne d'après les écrits johanniques*, chapter 4.

18. For example, an overtaking of man by himself in the search for holiness; cf. Pierre Blanchard, *Sainteté aujourd'hui*—or in the search for the good: see Henri Baruk on the function of the Good.

19. Cf. Reiner, "Ethik und Menschenbild," 284.

20. It seems thus for the law of love for Reinhold Niebuhr: *Interpretation of Christian Ethics*, 114.

21. Cf. de Quervain, *Die Heiligung*, 25.

Knowledge of the Good

ambiguous, and all the more deceptive since it will be generally situated in relation to a good defined by man. He cannot be convicted of sin if he is confronted with a good, a morality, a more or less abstract principle, but only if he is confronted by God.[22] Human transgression goes so far that, short of a divine manifestation intervening to prevent it, man can always listen to the thousand and one truths that he will be told about morality and the commandment of God.

This is why we cannot agree with Ricoeur when he makes the penitential experience of Israel—presented as a human experience, situated at the human level—the point of departure for all the notions (symbols) of guilt, sin, and for all the mythical constructions carried out on this basis. To assimilate the fear of the most Holy God to the "negativity of the transcendent" (*Symbolism of Evil*, 33), to say "conscience, not *finding* the manifestation of the law of retribution any longer in real suffering, *looked for* its satisfaction in other directions . . ."(42) or that "consciousness of sin advances and becomes boundless as historical insecurity grows" (57), etc.— this is to reduce, to natural human experience and natural human depth, something that only exists as a result of Revelation and in the presence of the Revelation of the Good (Justice and grace). And if this latter is true, then sin is no longer a symbol destined to give an account of an experience, but an objectively existing reality only discovered by Revelation, by man's being confronted by God.

Thus, because man is separated from God, and because in this situation he defines the good for himself, he lives in a radical incapacity to discern, love and want the good of God. And that is why when man claims to do good, he is guilty; when he alleges to be religious, he is an idolater. It must be concluded that either the revelation of God signifies nothing or man does not have natural knowledge of the Good. And the greatest witnesses of God know this well. After the word addressed by God to his people, consider the prayer addressed by his servant to God: Solomon, when he gains power and addresses God, what does he ask for? "Give me an intelligent heart to discern good and evil" (1 Kgs 3:9).[23] What would this prayer mean if he already had this discernment from birth, if the fruit of the tree had truly opened the eyes to the light of the good? Now, precisely, Solomon asks for this discernment because he must lead the people *of God*, a task that demands the true science of the true good, of the will of God that he conveys on the earth. And the one who asks this of God is—Solomon!

---

22. Barth, *CD* II.2, 747–48.

23. TN: The French text mistakenly refers to 1 Kgs 3:8. Verse 9 (NRSV) reads, "Give your servant therefore an understanding mind to govern your people, able to discern between good and evil; for who can govern this your great people?"

Solomon the Wise, the Just, he who has received exceptional discernment, as a gift, a grace—and it is a miracle that a man could thus know the Good. In Solomon's case, we see more clearly than for anyone else that the will does not respond to knowledge! How many times did the Wise One disobey the Good! But for him, the problem was not merely a problem of the will! For if he knew this good that he did not do, it is because the revelation of God had enlightened him, because God had opened his mind, removed the scales from his eyes, granted him Wisdom and the contemplation of the Good. But it required a prayer and a fulfillment—it took the submission of a man who, far from claiming to know the good, recognizes before God that he did not know it, that he is incapable of discerning this good and this evil on his own. We could even say that it is exactly when man recognizes this incapacity that there can be a revelation of the good from God. In effect, as long as man pretends to know the Good by himself, as long as he can declare himself master of this Wisdom, all revelation of God only produces a situation of conflict. God reveals a good that is not the good which man purports to proclaim: at that moment, the essential nature of sin comes out. And that is also why the Bible directly links the moral problem to the intention to sin. At this moment covetousness,[24] the source of sin, breaks out visibly. For this covetousness that Genesis speaks of was not so much the desire to possess the forbidden fruit as the pretentiousness to become like God, possessing the knowledge of good and evil: covetousness played precisely upon this latter possession. It is only when we possess this discernment that we also possess the power to justify ourselves.

It is because man has become the Master capable of declaring Good and Evil that—at that moment, by the same movement—he purports to affirm his own justification. The human thirst for justification rests on man's capacity to decide upon the Good for himself. But just as this thirst for justification is nothing other than the will to flee from the judgment of God,[25] so man's deciding upon the Good is nothing other than his refusal to be in communion with God: these are two aspects of the same revolt and the same "fall." This is why man cares so much about knowing the good: now provoked by sin, he can justify himself by invoking the Good—and if he

---

24. TN: Fr. *convoitise*—lust, desire, covetousness; Ellul develops this at length in *Éthique de la liberté*, vol. 2.

25. On this subject, see Van Peursen, "Ethik und Ontologie in der heutigen Existenzphilosophie," where the author proceeds to critique Existentialism from this viewpoint.

Barth, *CD* II.2, 726–27. Man is in all ways the transgressor of the divine law, and the very essence of all transgression of the law. The proof that man is a transgressor resides in the fact that man is always trying to excuse himself, to exonerate himself; this is sin *par excellence*.

is a Jew or a Christian, by invoking the law. It is here that the conflict with God is most obvious; this is also why only the man who knows himself to be incapable of this knowledge can find grace before God. He answers Solomon, the wise man—already wise to be inclined to pray this prayer, already enlightened by this coming light, but who alone learns, because it is a light *that is coming*, that he is in the night—the already-wise man, who knows that all wisdom is vanity. It is not by chance that Ecclesiastes was traditionally attributed to Solomon. For precisely, the Wise knows that he is not wise, and that if God does not grant him knowledge of the Good by his revelation, then he knows nothing and lives in madness.

2

The Good

So then, what is the Good according to the Bible? Theologians have written thousands of books on this topic. Our suspicions incline us to avoid analyzing these remarkably diverse theses, to refrain from entering this labyrinth, which has become endless (and for reasons that are not always linked to purity of faith). The biblical teaching seems relatively simple. As a preliminary remark, we note that practically all biblical texts (except for a few that we will examine at the end) are addressed to and speak of the People of God—whether the People of Israel in the Old Testament, or the people of the church in the New Testament. Consequently, they concern men and women who have received the revelation of God, for whom the Word of God is the word of life, a living word. These are women and men who *already* know that the Good relates to God. Therefore, when these texts speak plainly of the "Good," they cannot do so abstractly or indeterminately. Talk to an average Christian today (not a theologian, but someone with a living faith) about "doing good" and you will evoke ideas and images that point—variously and imprecisely, of course, but that point nonetheless—to Jesus Christ. Therefore, we must interpret these biblical texts in relation to those whom they address, since they are neither a philosophy nor a cosmogony, but invariably claim to convey a personal revelation that is only meaningful for those who believe and who already accept the will of God. In the Bible, whenever it is a question of the Good, it is because God is speaking.[1] When Cain is told to "do Good," this is not an objective and im-

---

1. The question of the good is posed within History and defined in concrete situations; these situations provide the occasion for God's formulation of his commandment.

personal formula: it is *God* who tells him to do Good, and thus who initiates the dialogue. Only in this dialogue does Cain learn what the good is for him and of his possibility of accomplishing it, since God is present in his word and appends his power to the possibility given to Cain *at this moment*. We see this precise pattern in Isaiah 1:15–17 and numerous similar texts: "Cease to do evil, learn to do Good": it is God who says this to this people, His people—the people who, because chosen by God, henceforth have the possibility of doing good, and who are awoken to this possibility by this word *hic et nunc*. And at the same time, only in this dialogue does the good receive its content: biblically, the good only has a content when God makes it known. "He has told you, O man, what is good" (Mic 6:8). Consequently, this is no spontaneous, intuitive, or *a priori* knowledge: for man to have this knowledge, God must intervene and make it known, reveal it and be revealed; this is thus the exact opposite of the knowledge won by Adam. Nor could Adam acquire and win *this* knowledge by his own efforts.[2] "He has told you . . ." This work comes from outside of man; it is a

---

The whole Bible shows us this relation. There are thus no "rules" or "exceptions," for example. As Bonhoeffer puts it precisely, "Good is not a quality of life but 'life' itself" (but only Christ *is* life); and again, "Being good means 'to live'" (but God alone is the creator) (*Ethics*, 253).

This relation between the will of God that is the good and its revelation in the Bible is strongly emphasized by Barth, CD II.2 §38, 706, in the following terms: ". . . *this God and the Bible*, His commanding and its commanding, are not to be separated. If there is no abstract authority in the Bible, there is no abstract authority in God. If the Bible is the living speech of God only in so far as it attests it, the living speech of God cannot be other than that attested by the Bible. It follows, then, that by the biblical witness we are not only called and set, as already formulated, in an analogous position to the biblical relationship and occurrence between God and man. We are not only invited to be contemporaneous and likeminded with the biblical men. We are not only exhorted to hear the command of God as they heard it. But at once the God who has spoken and acted in relation to them also becomes our God in virtue of their witness. And so the command given to them and heard by them becomes directly the command given to us and to be heard by us . . . [we should act] as the renewal and confirmation of the task laid upon them." [TN: Ellul's italics. I have added the quotation marks, which are absent in the French edition.]

2. Biblically, there is never really a question of natural knowledge of the good. Häring clearly demonstrates the opposing Catholic position in explaining how moral freedom presupposes knowledge of the good, which itself presupposes knowledge of the truth (*La loi du Christ*, 1:169). And there is no distinction between man as he was created, man as he is, and man regenerated in Christ. On the contrary, he regrettably alludes to the "normal" man. We thus find ourselves before a metaphysical anthropology founded on the conviction (about which little is said) that either the fall did not change very much or the kingdom of God has already been realized. Man can naturally contemplate and know the Good, but can occasionally or accidentally be blinded (1:178), while for us (and it seems to us in the Revelation) man is by nature blind to the Good but can be enlightened by grace: at this moment he sees the Good of God, and not its sinful homologues invented by man.

movement that comes to him. Indeed, when God speaks (and by this very fact acts on man) he "says the Good" (Num 24:13), and the prophet can do no more than repeat what the Eternal one says about good and evil. Thus, knowledge of the good is linked to knowledge of God's will; these two are always connected and even identified with one another.[3] "He has told you what is good: *and what does the Lord require of you*," says Micah (6:8). The Jewish people developed this notion in the direction of identifying the good with the law, with the latter being the totality of the revealed and definitive will of God. Biblically, an action is not good because it embodies certain values, nor because it conforms to a moral rule, nor because it is motivated by good intentions. It is good when it is the very work of God. As Søe (§19) says, "Man is never a star but always a planet, without any light of his own." Man only reflects the good that comes from God. Assuredly, if the good were distinct from the will of God, man could accomplish it on his own and claim it for himself. Yet the Bible never allows this perspective. If Jesus says, "*You* are the light of the World," it is *because* he says, "I am the light of the world." And no disciple can invert this relation and say for himself "I am . . ." Likewise, K. Barth says that "man's action is good in so far as it is sanctified by the Word of God."[4]

We will not develop this well-known theme here. Numerous texts remind Israel that in abandoning the law, they abandon the good (e.g., Hos 8), or again that by learning to know the law, children learn to know the good (e.g., Deut 1:39). But once more, the law in question is not an objective law *erga omnes*,[5] but the law as Word of God addressed to his people. We find this idea in Paul, for example, when in chapter 2 of the letter to the Romans, certain phrases seem to suppose an objective knowledge of the true Good: ". . . Glory and honor and peace for everyone who does good, the Jew first and also the Greek . . ." But the whole context shows that it is not a question of all men, but of those to whom a revelation has been made. When verse 5 speaks of "hardening," this term is reserved for those who reject the revelation of the word of God. The "perseverance" spoken of in verse 7 concerns those who seek honor, glory, and immortality; in Paul's mouth, these three terms take on a very precise content in direct relation with "His Gospel," not a vague and semantic sense referring to human concepts. Finally, Romans 1:32 is also very clear: the whole discussion

---

3. Against this conception, cf. Bois, "La crise de la Morale et la Christianisme," in *Le problème de la Morale chrétienne*. The arguments presented therein seem to misrecognize what the unity of the Good and the Will of God ultimately signifies.

4. Barth, *CD* III.4, 4.

5. TN: *Erga omnes*, a Latin term meaning "in relation to all," used in law to describe legal rights and obligations owed toward everyone.

concerns men and women who *know* the *judgment* of God about the things of which Paul has just spoken. This knowledge is precise, rigorous, and circumstantial, not intuitive or perceptible, and this knowledge concerns the judgment of God—that is, precisely a word of God, which no man can bear directly in himself, which is the most awful and intimate aspect of his relation with God, and which man only knows when he knows the love of God; because only by starting in this love can man learn to know what God detests and rejects. Thus, Paul perfectly confirms the point of departure that we discerned in the Old Testament: God, who reveals himself in his love, by this very fact teaches his will to man, and in this way man knows what is good.[6]

But let no one object: if the Good is nothing but the will of God, moral life will be purely incoherent, one act following another with no link, blind and contradictory obedience, etc. To say this is to have a strange idea of God! I know well that sometimes we can get this feeling by reading the Bible in a cursory manner, and from its apparently anarchic series of commandments. God is one; there is no division in him, no changing, no contradiction. And it is because he is One that his will is coherent, that our moral life is coherent. Because he is One, his commandments form a whole with no contradiction. Because he is One, our obedience is not absurd, and our life is not made up of isolated moments. And this is true even if our sensory experiences no longer teach it to us.[7]

---

6. This conception of the Good corresponds exactly to what Dietrich Bonhoeffer says on the Good and the ultimate Reality that is God (*Ethics*, 47); Prunet, *Morale chrétienne*, chapter 2, section 2, where he shows that a christological ethic presupposes that there is no other good than the will of God. See also Barth, *CD* II.2, 207. There are two absolutely synonymous notions here: first, God and God's commandment are good; and second, the good is God himself in his commandment. We cannot dissociate the good of God and his commandment. According to Barth, any dissolution of the notion of the Good to the detriment of one of its components (an operation that ethicists always perform) would entail the dissolution of the very notion of this God and of his commandment. It is certain that the notion of the good of the commandment of God holds absolute primacy over that of the good; because the good is a predicate of the function unique to God, God is the entirety of what is just and good. This means that the good has no preeminence over God; on the contrary, it is God who is and who speaks the good. And if it is thus, it is because God is love, and his benevolence toward man leads him to formulate the good for man.

7. On this topic, see Barth, *CD* III.4, 34–35, and de Quervain, *Ethik*, vol. I, 223.

This will of God that gives the good its content is not arbitrary.[8] In forgiving our sin, God does not call *good* what is *evil*, for God cannot lie. But God makes good what is evil in itself, healthy what is sick in itself, glorious what is wretched in itself, living what is dead in itself. We present ourselves evil before him, and we leave good; there is forgiveness of sins, but God never calls evil good.

What God decides has nothing in common with caprice; what he ordains for man to do or not do does not derive from the fantasies of a tyrant whose law coincides with his power.[9] The movement that regulates the relation of God with man is the history of the covenant of grace, throughout which God is faithful and constant. Consequently, the good is ultimately not incoherence. All of God's orders are situated within the framework of the history of the people of Israel and the history of Jesus Christ; all his prohibitions cannot be generalized, as they presuppose that the good coincides with the will of God.[10]

When God speaks, the Good does not remain a word or a notion. We could say that it receives a substance. But it receives its substance from God. The account of Cain's revolt is significant (Gen 4:6–7a): "Why are you angry, and why has your countenance fallen? If you do well, will you not be accepted?" Here, to act well thus means to cease being angry, to cease despairing, and to rule over Evil . . . but this is not a good *in itself*. Anger and Despair are not Evil. The real question is, Why is Cain angry and despairing? The answer is simple: because Cain did not accept God's decision to accept Abel's sacrifice and to disregard Cain's sacrifice. Cain did not accept the will of God expressed in this decision. He is angry and despairs because of this decision. He does not believe that God loves him in spite of his sacrifice; he thinks that God is unjust. Thus it is not Anger or Despair in itself that is Evil, but Anger or Despair in relation to this attitude of Cain toward God. The Good is thus to accept the decision of God, to believe that God loves him all the same—to accept the will of God whatever it may be, including when it prefers Abel. The Good is to be in accord with this will, and to conquer anger, despair, and evil on this basis. For this can only be done by loving this will of God without judging it, and anger, despair, and evil are products of a knowledge outside of the decision of God that we do not love. All other descriptions of

---

8. Barth, *CD* II.2, 757.

9. TN: In the French text there are no citations around this sentence, but it is found nearly verbatim in Barth, *CD* II.2, 676–77.

10. Barth, *CD* II.2, 675.

the good derive from this: according to Deuteronomy 30:16, the Good consists in loving God, following his word, observing his commandment, and worshiping him alone.[11] According to Psalm 14, it is seeking God, praying, calling upon him, and because of this, respecting men and not destroying those whom God loves. Significantly, Amos likewise writes in succession: (God says) "Seek me" and "Seek the Good" (Amos 5:4 and 5:14). Seeking God is fundamentally identified with the will to do what is good. But at the same time, it is to fear the Lord (a phrase that is often repeated), to formulate the truth (of God), to seek peace (with God—Ps 34:15), to place one's confidence in God, to have faith and hope in him, to be faithful to his love, and in his love, to find one's joy and delight in God's will and his presence (Ps 37:4). Thus, the Good is a certain relation with God, and it can only be formulated in relation to God. Nowhere is there a question of a good foreign to this attitude of man before God. And if the good is determined by the word of God, to do what is good is to believe in this word of God and accomplish it. This attitude toward God necessarily leads to a certain behavior toward men; this attitude, too, is never considered in itself, independently of Faith. Thus, the good will consist—*simultaneously* (but not separately)—in praying to God on behalf of others, interceding for one's enemies (Ps 35:12), accomplishing justice for men, and defending the poor, the humble, and the oppressed (Isaiah, Amos, Micah). We all know the duties proclaimed by the prophets as well as the virtues expressed by Paul that constitute the good, that describe good conduct before God. It is useless to insist on and describe them. What matters here is to remember that this can only be understood inside of the Good itself which is the will of God. Thus, we can summarize this notion of the Good in the Old Testament with the astonishing text of Micah: "He has told you, O mortal, what is Good; and what does the LORD require of you but to do justice, and to love kindness, and to walk humbly with your God?" (6:8). These three requirements summarize all the rest: to walk with God (in his presence, in the light of his revelation and with faith), humble and submitted to his will; to practice love of one's neighbor; to do what is just[12]—such is the Good. And what the New Testament (which, incidentally, employs this word with much more discretion) has to say about the Good does not contradict this at all. Paul often draws on Old Testament texts in this way. James defines the good as loving one's neighbor and putting faith in God into practice, accentuating somewhat the ethical character of this notion. In fact, the staunchly theological sense given by the Old

---

11. Recall the famous formula of Teresa of Ávila: "I do not seek virtue, but the Lord of the virtues."

12. On the concept of justice in the Old Testament, I take the liberty of referring to my *Theological Foundation of Law*.

Testament may leave us feeling that the good is an inward, mystical affair of intentions. This would obviously be a failure to recognize the realism of the Old Testament, but this misunderstanding is a real risk. The epistle of James brings us back to the heart of the moral problem by insisting on the practical level of these very elements that constitute the good (chapter 2). Again, all of this does not modify what we have said so far. The third epistle of John takes one step further: "Beloved, do not imitate evil, but good. The one who does the good is of God; the one who does evil has not seen God" (3 John 11).[13] This verse places us in a clearly christological perspective. "Imitate the Good": in effect, this formula supposes that the good is neither abstract information nor a simple attitude of man. Now (and this is new in relation to the Old Testament) there is a model of the Good. But this model is not a formula, a fixed or permanent idea, an object. Imitation supposes the notion of "following" found so frequently precisely in the Johannine writings. To imitate is to follow the one who is walking before us. If we view this text in its Johannine context, the imitation of the good should be assimilated to the imitation of Jesus Christ himself. That the author of this epistle calls Jesus Christ the Good is confirmed by what immediately follows this verse: the one who does the Good is of God. Now, John has precisely defined the one who is of God as the one who confesses that Jesus Christ has come in the flesh. And again at the end of the verse: the one who does evil has not seen God. But John said that we can only see God in Jesus Christ. There is thus a direct relation between the accomplishment of the Good and the person of Jesus Christ. This should not be surprising at all! But we must also see that there is no contradiction with the Old Testament. We could summarize this progression as follows: the Good is what God says in his Word; next, it is a certain attitude of man toward God, as a result and in function of this Word; then it is a certain attitude of man toward man as a result and function of the relation with God. But the Word of God is fully expressed, demonstrated, explicated, and revealed in Jesus Christ and in Jesus Christ alone, who is himself—and in-himself—the Word. Therefore Jesus Christ is truly the Good. Furthermore, the attitude toward God and toward man is proposed as a command, a call and a promise in the Old Testament; while in Jesus Christ this good is completely and fully incarnated and accomplished. The Good is thus an accomplishment that we have to enter into; yet for all that, the call and the command addressed to each one individually are not erased. But this can no longer generate anguish and despair. We are no longer completely (and exclusively) responsible for accomplishing the good

---

13. TN: Ellul mistakenly gives the verse reference as 3 John 2.

on earth; it is accomplished. But we are always incited to fill up anew the measure of the good for the very cause of the one who accomplished it.

This essentially agrees with the thought of Bonhoeffer, according to whom the Good has become reality in Jesus Christ (*Ethics*, 54). While all thinking dissociates a good from a reality, these cannot be dissociated in the event of the Incarnation; indeed, they only ever coincide there. And everywhere else, man is incapable of grasping the good, for he is always closed in by the real. The Word of God that speaks the Good is pronounced in Jesus Christ and nowhere else. To hear and to practice this Word of God is to receive Holiness as a member of the body of Christ. Holiness is a living relation with Christ.[14] If it is true that Jesus Christ alone is indeed the whole good, we thus learn three truths that are decisive for our life before God—three truths that we ought to receive and meditate on. The first is that the voice of Jesus Christ is the voice of the holy God himself. But because it is the voice of Jesus Christ, it is not just the voice of a God who limits himself to giving orders and making promises, who is only a transcendent and far-off God. We could never hear or receive the commandment of this God; it could only place us before nothingness and despair. Though it is the voice of God, the voice of Jesus Christ is simultaneously the voice of man; it is close to us. But this is a sanctified man—one sanctified in our place, who speaks the good in our place and who does, in obedience to his Father, what Adam wanted to do in disobedience.

The second truth situates us at the heart of the dilemma of faith and of the good: man always seeks a good that would be a determination of "doing"—while in Jesus Christ, it is always a matter of "being."[15] This goes against everything taught today under the influence of Marx—namely, that man only exists in "doing." But this is not the voice of the Lord.

The third truth brings us back to our powerlessness to accomplish the good: if any good whatsoever could reside in man or could be accomplished by man apart from God, this good would have appeared in Jesus Christ. Now, in Jesus himself, the love of God finds nothing worthy of being loved.[16] Jesus Christ himself has nothing to bring before God, nothing to show except our

---

14. On these different points, see the introduction and part 1 of de Quervain, *Ethik*, vol. 1, *Die Heiligung*.

15. On this opposition, cf. Barth, *CD* II.2, 606. We do not mean that this opposition is ontologically valid and permanent. We only observe the fact that in ethics man looks for what he should do and that, by contrast, the gospels and the epistles speak to us of what we should be, of a transformation of our being—which, of course, is not separate from doing; but this latter is secondary and follows as a consequence of the former.

16. Barth, *CD* II.2, 583.

sin, our transgression; in his person, man only exists as a renegade; the only Just one has no justice to present in our name.

This conception of the good, which seems to us to be rigorously biblical, allows us to respond very quickly to three classic questions of Morality:

—First, the question of indifferent acts (the argument concerning *adiaphora*). Between what is "commanded" and what is "prohibited," there is supposedly an immense domain of acts that concern neither salvation nor the good, etc. In reality, this is unacceptable in a Christian perspective: all of life should be obedience, and consequently no act is foreign to the will of God. A life does not consist in a series of separated acts in which each would be considered independently, but of a continuity expressed in each act. This unity of life is what Jesus Christ signifies in saying, "Either the *tree* is good or the *tree* is bad."[17] The fruits are only consequences. And consequently the fruits are not to be judged separately; none are without significance. Saint Paul says this directly: "Whatever you eat, whatever you drink, do *everything* to the glory of God." So the smallest act is significant. There are no "optional" acts, there are no "negative" or "positive" accommodations. There are no distinctions between a time of peace and a time of war, etc.[18] Everything is included in the determination of the Good as the will of God. Man is called to know that his entire life concerns God, and that it is his work in the global sense that is judged. "We can know of no human action which does not stand under God's command . . . We do not know any human action which is free, i.e., exempted from decision in relation to God's command, or neutral in regard to it . . . There is no neutrality in relation to God's command."[19]

—The second question is closely related to the first: are there autonomous *domains* of activity that do not concern the Christian life? Scientific, technical, economic problems, etc., seem not to implicate Christian ethics. One part of these domains is purely intellectual and includes no "moral" judgment. If the economy, politics, and sociology are phenomena of the same order as physics, if there are "laws" to these activities, where could we insert a moral decision? Another part of these domains is purely "natural"; there is no need to discern the good by referring to a "Revelation." A natural morality suffices. All theologies that admit a natural law seek to respond to this. And in a certain measure, this goes for theologies of moral conscience as well (even in Luther). But in reality, once the Bible convinces

---

17. TN: Ellul's paraphrase of Matt 12:33: "Either make the tree good, and its fruit good; or make the tree bad, and its fruit bad; for the tree is known by its fruit."

18. On all these points, see Søe, *Christliche Ethik*, §28.

19. Barth, *CD* II.2, 535 and 610.

us that the Good is God's will, this problem vanishes, for all the domains in question are part of God's creation. He is equally the Creator of politics as of economics, and consequently nothing escapes either his judgment or his grace; everything finds itself inserted into this decision of God that is the Good. No domain—no matter how theoretical, scientific, or technical it may be—escapes this determination of the Good, for the latter exceeds by far the reduced moral categories used in our appraisals. "The Good is Life." There are henceforth no domains where a natural morality would suffice, for this natural morality is defined by sin itself.[20]

—Finally, the third classic question is that of the autonomy of morality. Is morality a domain in itself? If we adopt the biblical vision of the Good, we are obliged to radically reject this conception. On the one hand, the world (and the morality of the world) wants to be autonomous, and every philosophical morality must proclaim itself autonomous, but only insofar as it revolts against the Will of God. On the other hand, the Revelation teaches us that if we take our creaturely condition seriously, it is impossible for man to pose a foundation for his ethics on his own, independently of the lordship of the creative and redemptive God. No ethic in accordance with the will of God can be autonomous.[21]

It was necessary for the Son of God to accomplish the fullness of this good himself, for man could never do so. The biblical teaching is clear and cruel. "There is no one who does good. The LORD looks down from heaven on humankind to see if there are any who are wise, who seek after God. They have all gone astray, they are all alike perverse; there is no one who does good, no, not one" (Ps 14). Nowhere in Scripture is this terrible judgment weakened; on the contrary, it is often confirmed. It is presented as a universal fact. "On the earth there is no just man who does the good,"[22] says the writer of Ecclesiastes, and Paul makes this observation one of the foundations of his theology. He cites Psalm 14 (Rom 3:10–12), then says, "The whole world is held guilty before God."[23] In this radical incapacity, there is no distinction between men. Of course, the "ungodly," the one who does not believe in God, *necessarily* does evil (Ps 36:4). This teaching is continually repeated. It is obvious if we think according to the conception of the good that we

---

20. On this subject, cf. Søe, *Christliche Ethik*, 29.

21. Cf. Prunet, chapter 3 section 2.

22. TN: It seems Ellul is referring to Eccl 7:20.

23. TN: Rom 3:19; the NRSV reads, "The whole world may be held accountable to God."

have indicated above. Now it is no less evident that the authors of Scripture were not stupid, and that they knew perfectly well that men who did not worship Yahweh, nor Jesus Christ later on, were capable of doing good. A lot of good was done in Egypt, and in Greece and Rome. They knew this. What man calls good was realized more or less, but all the same it was realized. Thus we need not talk of an ignorance or blindness in these declarations. No more should we talk of taking sides, or sectarianism; it is simply a different conception of the Good.

In the same manner, in the human conception of the good there are degrees—a greater and lesser good, a greater and lesser evil. And in effect, this coincides with the judgments that man can make, starting from his own conception (which he creates). But the Bible teaches us the opposite: there are things that are Holy and things that are not—no degrees, no border zone, no approximation, since what is Holy is really what is Separate. And in the same manner, when Jesus Christ declares that the one who has violated the least of the commandments has violated the entire law, he refuses the "more" and the "less." Now, this only makes sense if the good is not an objective reality in itself that man could know by his own means, if on the contrary the good is assimilated to the absolute of the will of God.

In summary, all of this boils down to saying: what men define and accomplish as good is not the good before God and according to God. The wicked man who refuses this God can know nothing of the good, not even the smallest thing; before God, then, he can only do evil. But we are not looking at a sectarianism! For it is not a question of dividing men *on this basis*, between the wicked who necessarily do evil and the believers who do or can do the good—alas, the Revelation is more rigorous and less simplistic! The Jews, even though they have received the Revelation, are no more *capable* of doing good than others. Each time that Israel, taking itself as a subject, conscious of the revelation that it has been given, wants to accomplish this good itself—every time, Israel commits evil before God. Thus the extraordinary provocation of God borne by Isaiah (41:21–24): Israel claims *to be* on its own (outside of its Lord) and to do the good by itself (outside of its Savior). God says, "Set forth your case . . . Tell us what is to come hereafter, that we may know that you are gods . . ." (Always the pretension of Eden . . . and Israel, having received the revelation, could certainly take itself to be a god!) "Only do something good . . . or evil! so that we could see and look at it together. But look, you are nothing, and your work is nothingness."[24] This

---

24. TN: I have held to the NRSV up until Ellul's parenthesized insertion; afterward, I have translated what Ellul cites, which corresponds to verses 23–24 of the French Louis Segond translation of the Bible (though the ellipsis and exclamation point are Ellul's interjections). The NRSV for this passage reads, "Do good, or do harm, that we

Israel of God is thus placed on the same level as the others, and Jeremiah reminds them of this fact: "Can an Ethiopian change the color of his skin, or the leopard its spots? Likewise, can you do good, you who know only evil?" Thus, even if they know in what the good consists, Israel is no more capable of doing it than the wicked. And their situation is even worse than that of the unbeliever, above all because they *know* what this good is, while the other does not. This knowledge is even the big difference between them; but since they know, Israel is therefore fully responsible. They are called into judgment before this very good. Moreover, Israel has the possibility of pushing Adam's sin to its fullness, since in them and in them alone can the supreme pretension of being like gods arise: to announce good and evil autonomously, even though God has revealed the good. This is what is meant by the chief text of Isaiah (5:20-21): "Ah, you who call evil good and good evil, who put darkness for light and light for darkness, who put bitter for sweet and sweet for bitter! Ah, you who are wise in your own eyes, and shrewd in your own sight!" Man wants to know good and evil on his own, to define them—fine. But in Israel's case, what is profoundly serious is that they hold onto this pretension even though God has revealed what is Good before him, and Israel tops it off by defining what *they*, these men, decree to be good and evil—concerning the very revelation of God, and in making use of it. And consequently, they come to decree as evil what God has revealed as good. This is clearly the gravest thing they could do! And it is fully realized, entirely accomplished when Israel says that the Son of God is sacrilege, that the innocent is guilty, that the Messiah is an Impostor, and that Good incarnate commits evil. Should we believe that these are Christian interpretations, that the line between the good and the wicked henceforth passes between Christians and non-Christians? Certainly not! As concerns the Good, Christians are treated no better than any others in the Bible! "I do not do what I want to do, I do what I hate ... What is good does not live in me ... I have the will but not the power to do good ... I do not do the good that I want, I do the evil that I do not want ... I find in myself this law: when I want to do the good, evil is linked to me. For I take pleasure in the law of God according to the interior man, but I see in my members another law which fights against the law of my intelligence and which renders me captive to the law of sin which is in my members ... Miserable wretch that I am! Who will save me from this body of death? Thanks be to God through Jesus Christ our Lord!" (Rom 7:14-25). Paul is talking about himself, but all Christians *should* say what he says concerning themselves. As with the

---

may be afraid and terrified. You, indeed, are nothing and your work is nothing at all." I have substituted a period after "together," where Ellul has a question mark.

Jew, we come back to the separation between the knowledge of the Good, which results from revelation, and the ability to do it: here, and only here, for the man who has received the Revelation of God, the distinction between knowledge and ability is legitimate. Thus this separation is situated in the life of the Christian, and not in the lives of all men, of the natural man, as certain theologians have interpreted it. Furthermore, this knowledge of the good further discloses this incapacity to accomplish it. For the pagan can delude himself: knowing nothing of the good according to God and setting a good for himself, he can, to a large extent, perform it and satisfy himself. On the contrary, the one who has received the revelation of the Good according to God should no longer delude himself. Despite all his efforts, he must realize his incapacity, judging himself against an absolute and not a relative standard, and he will observe his captivity to evil. And so the event of the accomplishment of the Good by Jesus Christ (and only he accomplished it, and he accomplished it completely) does not make things any easier for the Christian: this latter only has Jesus Christ and the revelation of the good and the revelation correlative to his sin . . . at the same time as the announcement of the joyful gospel of grace that is proclaimed to him! But this does not give him any intrinsic capacity to accomplish on his own the good promulgated by God. There is no permanent transformation of his being that would consist in this capacity to do the good of God by himself. On his own, he has no new, intrinsic possibility that would become a second nature.

Certain biblical texts nevertheless seem to evoke another notion of the good, a natural notion that would seem to belong to every man and woman. Thus, we sometimes see the formula "return good for evil," which is applied to everybody. For example, Joseph reproaches his visitors for having rendered him evil for good (Gen 44:4), but this always has a concrete meaning: one man does good to another, and the latter is perfectly capable of experiencing it as such. When I am hungry, there is no need of revelation for me to know that the one who gives me bread does good to me. All the texts of the Old Testament concerning a good discerned by natural man more or less pertain to this very practical, pragmatic, experiential sense. Thus in the Bible, there is a whole line of realist thought about the good. And without a doubt, this is also part of the Good. And it is probably *all* that natural man is *legitimately* capable of calling good. Perhaps we should also interpret a group of texts in the Epistles in this same manner: "Do not repay anyone evil for evil, but take thought for what is noble in the sight of all" (Rom 12:17); "We intend to do what is right not only in the Lord's sight but also in the sight of others" (2 Cor 8:21); "Do you wish to have no fear of the authority? Then do what is good, and you will receive its approval; for it is God's servant for your good" (Rom 13:3-4a); "For it is God's will that by doing right you should silence the ignorance of the foolish" (1 Pet 2:15). These four texts are related by the common idea that the good practiced by Christians can be perceived and understood as good by non-Christians. While they include different teachings, the first two nevertheless recommend seeking what is good before men—that is, doing not only what God requires, but also what the men and women of a given time and a given civilization call good. We will return to this below,[25] but it is essential to highlight that the second text precisely opposes two types of "good"—one that is good before the Lord and one that is good before men. Christians cannot limit themselves to the one while despising the other. They must *also* do what men call good, though it must not be conflated with the good according to God. Rather, we note that these words confirm the teaching drawn out above: the good according to God is not the good according to men. And Scripture says very little about this latter. It knows this good, recognizes it, but barely sheds any light on it that does not concern the salvation of man.

The third and fourth texts insist on a completely different aspect: in doing the good (and here we have no indication on the order of the good in question; it thus seems that we ought to hear it in its habitual biblical usage), the Christian will garner the approval of authority and will reduce senseless men to silence. Both cases concern pagans who become capable of perceiving the good performed by Christians. It is obvious that this is part of the witness that Christians must bear before men; supplementing their verbal witness, there must be the witness of life, of work and action. The two are inseparable, indissociable, as Jesus Christ teaches ("Let your light shine before men *so that* they see your good works" [Matt 5:16]), and the one without the other is worthless. It is possible that pagans could approve of and even admire the good according to God that is practiced by Christians; perhaps because it corresponds to their own concrete sense of the good that we have spoken of, and that is undivided, or perhaps a given act corresponds to the norms of the good in a given society. For there can be coincidence between what a society calls a good and the good according to God, whether this coincidence be accidental or voluntary (with "Christendom" falling under this latter type)—in which case there will be no difficulty. But there can also be opposition between the two: two different notions of the good with two

---

25. In chapter 5, we will examine the conciliation or opposition of the two moralities in relation with what we are saying here about the conciliation and opposition of the two 'goods.'

different contents. It is not inevitable or certain that pagans will recognize this good done by Christians. It is not assumed that the state will approve of Christian behavior; history has amply demonstrated this. In any case, we are on extremely ambiguous ground here. If men approve of the good done by the Christian because it corresponds to their contemporary notion of the good, there is no witness, since what is perceived is not the good according to God, the work for God; this is the confusion with humanism. It is strongly possible and even probable that Paul is alluding to this when he speaks of the authorities: they will accept and sanction the conduct of Christians because in many respects (do not kill, do not steal, do not commit adultery, etc.), the good revealed by God recalls a certain notion of the good contemporary to the Greco-Roman world. If, on the other hand, men find themselves in the presence of conduct that attempts to express the good according to God, and that would be surprising or shocking in their eyes, ambiguity reigns again; for nothing, on its own, can inform them that this is the good of God. On their own, they have no secret sense, no intuition that would permit them to say upon seeing a given act, "This is the good of God!" Left to themselves, their eyes are closed to good works, and the good does not directly come into contact with them. Even if they are capable of deeming this conduct good (and in the name of what will they deem it thus?), they nevertheless cannot directly receive a testimony about God in this manner. This judgment of the good cannot enlighten them as to the source of this good. That is precisely why the Word is indispensable: it is the light that illuminates these good works. Without the word that accompanies it, the work remains obscure and incomprehensible for those on the outside who see it. It must be explained; its ins and outs, its origin and its reason must be formally correlated. Thus these two texts remind us that practicing the good is a necessary part of witness, but it is completely insufficient and does not assume that the good will be directly perceived by men as a manifestation of God.

Everything that we have just said on the Good in the Bible, on what bears this name in the Revelation, demonstrates an extraordinary contradiction with the origin of morality, that is, the capacity of men and women to decide between good and evil. The Good according to God is not integrated in human morality and perhaps, as we will see, it cannot be the object of a morality. This latter is of man. It is not in accordance with the Good of God. It is of the order of the fall and of the order of necessity.

3

Morality Is of the Order of the Fall

We will keep using the term "fall" out of habit and practicality, but we know that it is unfortunate and imprecise. Ricoeur's critique thereof is undoubtedly correct.[1] But if we contest the term, we must at least hold to the event: that is, the rupture of the communion between

---

1. There is a tendency to minimize the gravity of the fall that is renewed in contemporary Protestant theology. One way or another, man always seeks to salvage his own dignity, wanting something to be left unscathed by this catastrophe. He wants to keep a dignity for himself, a freedom opposed to God. He wishes to be a being that is not oriented toward death. This heresy is an artefact of the pride of man, who cannot tolerate that everything is delivered to the grace of God. Yet there can be no disputing the fact that by virtue of the rupture with God, who is the Living one, man is rejected on the side of nothingness, cut off from life; he necessarily dies. God's act of freedom toward this man is not at all to have said that man, from now on, will die; rather, it is to have kept this "man for death" alive. If it were otherwise, Jesus Christ would not have had to die. To dispute that man is a being "for death" is to dispute the Incarnation and the Resurrection, to admit that there were other possibilities; it reduces the work of Jesus Christ to nothingness.

On the gravity of the fall, even Brunner with the orders and Bonhoeffer with the mandates recognize that these latter are not a remainder of the original purity of creation, and that they bear nothing divine "*in themselves*." They can only be recognized as such by faith.

On this perversion of the cosmos, see Prunet, *La morale chrétienne d'après les écrits johanniques*, 56. In the same work (154), we note the precise commentary on the difference in the notion of sin found in John and Paul (a fundamental state of man, expressed in his self-justification and self-vivification) and the notions found in the Christianity that followed after: a failure to live by the rules, a moral fault, a filth that man could wash himself, a superficial and relative deterioration, a parasite, a guilty attitude, a deficiency (in Arminianism, for example, etc.)—all notions that we find in contemporary Protestantism, even among orthodox theologians.

man and God. We have no intention of joining the discussion of the hundreds of doctrines interpreting what the Bible describes to us as an event. We will hold to the most traditional one, which appears to us to be the most closely conformed to the biblical account and to the irrefutable certitude that the rupture of the communion with God changes the totality of life and being. For either this communion is the very foundation of being, of life, and of the good, in which case its rupture modifies *everything*—or the modification is only partial, which implies that the communion with God was a secondary and nondecisive element. We cannot agree at all with those who try to minimize the importance of this event. In all cases, these theories really have only one objective: to accentuate the value of man, to preserve a grandeur, a good, a dignity for man on his own, and ultimately an autonomy in relation to God. All these theories distort the clarity of Scripture in ways that are often subtle and apparently legitimate, serving to justify man for being what he is; they rely on a presupposition of the validity of what man is and does outside of the exclusive grace of Jesus Christ. The latest undertaking of this kind consists in drawing (what we believe to be) abusive conclusions from the (perhaps only denominational) hypothesis that the Genesis account is a Myth. We dispute that there was a Before and an After, a passage from one situation to another (I will refuse Ricoeur's terminology: a passage from innocence to sin, for this is not what the text says—these formulae are anthropocentric and "essentialist"—however, it is certainly a passage from a communion to a rupture); that there was a precise moment of the inauguration of evil— and thus we describe the situation as a permanent starting over; a state of innocence and a superimposed (as opposed to a successive) state of sin: "In the Instant I am created, in the Instant I fall."[2] There is no anterior or posterior state, but two contemporaneous states, which means that man is not radically lost and evil; on the contrary, man is naturally good, innocence is primary, and evil is only contingent.

Despite the subtlety of this interpretation, insoluble problems remain (beyond the question of the unity of the biblical current, which is often cleverly dissociated, then minimized, and splintered into fragments of "blemishes," "nothingness," "guilt" and "myths"). Here are several such problems:

1. *Is* the world as we know it the world created such as God willed it? Ricoeur explains the inexistence of the fall for man, but the Bible tells us of a total degradation of creation (including things and animals): we find no response from Ricoeur. Now, if the world is not the one that God created, there necessarily must have been a before and an after.

---

2. Ricoeur, *Symbolism of Evil*, 251.

2. Ricoeur tells us that man inaugurates evil himself (and that there is no original sin) but that nevertheless, from the beginning of his life and act, he finds himself before an "evil already there, an evil already in place." I cannot follow this path. Dialectical thought can do many things, but it does have its limits. It seems to me that we are in the presence of an intellectual impossibility.

3. To say "in the Instant I am created, in the Instant I fall" presupposes that the problem of continuous creation is resolved; and on the other hand, we must ask ourselves, *Why* this necessity of falling? If there truly is no passage to the situation of sinful man, we must therefore believe that a man could possibly not be a sinner: at a given instant, could he *not* fall?

4. The entire doctrine of Ricoeur, like all doctrines that minimize the fall and the gravity of the evil of man, by this very fact minimizes the work of Jesus Christ. If at each instant man is created and falls, Jesus Christ is nothing more than a man who, at this moment, did not fall.

But if, conversely, Jesus Christ is what Scripture teaches he is, then we must be serious: if the fall and evil were not of the utmost gravity, do we really believe that God would have gone as far as the unthinkable sacrifice of giving his Son, to the point of performing this inconceivable denuding of himself? For the work of Salvation to have been so immense, the rupture in the fall must have been fundamental; *everything* must have been broken so that *everything* could be recovered, *everything* must have been lost so that *everything* had to be saved by grace.

There is thus no remnant of former innocence, for this very innocence would allow us to do without the reality of the work of God.

The Bible clearly shows us that the origin of morality is linked to disobedience. It is henceforth part of the order of the fall.³ What exactly does this

---

3. As Karl Barth has shown very well, in this order of separation, when it is known by man, the law of God is no more than the occasion for covetousness [*convoitise*]. The commandment of God is transformed by sin; the law does not give this man the starting point for a true knowledge of the good, but instead a sort of incentive to be like God, to "*self*-purification, *self*-justification, *self*-sanctification" (Barth, *CD* II.2, 592). Within the world of the fall, the law in itself is not the source of a true morality, but exactly its opposite, which is why Jesus directs his most severe attack against the Pharisees: "as a result and in prolongation of the fall, we have 'ethics'" (Barth, *CD* II.2, 517). Thus when Reinhold Niebuhr (*The Nature and Destiny of Man*) insists on the autonomy of (natural) ethics and affirms that ethical research is a human task, he is right! But while

mean? It really is a question of an order. It is not nothingness, nor the absurd, nor incoherence, but an order, an organization, a stability—containing those things necessary to maintain life (relatively) and creation (also relatively). Morality is one of these things. It is thus useful. We will come back to this. But it is an order of the fall, that is, of separation from God, in a world whose Prince is Satan and where sin has exclusive reign over the heart of man. Morality is not of some other essence, some other order, or some other nature. There is not an order of sin, on the one hand, and then a miraculously preserved morality, on the other, which would judge sin, would allow us to denounce and combat it. In reality, morality is in this order of sin, precisely insofar as it is knowledge belonging to sinful man. Morality is part of the world. It is part of the world of sin: it is included within sin and not the judge of what sin is, as if arbitrating from outside the conflict. Believing that the morality decreed by man, or experienced by him in his conscience, or obeyed by him in his action, could ultimately be a reflection of the will of God is to believe that man has not lost everything in the fall, that he is in some small way still situated in Eden. We are not looking here to revive the question of the *imago Dei*. We will not decide upon whether or not it remains in man to some extent, whether it is broken or disrupted but exists, nor even what this *imago Dei* is, for we do not need to resolve these problems to resolve our problem. It suffices to observe that whatever might subsist of the *imago Dei* can in no way be moral sentiment. In fact, the covetous desire to become like God and the will to discern good and evil were the occasion and reason of the temptation and fall; it is certain that this definitively could not have been upheld in man. He could have retained the *imago Dei*, but he certainly cannot have kept the crux and the heart of disobedience.[4] Otherwise, this would have been the ultimate victory of man over God.

---

this is a positive element in his eyes, it seems to us that he is only translating the fact that, in the knowledge of good and evil, Adam has become autonomous! The fact of wanting to know good and evil constitutes precisely the original sin "which separates man from God. And in this way it establishes something that man would prefer to deny" (Barth, *CD* II.2, 645).

4. This remark is even more pertinent if we accept the translation of the biblical text as "man was created in the image of God" and not "according to the image of God" [TN: Ellul proposes "dans l'image de Dieu" instead of the "habitual" translation "à l'image de Dieu"]. The habitual translation, as Crespy highlights (in *Le problème d'une anthropologie théologique*), signifies that there would be a sort of quality of created man, a quality of his nature; on the contrary, it seems that the Hebrew text signifies that man is created in the image of God, that is, as a promise, as establishing his destiny and his future. It concerns a destining of the being of man, the mission assigned him by God; but if this is so, as soon as man claims to take charge of the knowledge of good and evil himself, he claims precisely to take charge of his own destiny, and in fact that is what

Man cannot have a true religious perception, nor direct knowledge of God, nor an intact moral conscience, for these "goods" belong to revolt and autonomy.[5] Thus we do not have to look here for what comprises the *imago Dei,* nor that which could still comprise it; for our remarks, we only need to be assured that it cannot consist in moral Conscience. And consequently, what is given this name by man is not a reflection of God, a remainder of his original wholeness: on the contrary, it is a supplementary mark of his belonging to the world of sin, a manner of being in this world and not a memory of a past Eden. What man supposes to be the good and what he condemns as evil certainly have meaning and value, which we will look for. But they have no value for life and salvation before God. This good is included within disobedience and sin, and consequently is not a good of God and for God. We could say more or less that this good is no closer to God than is (what man calls) evil, since it is this man who claims to be God who decrees, "This is good," and in so doing, he reproduces the exact progression of Adam; he wants to know the Good, that is, to determine it, since he cannot know the true good that is in God. In reality, the entirety of man's moral undertaking is contradicted by the gospel. Never does Jesus Christ consecrate human morality. The gift of God in Christ is redemption, restoration of the life of man, the inauguration of a new life; it is founded in newness, and not a prolongation of a preceding good, or the crowning moment of a spontaneous knowledge of the good. If the condition of Christians is so often described to us as that of strangers and exiles, it is in fact because nothing really attaches them to this world, because *all* of this world is foreign to them—including the good determined by morality. And nothing in the life of these Christians corresponds to what

---

the Bible continually describes to us concerning the pretension of man—and God does not oppose this claim directly or by force! Consequently, we could say that from the moment that Adam lays his hand on the tree of the knowledge of good and evil, he is no longer in the image of God; and if the promise subsists, it is exclusively in Jesus Christ, who is now the only one remaining in the image of God. And by further consequence, we cannot draw any conclusions for the current situation of man from this notion of the image of God, which, as it were, no longer concerns us except by way of the fact that Jesus is Lord.

5. It is an obvious error of Bonhoeffer to consider that the modern world has attained autonomy in the domains of political life, art, or morality, and that only modern man has discovered laws of these disciplines independently of all that Christianity can say. In reality, at least concerning morality, we must recall that from the beginning (and in all civilizations), this tendency toward affirmation, toward the autonomy of morality is constant and corresponds to the exact situation described in the Bible. It is only precise to say that in contemporary society, we clearly rediscover the traditional situation that had been momentarily and artificially veiled by a religious conception of Christianity. [TN: Ellul revisits these themes at length in *The New Demons.*]

men call Good. It is not this good that characterizes the Christian life, but Salvation. This is not the good that must be accomplished, but the good received from God. The gospel does not create any moral distinction, but accomplishes a revelation of Grace; there is no normative ethic of the Good, but an ethic of grace, which is the complete opposite.[6] The gospel, consequently, far from confirming the morality of the world, overturns and contradicts it, just as much in what man designates as good as in his claim to judge evil. As a consequence of the event of the Revelation in Jesus Christ, a tension is established between grace, on the one hand, and the morality of men, on the other. Henceforth, a Morality that defines the Good is not a sort of bridge thrown down between the worlds of man and of God. The Good and the Virtue represented by Plato's superhuman ideal are of man and in man. The accomplishment of what man calls the good does not bring him any closer to God. Nothing can bring man closer to God. Recall that after Adam's rejection he leaves Eden, and henceforth the entrance to the garden is guarded by vigilant, flaming cherubim who cannot be duped. The quest for Eden is far more impossible than the quest for the Holy Grail; at least the Grail was still on earth. But here, nothing enables us to cross the absolute space separating Adam from Eden; nothing can appease the anger of these guardians. "Remember that God is in heaven, and you are on earth." No words are more pitiless than these. And the good that you perform, however ideal it may be, is never anything but the earthly good, having no common measure with the requirement of God, with what He calls Good. This Good exists, certainly, but it is beyond the reach of your hands.

The requirement of God is Holiness. Now, all accumulation of virtues, good works, lofty sentiments, right intentions—all this is not Holiness. Even the Roman Catholic Church, with its pronounced penchant for mistaking exceptional moral purity for Holiness, still avoids confusing them completely. Holiness is of another order; it is never a succession of just and pure acts, and these latter do not necessarily express it. All the good that man can do remains the good of man and never becomes the Holiness of God. Yet, this latter is what God expects of man, nothing less. There is an impassable abyss between the two. No value created by man,

---

6. "But this, the grace of God, *is* the answer to the ethical problem. For it sanctifies man. It claims him for God. It puts him under God's command. It gives predetermination to his self-determination so that he obeys God's command" (Barth, *CD* II.2, 516).

And in this sense we agree with Niebuhr's thesis (*Moral Man and Immoral Society*), according to which social life is amoral when considered objectively. (As far as Christian ethics, there is no social morality; only man can be the subject of morality.) But we do not agree with him if this is taken to imply that there is no morality in society, and that habits and traditions are outside the purview of morality.

no accumulation of such values can attain the Holiness of God, which is not a morality raised to the absolute level, nor *perfection*, but the very life of God.

This, incidentally, allows us to reject the argument of those who seek a proof or condemnation of Christianity in the good. "Christians do more good than others . . ." or, inversely, "What good is Christianity? You don't need to be a Christian to do good . . ." In effect, both of these attempts to measure the Christian life according to the standard of what men decree as Good can only lead to disappointment. We will need to discuss the extremely diverse conceptions of the Good among men; and what are accepted as universal standards of the good, to which Western adversaries of Christianity refer, are precisely conceptions stemming from a deformed and laicized Christianity. No, this good in no way permits us to sneak our way into paradise. There is no bridge that man can take up to God. Glory and thanks be to God: he descended to us, he came to the earth, he crossed the abyss, and it is here that we encounter him, even as he consented to enter the domain of our morality, submitted himself to its judgments—he whose condemnation has judged our morality and our justice!

And yet, man possesses a morality? Natural morality exists?[7] First of all, let us avoid a misunderstanding. It is obvious that a natural morality exists! The entire problem resides in the fact that some want to see this natural morality as righteous before God, or even better, as an expression of the will of God in nature—yet another bridge with Eden. We note that in the Bible, the word "nature" is very often used in a neutral sense: there is a natural order of relations between men and women; this means that it is ordered by biology. And likewise, it is in conformity with nature that women have long hair; this too is a matter of biology. We can take absolutely nothing from these several texts. When the Bible speaks of Nature in a sense that includes a moral or spiritual evaluation, we really must admit that the opinion of the Holy Spirit expressed in Scripture is rather discouraging. Nowhere are we told that nature is conformed to the good, or capable of bringing about the good. On the contrary, all men are children of wrath by nature (Eph 2:3), which is to say that conformity to our

---

7. This natural morality is certainly fragile precisely because of its natural foundation (Niebuhr, *Interpretation of Christian Ethics*, 50). It seems to us that the study of Vos (*ZEE* 6, 1958, 347) reestablishes neither the universality nor the solidity of natural morality. But what seems the most unsustainable in this study is the relation between natural morality and Christian morality.

nature merely destines us to suffer the wrath and retribution of God. Likewise, there is antinomy between nature and grace. Far be it from us to think of entering this theological debate! We will limit ourselves to what is strictly necessary for our ethical questioning. So then, Paul reminds us (Rom 11:24) that nature never merits grace. Even if nature could lead us to perform what we call good, this is worthless for obtaining the grace of God. And when man remains natural man, we know for certain that he does not welcome the Spirit (1 Cor 2:14), and this is also what Jesus says to Peter right after he confesses his faith . . . and Peter is very well-informed about nature when he writes, "like brutes who abandon themselves to their natural tendencies . . ."[8] (2 Pet 2:12—granted, this epistle was probably not written by Peter, but this matters very little). We could multiply citations of this kind; what matters is understanding that from the biblical point of view, a thing is not good simply because it is natural—quite the contrary! Here we are precisely at the polar opposite of modern thought, which considers an act legitimate as soon as it conforms to nature. The Bible reveals to us that nature has nothing to do with the good (according to God) and that the fact that a morality might be natural in no way guarantees that it correctly defines the good or could guide us to it! Once again, quite the contrary! From the biblical point of view, a natural morality is in fact exactly what we are talking about when we describe a morality of the fall: natural morality does not define a good and evil "from before the fall," in a sort of miraculous knowledge related to the EAST of Eden; it defines a good and an evil within the fall and disobedience, and consequently foreign to the will of God. Incidentally, it must be noted that the Bible—which speaks of nature—nowhere alludes to a natural morality. This question is never raised; it is an invention of theologians and philosophers. Nevertheless, we must examine the only text where we might see an allusion to this infused science of the good, which according to Catholic theology and Protestant liberalism belongs to man by nature—the sole text upon which we have built the entire construction of natural morality, moral conscience, natural law, etc. So much rests on a sole biblical text, which is not confirmed anywhere else in the meaning that has been attributed to it. We are referring to the famous text of Romans 2:14–15: "When the pagans, who do not possess the law, do naturally what the law requires, these, though not having the law, are a law to themselves. They show that the work of the law is written on their hearts, to which their own

---

8. TN: I have translated Ellul's citation directly, which emphasizes the abandonment to "natural" instincts. The NRSV reads, "like irrational animals, mere creatures of instinct, born to be caught and killed."

conscience also bears witness . . ."⁹ This is interpreted in an elementary manner by saying that natural man (the pagan), spontaneously and by following his nature, can accomplish the commandment revealed by God in his law; which proves that we do not need this revelation since this law is written in the heart of man, and that he need only listen to his conscience. In addressing this text, even Calvin admits that natural man retains some scrap of justice, some natural glimmer of the good, a view and a judgment that allow man to discern between wrong and right, between uprightness and wickedness. To us, this text does not appear so certain and convincing at all. Pointing out that this text is the only one of its kind will not be welcomed, I think. And yet, it must be said. The agreement of biblical texts is essential. One text must be interpreted by the ensemble of others, and when taken from its theological and historical context, one text does not have a decisive weight. Nevertheless, of course, there can be no question of setting it aside, nor of bending it to square it with the rest. It is possible that there could be contradictions in the Bible, that there would be contrary currents of inspiration; but it is very unlikely that these contradictions would be found in the same author's writings—and almost impossible that they would appear in the same book. Now in the epistle to the Romans, we see that concerning the pagans, Paul affirms first of all that they are totally perverted (1:18-32): man is delivered to his debased mind. And there is no exception to this statement. Then: all men are under the power of sin (3:9), the whole world is guilty before God (3:19); and our text is situated precisely within this framework! Can we imagine a more glaring contradiction: in chapter 2, Paul says that the pagans spontaneously carry out the will of God, in chapters 1 and 3 he says they are incapable of doing so? It would be rather difficult to accept. First, let us consider this text by taking the word "pagan" in its obvious sense. We can immediately note that in reality, it is not said that there is a natural law written in the heart of all men; on the one hand it is the *work* of the law (*ergon*) that is written . . . that is, not the will of God in itself, but a work, a consequence. There is no "forensic," intrinsic knowledge of the law itself; there is only an execution of the work demanded by this law, and this putting-into-practice, this work accomplished for motives that might be very diverse, only demonstrates a coincidence between the revealed will of God and the action of man—who can be perfectly unaware that in doing

---

9. TN: In order to make sense of the following discussion, I have modified the NRSV text at three points to reflect the French translation given by Ellul: first, I have substituted *the pagans* [*les païens*] for the NRSV's "Gentiles"; second, I have substituted *naturally* [*naturellement*] for the NRSV's "instinctively"; and third, I have substituted *the work of the law* [*l'œuvre de la loi*] for the NRSV's "what the law requires."

so, he accomplishes the will of God. But when they perform this work, in doing so they demonstrate that they are a (just) law for themselves; Paul's formula is very clear. He does not say that they have the law of God in them, but that they *are a law for themselves*. In short, the work that they accomplish transforms them into a law. This has nothing to do with a natural morality written by God on the heart of every man and woman. On the contrary, this recalls[10] the parable of the man with two sons (Matt 21:28, in which the son who says *no* actually *does* what the Father asked), and even more precisely, the parable of the last judgment (Matt 25:37) where the just are unaware of what they have done, having accomplished the work of the law without it effectually being a law for them at all, neither a revealed law nor a natural law. And it is true that this coincidence can take place, and that—for very diverse motives, of a natural order, and sometimes very bad—in his acts, man accomplishes a work that God adopts as his own, in his love. On the other hand, it does not say that "Man" has a law coming from God in his heart, as part of his nature; only that *when* it happens (in short, by chance) that the pagan accomplishes the will of God, *then* he shows that he *has* the work of the law written in his heart. But this text is thus doubly restrictive: first, it in no way concerns all men, but only the one who accomplishes the law; we therefore cannot take this to say that everyone has the law written on their heart, and that they obey or disobey it. Next, when this act is performed, it is shown that the work is written on the heart; not that "man had the law in his heart" (with the implication that he obeyed it), but "he *has*..." from the moment where he accomplished this will of God. And this corresponds to the formula "They are transformed into a law for themselves." Consequently, in all this there is never a question of a general natural law valid for all men, or of Man. Finally, we should highlight that this law which Paul speaks of is not just any moral law whatsoever, but the law of Justification. Our text comes after verse 13: those who put it in practice will be *justified*—and before verse 16: "It is this which will appear one day when God will judge the secret actions of men by Jesus Christ."[11] Now, Paul's entire moral teaching affirms that the accomplishment of moral works and the application of the law are incapable of saving us. We are saved by grace in Jesus Christ. Here, it is a matter of this salvation, of this justification. How could we believe that the justifying law is written in the heart of each man, in his nature, by

10. TN: At this point, the 2013 French edition makes a small correction, changing Ellul's "this recalls either..." [*cela fait penser soit*] to "this recalls..." [*cela fait penser*].

11. TN: Verses 15b and 16 in the NRSV read, "and their conflicting thoughts will accuse or perhaps excuse them on the day when, according to my gospel, God, through Jesus Christ, will judge the secret thoughts of all."

origin and without conversion, without grace? Paul's theology never lapses: Jesus Christ alone justifies, the law only condemns. How could we believe that here he intended to tell us of a law that justifies? And this brings us to the well-known, very strong interpretation of the text by Barth in his *Römerbrief*. According to Barth, the pagans in question here are the "pagan-Christians." In effect, it regularly happens that Paul refers to these Christians of pagan origin by the shorter term "pagans," as opposed to the Jews (for example, Rom 11:13; 15:9). Henceforth, the ideas of the "heart" and nature are explained. The heart upon which the work of the law is written is precisely the transformed heart, the heart of stone become a living heart, the heart where God has engraved his will according to the prophetic promise of Jeremiah 31:33 and Ezekiel 11:19. But this is no longer the natural heart; it is the heart from which grace itself has ripped out the roots of sin and planted life in Jesus Christ. The nature according to which these pagans accomplish the will of God is not the nature of the flesh, but the new nature; it is not the nature that is oriented toward death, but the new man who is moving toward life, the nature of the olive branch grafted onto the elect olive tree. Thus there is no natural moral law. The pagan who has converted to Christ does not need to learn the Jewish law or be circumcised; this is the meaning of this text. And the parallelism between the law of circumcision established by Paul in verses 15–25 is very illuminating in this regard. Just as these pagans need not be circumcised to be saved in Jesus Christ because they have the circumcision of the heart, so they need not learn the law of Moses, since they now have (because of their faith in Jesus Christ) the work of the law written on their heart. Thus they are, in fact, a law for themselves: God gives them his Holy Spirit, and by the same token, a new heart that knows the divine will, in such a manner that these pagans, too, can live according to this will. Thus this is inscribed within the entire general theme of the epistle to the Romans: relations between Jews and Christians. As for the Jews, they know the law directly, intellectually; but they resist grace, they do not accomplish the work of the law, they do not obey the will of God. The pagans who have converted to Christ are not well informed concerning the law, they have not learned it, but they accomplish its work because Jesus Christ has sent them the Holy Spirit. To us, this in-depth grasp of these verses seems perfectly convincing since it is inscribed in the general line of Paul's thought, and in the precise context of chapters 1–3 of this epistle. We know, nevertheless, the reservations that one may have in this regard. But we would like to point out that even if one does not accept this interpretation, and if one wishes to hold to the idea that Paul is speaking purely and simply of pagans, this in no way leads one to believe that this is an allusion to a natural morality: the entire first part of our argument stands. Consequently, whether we adopt one or the other interpretation of the word "pagan," it amounts to the same thing as concerns the notion of a natural morality, taken in the sense of a knowledge of good and evil infused in nature, and of a natural power of man to discern and accomplish the good.

Theologically, the construction of natural morality rests on a philosophy; it is a will to find an accord between the facts of the world and theological facts. This perspective invites (or presupposes) several serious errors: in all formulations of natural morality, there is *no* mention of Jesus Christ. In reality, we do not see what the work of God accomplished in Jesus Christ could really do in this construction. Neither the Incarnation, nor the Death, nor the Resurrection have anything to do with a theory of Natural Morality: we thus find ourselves before a "Christianity" without Jesus Christ. For if man is capable of naturally "compensating" for sin by his good conduct, if the fall is only a "weakening," well, there really isn't any need for Jesus Christ; Buddha, Socrates, or Nietzsche do just as much for the moral or religious uplifting of man conforming to his nature. This leads us to observe a second error.

We are led to eliminate the doctrine of Justification, for precisely this doctrine annihilates every claim of man to know Justice naturally, on his own—much less to effectuate it. If God alone is just and he does not confer his Justice on man except by Justifying him, and if he does not make his work of Justice known to man except by revealing himself to him, then this means that man knows nothing of Justice outside of this revelation and that there is no justice inscribed in his Nature. The Doctrine of Natural Morality is an aspect of the incessantly rebirthing heresy in which we seek to harmonize Grace and Nature by promoting the latter.[12]

The third error is one of method: it is the transposition of the theological into the philosophical—that is, the transformation of the living Event of Love and grace into a Principle of systematic construction and the elaboration of an explanation. It is a utilization of Revelation for the satisfaction of man, which crystallizes, immobilizes this revelation in order to insert it into its system, and in doing so removes all of its value.

Finally, we must address one question: the doctrinaires of Natural Morality believe in the existence of a Nature of man. We talk endlessly

---

12. "The permanence of natural law holds to the unity of human nature; its relative variability holds to the relative variation of this same nature." Sertillanges, *La philosophie morale de saint Thomas d'Aquin*, 113.

about "the essential Nature of man." But from where do we get this, and who makes it known to us?[13] If we are talking about a philosophical concept (which is in fact at the origin of the notion of Natural Law with Aristotle and the Stoics), we must recognize that modern philosophy (existentialism, phenomenology) rejects this concept, and perhaps there are grounds for reconsidering the problem. If it concerns a notion taken from the sciences (psychology, history, sociology, for example), here too we must proceed carefully; for these very sciences that affirmed the existence of this human nature half a century ago dispute it today. Modern psychology and even contemporary history no longer admit the idea of a permanent, stable, etc., human nature at all. If, finally, we claim to find this idea of human nature in the Bible, we have already examined that question. Incidentally, in placing ourselves in the perspective of these authors, we recall that the Bible is taken here to be the decisive authority. But this implies that we must accept its authority in other domains—including questions of Morality! Now, the Bible tells us nothing about a natural Morality. Consequently, if we build our idea of a human nature on the Bible, we certainly cannot assert the existence of a natural Morality on this basis.

In all cases, we can maintain that the will to construct a natural Morality corresponds to a valorization of man and to a diminishment of the work of Jesus Christ. There is a fundamental contradiction between the intimate content of Revelation and natural Morality. For the church, this latter is always one mode of conforming herself to the World.

---

13. Despite his nuanced approach, Häring converges with this approach in this formula: "The fundamental principles of the natural moral law can be known with certainty by every normal man who possesses his reason, for they are self-evident" (*La loi du Christ*, 1:374). Here, it is a question of principles, that is, of coordinates knowable by reason, which have nothing in common with the action of the Holy Spirit revealing the work of God in Jesus Christ.

And yet, a moral conscience exists?[14] It is true that on several occasions the New Testament speaks of conscience,[15] primarily Paul. Again, we must be clear about the meaning of this term: the Greek word *syneidesis* employed here means "conscience of one's thoughts and of one's acts"; it indicates that one is conscious.[16] The majority of the texts in which Paul uses this word very clearly entail this application: my conscience bears witness (Rom 9:1), a weak conscience (1 Cor 8:7), my freedom cannot be judged by another's conscience (1 Cor 10:29). Our conscience bears witness that we have behaved in holiness (2 Cor 1:12). And even the texts that speak of "motives of conscience" (Rom 13:5; 1 Pet 2:19) must also be included in this perspective: to be conscious of . . . Thus, "conscience" here is not a moral quality, an interior value; rather, it is perspicuity. And the majority of these passages demonstrate a relation between faith, knowledge, and conscience. In effect, faith gives us a light that allows us to clearly understand ourselves in relation to Jesus Christ, in whom we believe. The knowledge of the gospel gives us the means to be conscious. It is a question of being aware of what we are doing, of our passions, of our sin, of our acts—as well as of our intentions—and also of our holiness. Conscience is a clear vision that allows us, for example (but this is not all it allows us), to perform . . . our examination of conscience! A weak conscience does not mean a weak disposition toward doing the good, but an insufficient knowledge of the gospel, a knowledge that does not allow for true judgment (for example, everything Paul says about meat sacrificed to idols is very clear on this subject). When Paul commends keeping faith

---

14. So much has been written on this moral conscience . . . "inner agent of the good," "judge of our acts," "receptive organ of the call of Christ"—and these are only the least of its virtues! It is the "sense" that allows us to hear the word of God (Häring, *La loi du Christ*, 1:188). And it is also held that all peoples accept the existence of moral conscience because Socrates spoke of his daemon, and because the Stoics made *syneidesis* a participation in the eternal law of harmony.

For a description of the formation of the moral conscience, see Søe, *Christliche Ethik*, §5, §7. However, he wonders if Paul already had this interpretation, which we doubt. On the other hand, he does well to note how moral conscience is a human phenomenon which in no way refers to Revelation; it is not the "place" where God speaks (§9).

15. Only by abusing the texts can Häring speak of conscience in certain texts of the Old Testament (Gen 4:12; 2 Sam 24:10; etc.). He attributes to conscience what is very clearly the event of the presence of God. It is not his conscience that accuses; it is in the presence of God that man discovers he is a sinner. And only a very cursory view of the texts of Paul allows us to see in them the contemporary concept of the moral conscience. Furthermore, to claim that acting according to faith or according to conscience is the same thing on the basis of Rom 14:20–23 is to go too far, for there is obviously no question of conscience in this text.

16. And the verb that this word comes from confirms this meaning: *synoida*, which is either "to know with an other, to be confident of . . ." or "to know in oneself, to be conscious of . . ."

and a good conscience (1 Tim 1:18–19) or holding the mystery of the faith with a clear conscience (1 Tim 3:9), he means precisely that faith must be linked to a conscious doing, to a becoming-aware,[17] to the examination of one's life in relation to the faith. And the good conscience spoken of by Peter or Paul (Acts 23:1; 1 Tim 1:5) is the consciousness of doing good, that is, of living in Christ.

This is emphasized by M. H. Roux in his commentary on the pastoral epistles,[18] when he writes, "This totalitarian character of the Christian faith makes it the creator of good conscience in man; the liberation of man by Christ and in Christ implies that he would have a completely new awareness of himself and of his entire existence, and particularly of his relation with men.[19] He is called to see, and thus to know and understand; and first of all in relation to himself. This new self-consciousness is truly good for the Christian, for it does not come from his own heart nor from a natural light; it comes from the one who, by coming into the world, sheds light on all men. The Johannine theme of sight and light translates (in its own manner, to be sure) this direct relation between faith and a new moral conscience, a right discernment of lived conduct. Such a good conscience, guaranteed to judge correctly and to choose the will of God, can only be held in faith, i.e., in Christ. Finally, this good conscience remains the touchstone of the faith, which allows us to hold it sincerely and without hypocrisy; only this good conscience can inspire good works, can produce a love, a justice and a holiness whose authenticity is guaranteed by Christ himself."

Conversely, the author of the epistle to the Hebrews shows us that conscience is also consciousness of sin (Heb 10:2) in indicating that if the sacrifices recounted in the Old Testament had really purified man, he would no longer be conscious of his sin. It is worth reflecting on this epistle, for it contains a truly remarkable teaching: on the one hand it teaches us that the ritual worship ordained in the law, the sacrifices, etc., cannot make us perfect in relation to conscience. This is a question of worship; it thus does not concern *moral* conscience. It is a spiritual consciousness. It also concerns a conscience that can be better or worse, perfected (or not); this is in no way a natural conscience. There is no conscience of this order in the nature of man. The ensemble of the epistles show us that this conscience is the fruit of faith, a consequence of revelation. We can lose it in losing the faith (1 Tim 1:18–19). And the epistle to the Hebrews tells us

---

17. TN: Here and in the following pages, "becoming-aware" translates Ellul's key term *prise de conscience*.

18. Roux, *Les épîtres pastorales*.

19. TN: I have added this period; the French edition lacks a break in the sentence.

that Jesus Christ purifies our conscience from dead works; this concerns the works of the law. The law was a revelation of God; it thus provoked conscience. But it committed man to a sterile path of works, of practices that precisely tested the conscience in relation to false criteria, engaged it in false judgments. Only the total revelation of God in Jesus Christ brings full light, true perspicacity; it allows us to see ourselves in the love of God, which fills us with joy and embarrassment at the same time. And our becoming-aware is no longer based on our works, the works required by the law, but on the love of God revealed in Jesus Christ crucified. Only at the foot of the cross does conscience become true, and only here can it—potentially—be good. Everywhere else, it is perverted and can only be bad. To summarize this teaching, then, we will say that conscience is above all the fact of being conscious of what one is. This conscience can thus be a neutral quality of man, but usually this becoming-aware includes judgment, or at the very least serves to formulate judgments. But the judgment that conscience performs depends on the criteria that the conscience will apply.

In this dialogue, natural conscience only uses human elements. We could say that there is tension among the various tendencies and influences of man. It is difficult to affirm that there is a "better" which judges a "worse" according to fixed and certain criteria; current psychology tends to dissolve this notion.[20] And when we judge ourselves, it is always according to our own criteria, which really gives us a definite advantage. Whence the validity of Paul's declaration: "I do not even judge myself. I am not aware of anything against myself, but I am not thereby acquitted. It is the Lord who judges me" (1 Cor 4:3–4). And here we have a second element of becoming-aware: the criteria in relation to which we are called to judge. We might say that conscience bears on reality (the first element) and on truth (the second element). This can only happen when the conscience, illuminated by revelation, receives knowledge of the truth from God. Still, man must bring faith to bear for conscience to make use of this knowledge. We thus see that conscience will lead him to his own "self-critique," to consider his acts and words in relation to revealed truth. It is indeed an instrument of judgment, but only in a subordinate manner. This allows us to reject the majority of moral definitions of conscience; conscience is not the place where the good is naturally inscribed in man.

The doctrine of grace eliminates the possibility of a meaningful moral conscience. Conscience is neither the reflection of God (who only reveals

---

20. Henri Baruk's notion of conscience (*Psychiatrie morale expérimentale*) is very close to what we are describing here. "The moral conscience corresponds less to a commandment than to an interior judgment . . ."

himself in Jesus Christ); nor the place where God speaks (for we cannot dissociate the encounter with God in Scripture from the encounter of God in one's being by the Holy Spirit); nor the voice that judges us (since our true guilt is revealed by God in the moment that he gives himself to us); nor the receptacle of truth hidden in us, which revelation only brings to light (without grace, we cannot even believe in the gospel; how could it preexist in us?). Conscience possesses no knowledge; the Holy Spirit moving in us establishes a dialogue which is different from that of conscience. Accepting the validity of the moral conscience ultimately evacuates the entire doctrine of grace.

There is no voice of conscience identical to the voice of the good. Conscience is not the discernment of good and evil as objective and independent entities; it is not a natural capacity of man to grasp the good and to judge himself by the content of conscience. Of course, all of these ideas can be endorsed; they have been numerous times, they are respectable—but there is nothing Christian about them. For the Christian faith, there is thus no moral conscience. Karl Barth highlights that "the concept of conscience . . . cannot be classed as an anthropological but only as an eschatological concept. It is only in the light of the integral connection of our existence with that of Jesus Christ, in the light of the future consummation . . . that conscience . . . can be understood and claimed as . . . the organ of our participation in the good." The conscience is nothing by itself; it "cannot possibly be interpreted as an independent 'voice of God' . . . we are not made judges" of good and evil, but simply "witnesses to the judgment to which we are subjected."[21]

Thus far, we have primarily spoken of the conscience of the converted man, which is evidently the conscience that most concerned the apostles. Nevertheless, two texts speak of the conscience of unbelievers. It goes without saying that this capacity of becoming-aware is not exclusively reserved for Christians! The first of these texts is categorical and very harsh: "Everything is pure for those who are pure, but nothing is pure for those who are defiled and unbelieving; their intelligence and their conscience are defiled" (Titus 1:15). The unbelievers in question here are either Christians who have turned away from the faith or Jews, as the preceding verses show. Here, conscience is thus perverted, that is, it is incapable of producing a just evaluation of conduct; since it has turned away from the truth (from a Christian point of view), it no longer has authentic criteria. This conscience is defiled because it will use other criteria than the gospel, which necessarily take part in evil; thus, the judgment of conscience will involve the entirety of

---

21. Barth, *CD* II.2, 668.

man in evil, since his becoming-aware is absolutely ineffective as such. The other text is the famous text of Romans 2:14–15. We have already examined this text concerning natural morality; let us examine the only passage that concerns the conscience. The pagans "show that the work of the law is written on their hearts, to which their own conscience also bears witness; and their conflicting thoughts will accuse or perhaps excuse them . . ." Basically, this text sheds no additional light on the conscience. There is no question of a moral conscience or the voice of the conscience, no more here than anywhere else. With the work of the law of God written on the hearts of these men, conscience refers to this work, and, proceeding to this discussion of judgment and of becoming-aware, it bears witness to just action in relation to this work of the law. Thus it means exactly the same thing here as what we have seen already. Thus, biblical thought knows nothing of this alleged moral conscience. Conscience is not an intact piece of man recalling the heavens . . .[22]

---

22. We will conclude this section by recalling two studies on this problem: Dietrich Bonhoeffer rightly notes that the conscience is a phenomenon of duplication of being which in reality is a product of the fall (*Ethics,* 307). The criteria of conscience is man's agreement with himself, but this is the situation of sin. Thus conscience in no way implies a relation of man with God; and instead of leading man to find his unity in the covenant with God (an act of grace), it purports to allow man to find his relation with God in interior peace with himself. This is the very inversion of the decision of God. Thus, conscience leads man to an analysis of self and to a radical inability to grasp the will of God. It is the center of man's autonomy (*Ethics,* 277); it thus must be vanquished in its identity so that man can be submitted to Christ. Therefore, man responsible before God takes the place of the phenomenon of moral conscience.

Second, and in the same line of thought, we are entirely in agreement with Ricoeur (*The Symbolism of Evil*) when he analyzes the relation of conscience and the gaze of God. "My own observation of myself is the attempt of self-awareness to approximate the absolute view; I desire to know myself as I am known" (85). "With guilt, 'conscience' is born; a responsible agent appears, to face the . . . demand for holiness" (143), but this conscience degrades into a moral conscience that judges good and evil, that becomes, in itself, the reference for the good: ". . . let the *before thee* be even forgotten, and the consciousness of fault becomes guilt and no longer sin at all; it is 'conscience' that now becomes the *measure* of evil in a completely solitary experience" (102, Ricoeur's italics). "While it is indefinite, the guilty conscience is also a conscience that is shut in" (146). "To become oneself the tribunal of oneself is to be alienated" (145).

4

Morality Is of the Order of Necessity

As a consequence of the fall, necessity is introduced into the world. Determinism, Mechanization of History, scientific law, Destiny, Ananke—whatever name might conceal it, under whatever form man might recognize it, necessity is always the same. There is no great difference between the deep sense of implacable fatality that weighed on the family of the Atreidae[1] (who serve as a type of all humanity), which inevitably ran its course through the ignorance, unawareness, and apparently free decisions of each member of this family, and the Law of Large Numbers weighing on modern crowds, which is expressed in man, in his apparently free decisions, and in his spontaneity, reducing him to a generic pattern. There is no great difference between the blind, immobile *Ananke* which enforces its standard even on the gods, and scientific law which comes to fruition and fulfills itself, cutting across all our pretensions to freedom and leading us to say,

---

1. TN: In Greek mythology, the Atreidae were the descendants of Atreus, a cursed and corrupt king who partook in the murder of his stepbrother, Chrysippus, and was eventually himself slain. The stories of his lineage reflect similar curses; for example, his lineage begins with Tantalus, whom the gods confine to a pool of water under a fruit tree. Whenever Tantalus tries to satisfy his thirst or hunger with the water or fruit, they recede before his reach. Necessity of this type—a fatal inversion of the best of human intentions that results in their opposites—is indicated (and sometimes personified as a deity) by the Greek word *ananke*. This necessity is a long-standing theme in Ellul's life and work, especially regarding Western political aspirations. In addition to the following discussion, cf. *Violence: Reflections from a Christian Perspective*; *The Political Illusion*; *The Ethics of Freedom*; "Les structures de la liberté"; and Clendenin, *Theological Method in Jacques Ellul*, especially 57–86.

"Therefore, God does not exist." And in so doing, we confuse the creation of God with the order of the fall.

As a creation made for the love and joy of God, it was the very locus of liberty, for nothing could have expressed God except the freedom of his creation. Nothing could have responded to God except gratuitous spontaneity. Nothing could have loved God, except the free play of a creature turned toward its creator—neither duty, nor constraint, nor organization. There could be no necessity in this creation since God is not subject to necessity; what he creates is not the fruit of a torturous and implacable will, but of love. Everything in this nature is spontaneous, because it is all a response to the spontaneity of God. Each thing has a function, but this is a free compliance with a word offered it by God. Everything is gratuitousness, because it is all a response to the gratuitousness of creation (since God creates not out of necessity, but out of pure gratuitousness) and out of his love: if he loves, it is not because . . . He loves gratuitously. There is nothing that must be done, established, or given. There are no constraints or duties to fulfill. Precisely, there is only the play of a life that gives because it has been received, that has significance because it is before God. But no less precisely, Adam's rupture with the Father provokes negation, chaos, and risks returning everything to nothingness: when this freedom is no longer in love, it is the great Tohu Bohu.[2] Love is evacuated by the will to power, and so the significance of everything changes. The order laid down by God ceases to be gratuity and becomes an outer constraint. Were it not persistently maintained, creation would disappear. The function proposed by the Word ceases to be spontaneity and becomes obligation. Life is no longer play but becomes work and exertion. And man bends under necessity because he could not live in the freedom of love. Thus, this very creation enters the order of necessity.[3] And from this very moment man knows very well that he is subject to *fatum*,[4] that

---

2. TN: *Tohu bohu* is the transliteration of the Hebrew text in Gen 1:2, which the NRSV translates as "a formless void."

3. The passage to the order of necessity is much more than a "tarnishing of freedom." Whatever the dialectical relation between contradictory themes may be, they are still exclusive of one another. Where there is freedom, there is no power for evil, for freedom is only found in Christ. It is impossible to say that sin inaugurates an era of freedom (Ricoeur, *Symbolism of Evil*, 254). It is impossible to say that a country which falls into enemy hands intact can still control itself (ibid., 156). (Comparison is not reason.) Whatever truth there may be in the proposition that evil cannot be as original as Good, it is no less true that slavery (real slavery, not a Symbol of thought) is not freedom, and that the rupture with God leads to this slavery which translates into the order of necessity. We thus cannot agree with Ricoeur's explanation of the servile will, among other items (ibid., 151–57).

4. TN: Latin for *destiny, fate*.

a destiny has been inscribed in nature, around him, in him, a destiny that no one escapes. Everything is written. It must be so for the world to continue. The tiniest atom of freedom threatens the very existence of the world. The littlest *real* political liberty likewise threatens society and the state. After the fall, man's true choice is no longer "Liberty or Death," but "Liberty or Life."[5] Life can only be maintained through a complete and painstaking network of constraints—from the unknown constraints governing Matter and Worlds, to juridical and social constraints. Everything is maintained by an iron straitjacket. And freedom leads to destruction, since from now on, this freedom is situated outside of love. If a planet does not follow its orbit, if an animal wants to be free with respect to eating or reproduction, if man wants to be free with respect to law . . . at every level from top to bottom, necessity is the condition for the preservation of the fallen world; and in fact, we could say that when any freedom is asserted, it leads to death. The triumph of the tiniest freedom demands immense sacrifices, as we know all too well—the Martyrs of freedom!—and when this freedom is won (I am speaking of freedom in the illusory domain of politics and economics), it immediately deteriorates into new constraints. But those who fought, who knew the moment of freedom inscribed in their fight, are dead. Dead—that is, reduced to the most complete necessity. For the final point where necessity is inscribed, its most absolute sign, its irrefutable presence—is death. Death, the passage by which the one who could claim to be free becomes a Thing. At this instant, the victory of Destiny is unavoidable, and those who claim to escape it by way of freedom inevitably find it again in death. Such is this order that is not that of the love of God, but is nevertheless maintained by God since it is still preferable to nothingness, the negation of God.

Situated as it is in the order of the fall, morality is inscribed in the order of necessity. What does this mean?[6] Undoubtedly, it implies that morality itself

---

5. TN: A reference to the famous slogan of French revolutionaries in 1793.

6. Karl Barth forcefully describes this entry into the universe of Necessity by virtue of the knowledge of good and evil. "He is the one who not only can do this, but *must* do it . . . wherever he goes or stays, the line is drawn between good and evil. He is confronted on all sides by *sic et non*, motives and quietives, commands and prohibitions . . . subjecting him to the highest possible degree of unsettlement, assaulting him, grasping at him, forcing him in different directions . . . His eyes are now open but only like those of a victim of insomnia. He now has to choose and decide and judge on all sides. He has to try to hew a track for himself through the unending primeval forest of claims. He has to establish his preference. With the help of a classification of values he has to set up a little system of values which he thinks he can and should satisfy first . . . He will never

is already a constraint. Morality is always presented as an ensemble of duties and obligations, and no society or group of any kind could live without it. Of course, there is a hierarchy in these determinations! They are not all on the same level; not all are necessary and inevitable. Morality is situated among the least rigorous; it is even less constraining than juridical law. Nevertheless, it obviously represents an attempt to direct man, to impose a certain model of intentions and actions on him. Thus, among other things, the consequence of man's decision to be like God is that he is submitted to a certain good which, though it is not the will of God, constitutes part of the order that is necessary for the world to live. And the low necessity of morality (as compared to a higher necessity of scientific laws, for example) owes to its supererogatory character in the order of preservation of creation. If man does not follow the rules of life in a biological or chemical sense, if he claims to be exempt from them, he inevitably dies and vanishes.[7] If he disobeys the moral rules of his group, the necessity is not immediately or implacably recognized. There are delays, ambiguities, hopes of escaping punishment. Man can claim to be free from this moral law; he will not die. He may experience some disagreement, in his "conscience" (remorse, etc.), or in his social relations (the judgments of others). But it is not this man himself, but his group that is put in question by his disobedience. Moral law is a necessity not for individual survival, but for society. It is absolutely essential to consider that biblically, observing morality is in no way a condition of individual life or individual success on earth, any more than it is a condition of eternal life. The book of Job reminds us that, precisely, this accomplishment of the good has no relation with individual survival. On the natural level,

---

satisfy all claims, and he will not really satisfy even one. This is the divine likeness of the godless—of Adam, the man who would not first satisfy God . . . When man sins . . . against God . . . *he is delivered up*, like a hunted beast to the hounds, to what the world and life and men want of him, to what, above all, he himself must continually want of himself." Barth, *CD* II.2, 79 [Ellul's italics, except for the Latin phrase].

It is commonplace to speak of the slavery of sin, but in reality, this must be translated from the interior domain to apply to everything, in speaking of the order of necessity.

7. Despite the increasingly rigorous awareness of the existence of human determinations made possible by the sciences (including psychology and sociology), metaphysicians, moralists, and theologians continue to hold human freedom as a given, a fact of nature. They thus affirm it in the face of every observation, every demonstration, as a presupposition. Incidentally, the question is usually posed in the domain of behavioral and ethical problems. Among Catholics this is expressed, for example, in the formula "man is free in the image of God" (cf. Häring, *La loi du Christ*, 1:145), as if there were no difference between man as he was created and the one that now exists. But we immediately find ourselves obliged to make countless distinctions, for we are truly obliged to remark that this freedom is not: and thus begins a long casuistic on the "Troubles of freedom" (ibid., 1:54–168), which we ultimately cannot escape!

morality concerns the preservation of the group.[8] Everyone must respect certain taboos, perform certain acts, harbor certain sentiments, take part in this or that relationship, experience certain indignations, formulate this approval or that disapproval, because these are the facts of the world in which they live. If they disobey, they weaken the unity, cohesion, and equilibrium of their group. This holds true even for purely interior disobedience, for the group requires an internal adhesion manifested in the moral dimension of an act. What good is a soldier who fights without patriotic enthusiasm? What good is a laborer who works without conscientiousness for his job? What good is the citizen who obeys laws in a purely external manner, with no sense of civic duty? What good is marriage without faithfulness? The outward appearances of social life demand active and effective inward participation from individuals, without which the appearance is stripped of its efficacy and strength. The group can only endure by the perpetuation of virtues. And it is not insignificant that the Latin word *virtus* has the double implication of courage, strength, force, and then of virtue, of morality. Thus we see how morality participates in the necessary order of preservation.[9]

But to say that it is part of necessity implies much more than this: in reality, the good affirmed by morality is determined by necessity. It is not a good in freedom and gratuitousness. Despite all his moral, spiritual, or intellectual claims, man is remarkably determined. When he says that a given act is Good, when he develops an ethical system, he in no way enters the domain of the absolute, not even by one step—no more than he abruptly ends up in the domain of freedom. And so he continues to be conditioned by his heredity, by his biological life, by his milieu, by his education, by his human relations . . . thus, what he arrives at as Good and what he defines as Evil are completely relative, fundamentally variable notions. For it to be otherwise, man would have had to retain part of his original freedom, which he did not—or he would need direct access to the absolute will of God, which he does not have either. Consequently, the morality formulated by man never results from an act of his freedom. Constructing morality and defining the Good are ideological expressions of social and biological determinations in which the individual lives. The Good is determined by historical, geographic, and psychological circumstances. But of course, it is not only this. It is not only the mechanical translation of these necessities; it is also a protest against them. It is a refusal to recognize oneself as determined, an affirmation of the freedom of man. But let us not forget that it is

---

8. Cf. Bergson, *Two Sources*, 12–13, for example.

9. Despite its grandeur, Kant's Ethic particularly illustrates how Ethics belongs to the order of Necessity through the absolutization and impersonality of the law.

precisely when he is most determined that man wants to declare himself the most free! Of course morality expresses man's will—or at least his claim—to transcend his material conditions, and to attain an absolute that is beyond all determination. But even though he devises this means that seems good to him in order to overcome his condition, he constructs this ideal world in, and in relation to, this condition. The determination of conditions and circumstances weighs on morality positively, but negatively as well. Morality is directly conditioned by the environment, the economy, and sociological structures, not only as expression and choice of values, but still more as a protest against these determinations: it constitutes their counterpart, their counterweight, their negative image. But it is developed in relation to *this* recognized weight, to *this* unpleasant image, to the point that man still cannot escape necessity. He is limited to voicing a protest that is itself conditioned by what it protests against. He never manages to formulate a good in itself, escaping these concrete conditions; he never manages to formulate an eternal, immutable, universal good. If we examine the greatest moral declarations, it is easy to see how dated they are, how they are integrated in a certain time and period. For them to make sense again requires effort. They never speak to us directly, without mediation, as they could to their contemporaries. And it is only because we isolate several happy formulas, several rare pearls from an outmoded hodgepodge, that we can still relate to Socrates or Confucius. But when we dissociate and select like this—when we snip several threads that seem strong or shiny today, and that we therefore dub eternal values, from a woven fabric that was meant to be tightly knit—we act as a function of our own necessities, our own conditioning. An Indian thinker probably would not choose the same pearls, and two hundred years ago (or two hundred years from now), a Westerner would have been (or will be) able to treat as negligible what we see as essential. Because two thousand years ago, a Wise man said a sentence that still speaks to us, we exult in the permanence, the freedom, the absolute character of these values. But would this formula have spoken to a man in the Middle Ages? Or to a fifteenth-century Inca? Our decision is as arbitrary as theirs—not at all in the sense of indeterminate freedom in formulating values, but arbitrary in declaring the eternity and immobility of a given value. Even our moral attitude and our moral choices are determined by circumstance. When we forget this, we easily take ourselves for gods; and it is precisely in this that sin resides. Incidentally, when this morality is pronounced, once it is formulated, necessity appears very quickly as soon as it must be performed; for in the presence of this good that he must do, in reality, man always carries out an order of necessity. When morality directly expresses this necessity, there is no discord; in obeying his determinations, by this very fact, man does what is good. When the citizen of a Western country fulfills their draft duty, they act in accordance with the morality of their country, which has made the homeland into an absolute value and military sacrifice into one of the highest virtues. But there is moral conflict when the ethic is formulated as a protest against necessity: man is thus engaged in conflict.[10] But this is not a conflict of moral freedom against material necessity, nor of the ideal imperative against sordid interest, but a conflict of necessities—sociohistorical pressure, on the one hand, psychological refusal and resentment, on the other. When receiving their draft order, in their heart, the same citizen might experience the command "You shall not kill" (assuming that this is admitted as an effective moral rule in the society where he lives, which is not the case in France today, for example!). Most often, following the psychological rule of the economy of means, the individual will obey the most pressing necessity since he insuperably seeks to escape conflict and tension. Thus, on every level of the moral problem, we encounter the grip of determinations—which does not mean that morality is unimportant, of course, but only that it belongs to the world of the fall characterized by necessity.

Morality is always an ethic in a situation of necessity. Ricoeur has recently shown that the morality of our times is one of distress. In reality, all morality is always a morality of distress, because man is always confronted with situations that are bigger than he is. This truth is not limited to our times, and morality is one of the means that man uses to defend himself against his distress; it is a refusal to accept defeat. Along these lines, morality is not limited to expressing necessity, but most often will seek to integrate it. Undoubtedly, one of the biggest motivations for moral formation is man's attempt to subjugate necessity by submitting himself to it—to make necessity into a virtue. Akin to technique or politics (taken in different senses and with extraordinarily different means), morality is an art of the possible. When it is not a constructed theory, morality expresses possibility. What is necessary becomes good. When he is placed in a situation of necessity, we must admit that man cannot only observe the conflict; he must integrate it, translate it into different terms so that it would not render his life impossible. To make necessity into virtue is to reassert control over a situation that escapes us; it is to recover the superior dignity of man which consists in naming the unnamed. What was a purely blind event receives meaning and value because man imposes a name on it. He thus controls the thing, integrates it into a

---

10. Cf. Horney, *Neurotic Personality of Our Time,* on the psychological effects of conflict between accepted morality and social behavior.

system, qualifies it. But this is also a way of coping with the determination that overwhelms us, the burden laid on us by destiny. It is precisely the capability, by bracing oneself through a proclamation of values, to not give in except by integrating that which obliges us, of being able to proudly say (but in a completely different sense than the roman jurists intended it): *coactus voluit, sed voluit*. The will has integrated the constraint; the constraint has not forced the will. Morality always claims this domination, but never fails to include necessity by ordering itself accordingly. In this way all morality always takes the limitations of human nature into account. No morality could hold to the absolute demand of its commandments and the intransigence of its rules. Popular wisdom is adept at finding the route of reconciliations, but even moralists have formulated countless casuistic arguments in the same direction. We know that a rigorous moral rule is impracticable. Once the rule is set in its luminous intransigence, someone comes along to explain it, comment on it, and adapt it. They set out to know: when and how can it be put into practice? How far can we follow it? And so begins the slow process of elaboration in which, from *casus* to *casus*, ambiguity arises. None of the major moralities can escape it: Christianity, Judaism, Confucianism, Islamism . . . The work of moralists has always been to make principles palatable—for they have always been inapplicable; and a morality *must* be applied, or it is nothing. If we keep to the purity of its requirement and its formulation, it will remain a gratuitous and illusory intellectual system. If we want it to be applied, we must make it applicable; that is, it must be brought to the proper level of what man can do. Incidentally, this adaptation can happen without the participation of scholastic philosophers; sometimes it happens spontaneously. Thus the morality of Kant was perfectly adapted to the circumstances of the nineteenth century by the Western bourgeoisie, who probably never read Kant. And whenever a morality retains its integrity, in every case this is simply because nobody applied it—for example, the moralities of Nietzsche and Aristotle. So morality must be adapted, but to what? The response is easy: to the possibilities of man and his weakness—a concession that should not be made, that we should deplore, but that is part of morality itself since man is weak. In reality, it is not correct to speak of weakness, but of necessity. This adaptation, this process of making morality palatable always involves the integration of social, biological, economic, psychological, and historical necessity into ethics. The "limitations of human nature" that must be accounted for are in reality limitations owing to the conditions of one's life, to the conflicts in which one is engaged, to the weights pressing down from all sides. It is because we know in advance that we will not be able to surmount this conditioning that it is fitting to adapt the principles of action and life to this conditioning—in other words, to include this conditioning in the very imperative designed to direct action and life. Failing to account for these necessities would be to elaborate an inapplicable system, but we must always remember that an inapplicable (and unapplied) morality *is not an ethic*. The determination of pure values in themselves that are contemplated (and not lived) can be the occupation of a metaphysician, but it is never that of the moralist. The metaphysician who creates a perfect but unapplied morality succumbs to illusion, for morality is only serious and meaningful to the extent that it informs the life of man. Ethics implies behavior of some kind—whether act, intention, remorse or hope—but also that minimally, some moral claim which further includes an intention to provide orientation and direction to the individual, would be incarnated in a human reality. But when separated from applicability, at best, this intention can be a vain protest of philosophers and ideologues. Now, applying this condition of applicability to morality implies precisely that it must take into account the limitations and necessities of the life of man. It must integrate these determinations, or else it presents man with a discouraging and inassimilable absolute; man will shrink back from the excessive effort required, from the unattainable perfection that he cannot even attempt to reach, knowing all too well (even if only unconsciously) his own limits and weaknesses.

In the same perspective we note that, to a lesser or greater extent, necessity tends to become justification in all morality. At first glance, this appears outrageous! Do not the Good and Virtue consist precisely in refusing necessity, in saying that we must act according to justice and not determinations, and that giving in little by little is not a moral act? And yet, when it accepts the conditioning of man (and it cannot do otherwise), every morality turns this conditioning into a justifying value. We are conditioned by labor, so labor becomes a justifying value—and the same goes for our homeland, education, science, etc. In reality, the process consists of an evolution that leads man to declare that the necessity imposed upon him is "good," to make it a Value (which of course is not done arbitrarily or theoretically: not arbitrarily, for these are not just any necessities, but precisely the most constraining; not theoretically, for this is not the proclamation of a philosophy, but a sort of unanimous agreement, a collective knowledge). And at this moment, obedience to necessity becomes a justification, because it takes on the appearance of obedience to a value. It must be so, or else man would be a perpetual defendant against himself, accused according to a scale of values completely foreign to him—an intolerable situation that would cut off all action at the roots. But when, between the great military coercion of 1792, of which humanity had never seen the like, and the fierce desire to avoid being conscripted into the army (which was traditional), the

Value of the Homeland slips in—thanks to this value, the desire to flee can be subjugated, and man finds himself justified, with the same enthusiasm as the one who obeys the pure constraint of armed service. One way or another, according to various strategies, in all moral systems, necessity ends up as a value—and thus proves to be remarkably effective in allowing man to declare himself just.

However, we must examine the counterpart of this integration of necessity into morality: the latter will be subject to the same fate as everything else that is of the order of determination. Submitted to necessity, it is heading toward the normal end of all flesh, toward the supreme necessity—toward death. The death of morality, of moralities, of ethical systems, of values, is at once the sign and the consequence of their belonging radically, fundamentally, and inescapably to the order of necessity. All morality dies. Everything that man proclaims as good today is ridiculed and scorned tomorrow; or it simply collects dust, becomes anemic and deteriorates on its own. There is no greater proof that morality is definitively part of *this* fallen world ruled by fatality than the successive collapse of ethical values. Submitted to history? Inscribed in civilizations? And for this very reason fleeting and mortal? Yes, certainly; but not only this. There is more that can be said; we must see more clearly. For if morality is mortal, it is not only because it follows the course of history—hatching, developing, reaching a climax, then declining and finally dying. Rather, it is because ultimately, nothing in morality is capable of resisting the determinism of this process; nothing transcends this progression, no part of it endures *in spite of* everything changing around it; nothing is exempt from the common law of absolute fatality—death. As a work of man, it follows its own determinations, even if for a (short) time it raised a protest against this fatality, claiming to have escaped it—an illusory proclamation that experience has not confirmed thus far. My aim is not a simple declaration that morality is relative; we will speak of this fact later on. I aim to offer a different perspective here: the indisputable, unavoidable character of this evolution and its inevitable end are taken here only as evidence of morality's ordination to necessity. An ethic is never a proof of the freedom of man; when it claims to be this, it is at best an escape from reality, and a lie that death will reveal. At this point in our argument, it would be useless to object that the Just, the Good, and the Beautiful are continually affirmed; this is true. But since their contents shift with time and place, since the conduct that is declared good changes, we absolutely cannot deduce some permanence of the Good from them. The same goes for the content of morality as for its name! If I say "Thob" before a man who does not know Hebrew, this word will evoke nothing, no image at all, and will provoke no reaction. I will create the same misunderstanding if I think that saying "Good" before a Japanese man or an Indian from South America will produce the same image for both.

But I would like to briefly point out a final link between morality and necessity, even though it is of a completely different order than the relation studied thus far and will be examined at length further on. Morality is necessary. We need morality. Man cannot escape it. This too is part of the condition of the fall. Now endowed with this power to define Good and Evil, to formulate, know and claim to obey it, man is no longer able to renounce this power that he has won at such great cost. He must exercise it. He cannot live without morality. There cannot be a society or a group or individual life without it. On the one hand, the individual experiences an irrepressible need to live in a universe where things are divided into good and evil; this is part of his psychological structure. He has security only when value is attributed to certain things and refused to others. On the other hand, he needs to be given a line of conduct. He cannot live in the instant. He cannot submit himself purely to instinct; he cannot always be the man of the *Hic et Nunc*. And even when he has decided that it should be thus, he still only reaches this point at the end of a moral debate and a moral judgment. It is because he has decided that instinct is better than . . . and the *Hic et Nunc* has eternal value . . . He has thus reconstructed a morality. But this case is the exception. Usually man wants to have a line of conduct. He needs consistency. He cannot forgo it in planning what he will do tomorrow. And whether or not this involves planning a moral program, it amounts to the same thing: an action is chosen because it is judged to be a good action. This decision is made at the individual level, and morality can also be individual; each one has the power to discern the good. But most often, society or a collective affirmation will intervene. This is due both to an economy of individual strength and a collective need. First, an economy of individual strength: because if each individual purports to start from nothing—annihilating all value judgments made before and around him, then reconstructing it all himself after examining everything—there will be an enormous loss of energy. As experience has shown, very rarely does such an undertaking lead to an original and singular decision; most often it leads this hardy and adventurous spirit to well-beaten paths and time-tested values; it is obvious that such a waste of strength is not "profitable," and collective wisdom does everything it can to avoid it, moving in the direction of the lazy individual. It is a large undertaking with immense risks (for the entire life of man risks being consumed by it), and all for a result that, *a priori*, is rather paltry—especially since society scorns such results when they do not conform. A society only exists when there is a certain level of coherence between the behavior of individuals. Everyone must come together in calling the same things "Good" and the same things "Bad." We must be able to expect and hope for a certain behavior from others; no social relation is possible if reasonable behavioral expectations of others do not exist. This will be precisely the collective morality, the set of common values that provides for the possibility of both an identical appraisal of things and this behavioral expectation of others. Social life is literally impossible if it is not coupled with a morality that is social in its origin and implications, but individual in its applications. This is why an attack on shared values is the biggest disturbance against which a society defends itself with all its vigor; for along with a shared language, these values allow us to understand one another and to collaborate. By supplying a morality for the average individual, who is content to have this solid and practical tool, society can expect his or her obedience to it; it satisfies a need that is as individual as it is social. No society can forgo a morality, no more than any man can do without it. In itself, it is a necessity.

5

The Double Morality[1]

According to all that we have just said, we can conclude that Morality does not derive from the knowledge of the will of God.[2] The Good made known to us by Morality is not the same thing as the will of God.[3] It was thought that we could get out of this dilemma by positing a genuine division in the will of God itself. Thus on the one hand, we would have a redemptive will that manifested in Jesus Christ—the God of love who wills man's salvation. On the other hand, we would have the creative will—God the creator, who is manifest in his creation. The first will would be known only through revelation, while the second could be known naturally by contemplating Nature. We will not address the theological question but will refer, among others, to the study of the persons of the Trinity done by Karl Barth: there is no division among them; there are no different levels—neither in the person, nor the work, nor the will of God. He is one in all, and cannot be known except through and in his revelation. In its fallen state,

---

1. On this question, we can cite among recent authors: Søe, *Christliche Ethik*, §4 and §31; Bonhoeffer, *Ethics*, 121, 151, 159–60, 263, 399–400; de Quervain, *Heiligung*, 203, 214, 264, 275; Mehl, "Ethique et théologie," 31–51; Ramsey, *Basic Christian Ethics*, 192; Piper, "Die Mitteilbarkeit der christlichen Ethik," 125.

2. TN: Ellul added two somewhat idiosyncratic section numbers in this chapter, which I have removed. The first was inserted at the beginning of this sentence.

3. "Christian ethics [TN: Barth writes "theological" in place of "Christian"] . . . has not to reckon with man's possession of a kind of moral nature, with a knowledge of good and evil which is peculiar to him . . . It has, therefore, to be on its guard against a retrospective reinterpretation of the fall, as though the presumption of man in wishing to know of himself what is good and evil were only a natural inclination to do the will of God." Barth, *CD* II.2, 522–23.

nature gives us no knowledge of primitive creation, much less of the will of love that presided over this creation. This knowledge of the Creation and original Nature can only be acquired in Jesus Christ, in whom all things were made. The unity of the redemptive will and the creative will of God appear with particular clarity in the promise of the resurrection and of the new creation. But we will leave this aside, and we now remark that asserting natural knowledge of the creative will still fails to resolve the problem. In effect, we have tried to demonstrate that man cannot know the good according to God because this good is bound up precisely with the redemptive will and the person of Jesus Christ. But at a second level, one might possibly say that the good known by man and expressed in his morality comes from God, that it is a creation of God, that though it is not the Sovereign Good, the supreme good, it is a divine good all the same, and created in the same way as our sense of justice, human love, etc., are created.[4] This would mean that there is an ideal world mediating between the divine and human world, which is very precisely the world of values; we are in full-blown Platonism. We absolutely do not deny the grandeur and the value of the platonic ideal or of its philosophy. We are simply saying it is in no way Christian or compatible with Christianity. All conciliations attempted between the two have ended in evaporating the essence of Christianity. While it is possible to speak of moral values as a Christian (and we will see in what sense this is possible later on), we must always remember that they are resolutely in the domain of human phenomena, that they are in no way part of God, and that they are ultimately a creation of man, and not a manifestation of the "divine" in him. Moral values depend on the milieu, the economy, education, religious ideals, etc. They have no constancy, stability, universality, or even objectivity. If they exist, it is in a sporadic, fleeting, transitory manner, and they are certainly not shared by everyone. How could we see them as traces of God's creation? Yet they would have to be much more than traces, since these moral values created by God *in* the world of the fall (before the fall, they would have no purpose) would need to retain their full meaning and vigor. The argument of authority, incidentally, seems to us sufficient to assert that these moral values are not creations of God: the Bible never speaks of these values, nor of their creation. So if we consider Scripture as the rule of Christian faith, this is sufficient. But we must draw an additional conclusion from this consideration of the purely human character of the Good formulated by man and of values: this good cannot be a common measure between Christians and non-Christians. On the one hand,

---

4. To say along with Roux (*Les épîtres pastorales*, 95) that Jesus Christ is the criterion of the values is to say something that is very precise but that tends toward the elimination of values rather than their recognition.

Christians strictly cannot speak of an implicit Christianity among pagans ("Since you behave in this way, you are Christians without knowing it . . ."; many Christians were strongly tempted to view Gandhi in this way, as many are tempted to view communists today). What makes a man a Christian is his confession that Christ is his savior. Pagans may behave very well, but always only according to the human standard of the good; the objectivity of their work can never testify that it concerns the very will of God. For as we will see, only God can judge what is good in our works; it is not our affair, and we are not capable of doing so. On the other hand, we cannot accept any judgment of Christianity in the name of what men call good. This can be neither validation nor proof against Christianity. "Men can do good without Christianity, so Christianity is useless." Obviously men accomplish *their* good without Christianity! This only demonstrates that their good is not the will of God! I know that those who read this sentence will protest that this is the unbearable pride of Christians speaking, these Christians who believe that they have exclusive access to the knowledge of God himself! I will only pose one question: this good by which you claim to judge everything, where do you get it from? If it is of God, how, and in virtue of what? If it is your own, how can you claim to impose your human standards on the revelation of God? One would first have to demonstrate that God did not reveal himself in Jesus Christ . . . In fact, this is really a case of man wanting to reduce God to a human standard. This is the claim of the first temptation rearing its head. And this makes sense, since in formulating the good, man asserts himself as God's equal. It is thus natural that man would judge the revelation according to the norm of the good. But this is sin itself. And here, in the same line, we also run up against the anxieties and scruples of Christians. What men call good today does not correspond to Christianity. Social justice, the concern for efficiency, national dignity, class solidarity, grasping the direction of history, etc.—all that permits man today to know that he is on the right path and take himself seriously—on all this, Christianity has very little to say. Of course, through the wonders of interpretation, we can find it in the Bible. The prophets spoke to us of "social justice . . ."! In each era, we have tried to perform this operation. In the Middle Ages, honor, loyalty, service to the Lady, fidelity to the Lord, and military bravery were among the chief criteria of the good, and we attempted to align Christianity with them. Today, the idea of blessing weapons and killing infidels in the name of the faith scandalizes us, but what is really scandalous is the operation that consists of adapting Christianity to a temporary and temporal notion of the Good in a given society, under the pretext that when something is Good, it must therefore be Christian. The same operation today, regarding the liberation of the proletariat and people from underdeveloped nations, or raising their standard of living, or developing education (what man calls the Good today)—is equally destructive of Christianity and will probably be seen as absurd and incoherent in a few centuries. Of course, I am not at all saying here that these works are not valuable, that we should leave the proletariat in their slavery and not educate the illiterate. I am only saying that, even though it seems obvious to us, and despite certain biblical texts (liberate the captives, etc.), all this is no more Christian today than were honor, proper feudal use of weapons, or stoic, individualist scorn of wealth in the twelfth century . . . These too could be founded upon biblical texts, and yet for us today they seem worthless and out of fashion . . . Indeed, "out of fashion" is the right phrase—for it is a question of fashion and not of truth. And that is why it is unacceptable for Christians to want to modernize Christianity in adapting it to the moral fashion of their times.[5]

This morality—which is strictly human, relative, temporary and temporal, which is not in any way, shape or form an expression of the will of God—we have said that it is nevertheless necessary. The Christian who knows its limitations absolutely does not have the right to consider it as false or useless because of these limitations. Morality is absolutely not negligible, and as Christians, we must take it strictly seriously. It is good to remember that, as Christian as we might be, we have never attained the perfect stature of Jesus Christ, and that we are not yet in the kingdom of God. We live on this earth in a given time and a given place. We are men like the others. And by this fact, we share (and we must do so, for Christianity is not a school of inhumanity) the errors and knowledge, the hopes and beliefs, the values and judgments, the virtues and limitations of the men of this time and place. It is normal that we would judge as "good" (on the human level) what the men of this time call good. It is normal that we feel judged when we disobey this good. Paul advises us to pay close attention to the judgment that the morality of the world can make on us: "For we intend to do what is right not only in the Lord's sight but also in the sight of others" (2 Cor 8:21), and Peter tells us that we must be ready to give an account of the reason for

---

5. But in these conditions, the church must be precisely clear on this point: when it formulates an ethic, qualities of the ethic according to the world are necessarily present therein; the problem is thus one of ensuring that the values chosen by a given society do not become the values of the Christian ethic. That peace should be the central Christian value in popular republics, or equality in the U.S.A., and that authors uncritically demonstrate that the ethic should be built around this value—this seems unacceptable to us!

6. TN: The second of Ellul's section numbers has been removed from this location.

our hope to those who ask (1 Pet 3:15). The judgment applied to us in the name of morality must put us seriously on guard; it should lead us to pose the question of the orientation of the value of our acts, to ask ourselves if our disobedience to morality is obedience to God or to our sin. We ought to have a very strong motive to deny human morality, and we must be clear about this motive. We do not have the right to carelessly brush this morality aside simply because it is human. Certainly, the judgment applied to us is not the judgment of God, but it is very important as a sign of the value or non-value of our life, and even more of the quality of our witness to Jesus Christ.

The two texts cited above remind us that following customary morality and accomplishing what men around us call "good" is one of the elements of the Christian life itself. This morality constructed by men thus has value before God. Though it is within the fall, though it has no common measure with God's will, it is indispensable if (and because) it is relative. The fact that Paul employs the phrase "before men" on two occasions shows that the good in question is relative, and even though we are called to testify to another commandment before men, we must not make refusing their morality a prerequisite for this testimony. On the contrary, we should be careful that the refusal of human morality does not create a useless scandal, for this scandal can be satanic even when it is accomplished in the name of God. If we reject human morality in the name of the gospel, we must take care not to polarize the entire testimony and debate around the sole problem of moral content; in which case the whole content of the gospel evaporates and the testimony of grace becomes impossible. The churches have constantly erred by entering pagan countries and demanding transformed behavior *as a prerequisite*, focusing on polygamy, nudity, homosexuality, and fighting against morals that do not conform to Christian morality: at this moment, preaching the gospel is impossible because the heart of the struggle is misdirected. This is why Paul reminds us, "To those outside the law I became as one outside the law," etc., *"that I might by all means save some . . ."*[7] Scandalizing human morality can sometimes be necessary because of Jesus Christ—we shall see within what limits—but always within the preaching of the gospel, and never as a struggle between two moralities. You can obey human morality, and normally you should. We particularly note that the Bible nowhere condemns this morality! It is very remarkable that the Word of God is so intransigent regarding religions, magic, and idolatry, that it condemns the

---

7. It is only in this sense that we accept the idea that the Christian has to choose among the values of the world (Roger Mehl; Ricoeur, "Discerner pour agir"). This is true on condition of knowing that these values do not express the truth, nor the specificity of the Revelation that must be lived.

smallest spiritual diversion without forgiveness or leniency, but never concerns itself in the least with the diversity of morality. It addresses moral conduct only as a consequence of a spiritual attitude, of a heresy, an idolatry, and only as a sign of these latter does moral conduct become important. This type of tolerance, this kind of modest reserve toward moral decisions is astonishing. Yet it is understandable if we consider that, fundamentally, morality is so directly linked to man that to deny morality, to reject it, is purely and simply to deny man himself; it is to abolish his condition.[8] After the fall (and because of it), man is in a moral universe from which he cannot be dissociated. The occasion of his rupture with God has become his reason for being and his life itself. We must not think that tearing him from this universe could reconcile him with God! To claim to deny the morality made by man is either a demonization or an angelization: demonization, because rejecting man puts him in the situation of demons, who have no moral life but only opposition to God; angelization, because the Christian who does this claims to escape the condition of man and to have attained the situation of Adam before the fall. Denying or refusing to respect human morality is ultimately a failure to recognize man for what he is; it is a failure to see oneself as a man. And doing so would in no way help the Christian to prepare the listener, who is now reduced to nothing, to hear the gospel; on the contrary, it would decisively cut them off and abstract them from their reality, for despite our negation of their morality, they continue to be what they are. We must consider, moreover, that if this morality instituted by man—the very location of the decision of sin—is nevertheless accepted by God, it is equally in recognition of its usefulness for man. We have said several times that man needs this morality to live, that each social group is constituted and expresses itself in morality. Life is possible within an ethical system, but without it life would be a continual war and interpersonal relations would be inconceivable. We should thus respect this morality because of its usefulness, and because it is useful to man.[9]

---

8. Moreover, it is certain that we must recognize the considerable value of natural ethics when it expresses "the finite spirit's understanding of its own finitude" (Niebuhr, *Nature and Destiny of Man*). Whenever it is the recognition (whether explicit or not) of the insufficient and dependent character of life; when it testifies to a lack, an absence; when it expresses a normality whose implementation leaves room for bad conscience—natural ethics can, in effect, do these things. (But this thus implies the abandonment of any claim to attain the Good in itself, or the strict rationality of norms.) And in these cases, it testifies to the failure of the adamic project; in these cases, faith can also welcome it with utmost seriousness.

9. This idea of a useful morality comes close to the formulation of Eric Weil ("Raison morale et politique") when he demonstrates that "the moral principle has the significant weakness of never saying what must be done in practice, and this enormous

We find ourselves here on the level of a morality that is useful, that man knows both how to construct and observe—useful, but not necessarily reduced to utility. In this sense, we accept Bonhoeffer's idea of the Natural, despite several reservations regarding his choice of term.[10] Materially, this Natural is the form of human life directed toward its preservation; ethics corresponds to this, and using reason to express it is indispensable and right, and Evil is always a form of destruction of life. And formally, this Natural is determined by God's will to preservation. The non-Natural is that which tends to oppose this will. Of course, we must take into account that the will of God can sometimes be a will to destruction, and thus can make use of the "non-Natural" (cf. the plagues of Egypt, the Assyrians, etc.); which thus implies that the categories of Good and Evil established according to what is Natural, Useful, and Pragmatic certainly cannot be imposed on God!

We cannot wish that humans would be placed in more inhumane living conditions. The existence of this morality does not bring man closer to God, and it is not for this reason that the Christian ought to respect it. But it allows man to continue existing, and this is important if we believe that God does not want us to reap the harvest prematurely, but instead that it is fitting that the world where we are placed should live and be maintained in living order. It is radically wicked, yet it must remain livable. Breathable air, sufficient food, a coherent order, a possible relation between men—these are humble, but essential tasks—we have to take them seriously to avoid dishonestly retreating into abstraction. The Christian (because he is a man) must help others to make this world livable, and morality is part of this task: common morality, group morality, interpersonal morality, which we must at once respect, construct, and consolidate with the others—and even more, since in all this elaboration we will encounter values that cannot leave this Christian indifferent. We have said that after the fall, man knows that there is a good. He does not know what it is. But each time that man constructs a morality, enacts an ethical choice, or makes a decision, there is a hope, an expectation, and a call. For want of the good of God, man decides on this good because he cannot do without it, but also because he expects and indeed hopes for the sovereign good without knowing it, without knowing that it could even exist. But this man births into existence when he decides upon the good, since he exposes his hope, toward which he is striving in this way. Each time, man is convinced that this system will be the perfect

---

power of absolutely prohibiting certain procedures. The positive value that it indicates is not positively defined [TN: Rognon and Müller note that Weil adds the word "materially" here, but Ellul removes it] . . . it will have to be brought back to reason which teaches what is possible and what is not under given conditions . . ."

10. Bonhoeffer, *Ethics*, 171–218.

realization of his desire; each time he is deceived, because only perfection could satisfy it. This expectation, this call of man is thus expressed in the tirelessly renewed attempt to develop a morality (but not only in this, of course). For this reason, the recipient of the Revelation of God must pay attention to the hope of men—not to tell them that they are deceiving themselves by responding to it on their own, nor to assume a position of superiority, but as a midwife helping to deliver their hope, to formulate what they call good today and to obey it, holding to it as a requirement, never allowing it to get stuck in a dead command, and continually bringing it back to what it is: a cry of man in the night, to which man responds.

If we are thus led to positively consent to the existence of this human morality, then this means that for Christians there are two moralities (insofar as we can even speak of a Christian morality, which we will examine later on). On the one hand, there is the Revelation of the Good according to God and everything that follows from it; on the other hand, there is man's production of a morality in given circumstances.[11] These two phenomena are opposed to one another on every level.[12] Concerning their origin, on the one hand we

---

11. Whether we like it or not, we must choose to center everything on Revelation or on man. Mixing the two is impossible. All natural ethics start from man. We see the difficulty for Catholicism particularly well in Häring's *Théologie morale generale*. He posits just principles: "Moral Theology can only be the doctrine of complete commitment to following Christ, its point of departure can only be Christ." "We must not separate anthropology and Christology" (1:95). But having said this, he then engages in an ontology of man—natural man, not man regenerated by grace—and it is upon this that he makes the possibility of Christian ethics depend (1:97, 268). In the guise of nature, man is the director of true moral values. Ultimately, once we seek a compromise between man and God, the weight of the discussion shifts in the direction of man!

But in opposing two moralities, we must particularly avoid saying that the one which comes from God is a religious morality. This is a terrible confusion (which is to be expected) on the part of all Catholic authors (and recently by Häring, vol. 1, despite his excellent theological point of departure), but many times, also, by Protestant authors, which is more astonishing—e.g., for Niebuhr (*An Interpretation of Christian Ethics*).

12. I know very well the difficulty involved in recognizing the existence of two moralities, and that we risk falling prey to the all the critiques of Luther for his theory of the two orders. We will return to this problem later on. Nevertheless, I will insist on the fact that it is not a question of total separation or dualism between two moralities, where the one would be good and the other simply wicked. Likewise, there is no question of suppressing all contact between God and his creatures, though we must recall that in truth this contact only exists in Jesus Christ. On the other hand, to refuse the existence of two moralities, to seek to establish a monism at all costs, is to enter into a completely imaginary idealism. All doctrines claiming that human moralities contain more or less divine elements disregard the reality of the existing world—for example, disregarding

have spoken of the Revelation, of the attitude adopted by man first toward God, then toward his neighbor as a function of the word of God; and on the other hand, of man's creation of rules of conduct or judgment, whether by an individual or a collectivity, according to very diverse processes and with equally shifting contents.[13] What is called good differs from one case to another; we need not go over this again. But we could also say that in both cases, the moral process itself is different and opposed. If we leave aside the perfectly fictitious vision of Sartre, we can concretely say that the moral process unfolds in two steps: settling on a good to accomplish, then accomplishing (or not accomplishing) this good following a choice or a decision.

---

the reality of politics, judging only according to carefully selected exceptional examples, or again limiting themselves to considering only one aspect of the real, rejecting with ease everything that does not square with such monism. On the contrary, we aim to consider the complexity and the entirety of the real, and in doing so we are led to observe that the biblical doctrine of two moralities is the only one that corresponds to the reality of the world. An example of this opposition that is at once tragic and very clear can be found in the debate that took place regarding the subject of the condemnation of Eichmann. It is obvious that from the viewpoint of the survival of the human community, the viewpoint of civil justice, and the viewpoint of natural sentiments, Eichmann should be condemned to death; for as we have said, to let a murderer go free is to completely overturn the principles of justice, the laws of civilization. But opposed to all this, a Christian conscience is obliged to ask if forgiveness is a purely individual affair, or if it also concerns collective crimes, and if forgiveness would not imply that Eichmann should be liberated. This was upheld by Victor Gollancz, who wrote, "Six million human beings have been killed, but what good is it to kill one more? Will this measure tear the veil of hatred and cruelty that Auschwitz has thrown over humanity? Eichmann belongs to God and God alone can judge him. It is not the mythical idea of retributive justice which must guide us, but the idea of spiritual retribution which is closer to us; the more odious the evil, the greater must be our mercy; the extreme wrongdoing of Hitler calls for an extreme act of mercy. Only mercy and forgetting can bring a ray of clarity into this darkness" (Gollancz, *The Case of Adolf Eichmann*). And Gollancz ends by suggesting Eichmann's liberation with these words: "Go and sin no more." It is obvious that applying this morality would be disastrous for collective life, but it is no less evident that this attitude corresponds to the demand of love for neighbor, or more exactly of love for one's enemy; we perceive here the contradiction of the two moralities, and we should point out with somber humor that the morality of civil justice was upheld by a Dominican Father, and that the morality of love for one's neighbor in God was upheld by an Israelite. [TN: For more on this trial, see the influential treatment in Arendt, *Eichmann in Jerusalem: A Report on the Banality of Evil*.]

13. Karl Barth marvelously defines the opposition of the problematic itself: "The problem of ethics generally—the law or good or value which it seeks . . . the problem of truth and the knowledge of the good—is no problem at all in the ethics immanent in the Christian conception of God . . . And, conversely, that which is no problem at all to ethical thought generally . . . the actual situation of *man in the face of the question by which he is confronted when he answers* the ethical question, his actual commitment to the good, his actual distance from it . . . this is the burning problem in Christian ethics." Barth, *CD* II.2, 519 [Ellul's italics].

We could, as it were, speak of a general and a particular ethic. The fixation of the good can be collective, individual, totally predetermined, or elaborated through practice itself; in any case, the good appears as a goal to attain, or as a value to realize, or as a principle whose implications we must derive, or as a commandment to incarnate—in all cases, a predetermined abstract item that man must live or apply. Man's responsibility is situated at the level of this application, the level of action. Even phenomenological thought, however refined it might be, comes down to this—for example, with the idea of the "aim of values." Now, precisely this process of moral action has nothing to do with Christianity; or rather, when we describe Christianity in this manner (which we do very often), it has nothing to do with the Revelation of God. To say that there is a law of God which we must accomplish, that there is a Christian morality (described, for example, in the epistles of Saint Paul or the Sermon on the Mount) whose requirements we must obey, that there is a Sovereign Good that we can mystically contemplate and then apply, etc.—all of this imports experiences, judgments, and interpretations from the morality of the world into Christianity. The moral process of faith is completely different.[14] In effect, there is no presupposition or determination of an objective good. We will see that the law of God itself is not this objective good. There is nothing but a personal relation with God for each one, in which the good is revealed as the will of God. Now, this good is not a goal to attain, which we can approach little by little through feats of asceticism. On the one hand, we learn that this good is accomplished in Jesus Christ; on the other hand, we have to choose our present conduct not in function of a goal, but in expressing the love and glory of God. We could say (from the ethical point of view, and not in the soteriological sense found in Philippians or Colossians—"not that I have already attained the goal") that the Christian acts by virtue of a personal impetus that they receive, and to testify to a truth that is not ethical, that they must make present, current, and living. They act not through successive approximations of an immutable perfection, but in a decision that is total at each moment and new at each moment. They are not on a path with successive stages that express progressively higher moral accomplishments. The path and the growth in question in the Bible are those of faith, not of morality. The moral work of the Christian is full in each moment; it is indivisible. In it they express what they *are* in this moment. There is no addition of yesterday's work onto today's work. There is only a renewal of the being by growth in faith under the power of the Holy Spirit who is at work in us. And this renewal of the being expresses itself in works

---

14. TN: At this point, Hopkin's translation adds a footnote, "*Ibid.*," which is absent from the 2013 French edition.

that are actually always new. I judge these works myself, today, in relation to the will of God that was revealed to me, and I learn that in fact they are not a worthy and just expression of this will. In a certain way, then, this means that there really is not a Christian morality. And this leads us to highlight another difference: all morality rests on the presupposition that man is free, since in the end it resides in the choice that man makes between good and evil. If this man was not free, it would mean nothing. Thus, freedom is truly the condition of morality.[15] By contrast, Christianity speaks to us of a man who is bound by a personal will, a man whose life is fundamentally obedience; it teaches us that this obedience is the prerequisite condition of freedom, which is perfectly incomprehensible from a human viewpoint. From this viewpoint, the idea that the moral life and just behavior could be the fruit of accepting that we belong to someone is an impossibility, a veritable scandal for all independent morality. This latter always tends toward a greater self-mastery, toward individual autonomy, while the Christian life is a continually deepening belonging to God—which from the humanist point of view is alienation, yet which in truth is the very accomplishment of the only complete freedom (we will study this is the second part).[16]

Finally, another opposition between the two moralities holds to the fact that, in contrast to all moralities of the world, the orders that God gives never seek to lead man to realize an ideal. The commandments of God are always related to an action linked to the establishment and proclamation of his covenant, to his kingdom that is promised, and that has now come near. Consequently, in a Christian ethic there will never be a question of doing just any good, but of executing a certain task relating to the kingdom of God and the testimony that God asks of us.

In the Christian Revelation, there is no moral ideal, no typology of the good, and still less a symbolic expression of the good! There is a Revelation of the spoken Word that calls man to obedience because God accomplishes his salvation. Consequently, the Christian is not called to create his behavior at each moment, any more than he is called to create his own being, as in

---

15. See the very classic study of the relation between Morality and Freedom in Häring, *La loi du Christ*, 1:143. And, by contrast: "As this Elect, quite apart from any choice of His own between good and evil, He is concerned only with obedience. He does not crave to be good of and for Himself . . . he is subject only to the will and command of God who alone is good. This is how the good is done here. This is how the ethical question is answered here—in Jesus Christ. What has taken place in this way—*in antithesis and contrast to all human ethics*—is divine ethics." Barth, *CD* II.2, 517 [Ellul's italics].

16. TN: that is, the second part of Ellul's planned ethical project; cf. *Ethique de la liberté*, vol. 1 (*Ethics of Freedom*, ch. 1).

existentialism; he receives the entirety of his being in his encounter with Jesus Christ (and not with the neighbor!).

In any case, these elements allow us to understand the essential divergence that can exist between the two "moralities" that we have identified. The most common viewpoint consists of admitting that there is a certain difference between Christian morality and other moralities—for example, a difference in content, or a difference of expression. Thus the moralities of Confucius, Socrates, Kant, and then the Christian morality are analyzed alongside one another. In fact, for natural man Christianity can appear as a religion among religions, an anthropology among anthropologies, a philosophy among philosophies and a morality among moralities. On many occasions, incidentally, Christian intellectuals (with their philosophical preoccupations) and clergy members (with their religious or moral worries) have allowed these interpretations to take hold, permitting these assimilations. And it is precise to say that in its psychological or sociological expressions, Christianity has appeared as a religion; likewise, in its will to ameliorate human life, it has appeared as a morality. Now, just as there is an irreducible opposition between Christianity and religion (as Barth has demonstrated), there is an irreducible opposition between Christianity and morality. In a certain sense (which we will explain in detail further on), we could say that Christianity is an anti-morality: while it gives birth to phenomena that can be analytically classified as moral phenomena, this in no way justifies its inclusion among other moralities. This is not simply a difference of language or content: we could say that what we might call the Christian ethic is the opposite of everything which generally constitutes morality.

In all moralities, there are common qualities that allow us to speak of a general phenomenon of *Morality*. Now, it is precisely these common qualities that the conduct of the Christian life lacks. This life manifests a specificity that is irreducible to any morality.[17] Thus this is not a matter of one or several discrepancies in detail or content; it is an opposition at the very root of the phenomenon. We could say that on one side, there is the range of moralities that present common qualities, and on the other side,

---

17. On the specificity of Christian Morality, Niebuhr is right when he demonstrates that each time Christianity abandons this specificity, it loses the power to discern the ethical aberrations of the world. But this means that Christianity must defend itself on two fronts: against an idealist dualism and against a naturalist monism, against an optimism that allows for the validity of the world in itself and a pessimism that reduces historical existence to an absence of signification. Such is the precise uniqueness of this Ethic, comparable to no other, which is clearly expressed in the successive myths of ancient Israel. In the same way, Christian love is at once different from moral love of a monistic character and from love as a mystical essence (cf. Prunet, 25).

there is Christianity, which has no common measure with any morality. The very essence of the revelation is opposed to all ethical systematization and to all assimilation to another morality. The Christian life does not conform to a morality but to a revealed Word, that is present and living.[18] This singularity of the Christian ethical phenomenon will become more and more clear as we continue, but at this point in our treatment, we must draw attention to this important fact in the form of a proposition. Of course, this leads to great difficulties. And Christians are continually tempted to build a bridge between the Christian life and the moralities of the world. Whether because we do not know how to formulate the rule of the Christian life in any other way; or because it is difficult to accept this divorce; or because from the point of view of charity or humility, it seems unacceptable to exclude what is not Christian from the domain of truth; or, finally, because the spirit of the world is creeping into the church—or for still many other reasons—the process of rapprochement and identification between Christianity and Morality (or a given morality) is endlessly repeated.[19] Now, we must never forget that the biblical ethic can be confused with other ethics. Alongside the Commandment of God, there are other directives coming from society, nature or history that we can also take for commands from God; all the more since in revealing his will, God does not act in his crushing omnipotence but presents this will like any other requirement, just as in Jesus he presented himself like any other man. But Karl Barth highlights that what ultimately differentiates this Commandment of God is that it is not an obligation, but a permission.

The Commandment rests on the event of the liberation of man in Jesus Christ, on the fact that man becomes free by grace received in faith, and the commandment itself appears as a sort of guarantee of this freedom. This

---

18. It is certain that the confusion caused by many theologians comes from the fact that the Ideal, Duty, and Conscience can lead natural man, in a theistic perspective, to conceive of God as requiring the Good. But this is not what we learn in the Revelation, which unveils God as acting toward us in the way he wills for us to behave toward others (Søe, §4). A typical example of this confusion is Bois, *Le problème de la Morale chrétienne*.

19. This resemblance often provokes confusions and temptations. As Hillerdal has done well to note (*ZEE* 1, 1957), in many cases very little separates certain parenetic passages of the New Testament and a given philosophical or humanist morality. This "very little" is only the phrase "in Christ." How strong, then, is the temptation to remove it to arrive at a *consensus omnium*! If instead of removing it, we *start from* this phrase, the separation with all other moralities becomes radical.

Roux (*Épîtres pastorales*, 179) gives us a very typical example of this confusion. We will have to respond to the problem by examining the specificity of morality for Christians.

commandment authorizes man to finally live as he was called to live in creation. In all of this, it is rigorously different from all other moralities.

And yet, Christian Ethics can be similar to non-Christian Ethics.[20] Likewise, the behavior of the Christian, in good and in evil, can be very similar to that of the non-Christian. During the Crusades, for example, we know that one of the points of rapprochement between Christians and Muslims was asceticism: Islamic asceticism admired Christian asceticism, and vice versa. Similarly, today it is a commonplace to say that militant communists demonstrate a greater sense of justice or spirit of love than Christians. And the interrogation of Celsus is endlessly repeated: "What distinguishes Christians in the domain of virtue?"

Effectively, we really must remember that Christians are distinguished neither by *better* conduct nor by a higher intelligence. To find a common ground by comparing one asceticism to another, to compare faith and faith, religion and religion—all of this is simply a comparison and correlation of human things.

The asceticism that is called Christian is the same thing as Islamic asceticism, and "Christian" social love is the same thing as communist love. What does this mean? That Muslims or communists are Christians? Absolutely not! In reality, only from the point of view of the "natural" man, the son of Adam—that is, the one who lives by his own decision, or in his self-determination and independence—do these things resemble each other. And when a Christian finds that Islamic asceticism is similar to Christian asceticism, this is true insofar as this latter really is not Christian, insofar as faith is infused with the religious spirit of the world, insofar as the Christian ceases to belong to his Lord and begins to judge on his own what is good—that is, as he reproduces the sin of Adam. When a Christian finds that the love of the communist is similar to *agape*, this is true insofar as this latter has been transformed into a social humanist love, exhibiting the same infusion of the *Weltgeist* in the Revelation. Here again, the Christian has decided for himself what love is and has ceased to be what he is called to be. Of course, in this latter case, we note that this transformation did not take place under the influence of the communist! No infusion from the outside is necessary; the evolution happens from the inside. And it is because the Christian already no longer knows what *agape* is, because they follow the sociological trend of society, which tells them, "Here is what true love is, here is true humanism, etc.," because they listen to this social voice rather than the voice of their Lord—for this reason, they discover a love in a given

---

20. For modern times, Karl Barth has admirably shown the influence of systematic ethics on the Christian ethic and the subsequent adaptations of this latter to the ethical ideas of the world (cf. Barth, *CD* II.2, 521).

human movement or human model that they humbly but rightly recognize as superior to their own.

Well then, what is it? It is the person of Jesus Christ that makes Christianity. Everything derives from the fact that Jesus is God, that Jesus Christ is Lord and Savior: outside of this, the rest is only talk. But we discern, then, that the problem is above all a problem of Truth. And only in this recognized and assumed truth can the ethic take shape. (We will come back to the link between heresy and bad conduct.) For the Christian ethic is the relation between the person Jesus Christ and a person who recognizes him as their Savior and Lord. And here we come back to the Good that God says and accomplishes. Now, this good is rigorously impenetrable, incomprehensible, and unattainable from the perspective of what man calls the good. There is no possible comparison. The man who does not recognize Jesus Christ can only make judgments on the good from his own point of view, from what he calls Justice or Love at a given moment, in a given civilization. Consequently, most of the time he will view Christian behavior as incomprehensible, absurd, and sometimes bad. He can only render the judgment recalled by Paul's phrase: "a stumbling block for Jews and foolishness to Gentiles." It is always a scandal for humanists, politicians, the virtuous and the religious. It is always idiocy for philosophers, intellectuals and technicians. It is a question of expressing this singularity of Christian conduct in faith, starting from the person of Jesus Christ. But certainly, this does not mean that we must pursue originality at all cost, or again, that we must reject all human conduct *ipso facto*; these moralities can coincide accidentally or temporarily on the level of behavior. Nevertheless, their coincidence will often appear even more strange when a given behavior, in which man recognizes himself, finds itself inserted into an unexpected context, and again when the two moralities separate at the end of a short time. Many times, it is a scandal for non-Christians, who think they are on common moral ground, to realize that for Christians it means something completely different. These misunderstandings ought to be cleared up at the moment that such alliances are made, or at the beginning of a stretch of road shared that may be walked together.

How many times have Christians failed in this way, deceiving and scandalizing their companions by calling "love and charity" what was only cowardice, lack of foresight, and betrayal of the Truth! Various Christendoms are always reconstructed on the foundation of these particular ambiguities. Intellectually, then, it is easy to formulate a perfectly orthodox theology; but as soon as we enter the realm of practical life, in the lived and concrete expression of Christianity, we realize that the most orthodox theology is of little help and does a poor job of taking on flesh. Confronted with the necessity of incarnating the faith, we feel the need to formulate Christian truth in such a manner that it could actually be lived out. And from this moment, we witness theological work that leads to heresy. Barthian theology is currently confronting this very difficulty, and we are witnessing the reappearance of attempts to reconcile it with the moralities the world: either Barthians adopt extremely indecisive positions conforming to sociological trends (for example, regarding socialism in politics), or they have already attempted moral systematization. In both cases, it can only lead to a new theological formulation of the truth. But the problem of Christian conduct is one of the insoluble problems which we ought not to resolve, yet which we always try to resolve by modifying theology. Once again, let us forcefully remember that faith, not morality, makes the Christian life; and that faith is not centered on the Good, but on Jesus Christ. Here, the Christian ethic breaks off all *possible* relations with any and all morality.

If we are led to recognize the existence of a double morality for the Christian, what consequence can this have? Obviously, there is a relation between the two; but what kind of relation?[21]

1. Exceptionally, there can be agreement between the two in immediate action. A given attitude, decision, or judgment deriving from a platonic or socialist morality can be fully acceptable for a Christian, and similarly we have seen that from their own point of view, pagans can adopt a given work of faith and judge it to be good. But this agreement can only happen at the level of concrete and fragmentary works. As Niebuhr emphasizes (*The Nature and Destiny of Man*), the search for justice, resistance to tyranny, and the call to peace are legitimate means of moral judgment, but they are always mixed with elements of violence and hatred. Likewise, the exercise of power, which is always violence, is also mixed with a certain pursuit of justice and order. Those who thus speak of a possible "common stretch of road" that communists and Christians may walk together are not wrong, from this perspective. This does not entail adhesion to the general politics or doctrine of communism; we are only admitting the existence of a coincidence on a

---

21. On the diverse relations possible between the two moralities (cf. Barth, *CD* II.2, 522): neither apologetic, nor compromise, nor division of roles. Karl Barth rejects differentiating the two on the basis of the ethical criteria of the world. But we also recognize Barth's standpoint in considering that "[ethics] has to take up the legitimate problems and concerns and motives and assertions of every other ethics as such, and therefore after testing them in the light of its own superior principle . . . To that extent its attitude to every other ethics is not negative but comprehensive. But just because it is comprehensive, it is fundamentally critical . . ." Barth, *CD* II.2, 527.

particular problem between the demand of faith and communist tactics.[22] It makes perfect sense that Christians were able to affirm certain commandments of Roman law (the command of good faith, for example), or the Stoic morality. But this agreement cannot extend to Roman law in general or to Stoicism. The error takes place in passing from the concrete work to the system. When a non-Christian claims that Christianity can be assimilated to this or that moral system, this does not matter very much; it is an inevitable misunderstanding, since natural man absolutely cannot grasp the irreducible novelty of the Christian truth on his own, and he knows nothing of the double morality. In his perspective, Christianity can only be a religion and a morality like the others. He has no way to judge matters differently. The error is grave, however, when it is made by Christians, when they confuse the consequences of the faith with a given human virtue or human ideal. At this moment, they renounce the rigorous relation established by Jesus Christ between the "Words that I say" and putting them into practice. In particular, there are two prominent types of conciliation that Christians will seek. In the first, the morality of the world is a minimum threshold that is not opposed to Christianity; Christian morality simply includes this morality of the world, and goes beyond it. In this schema, Christianity would therefore be an additional requirement; furthermore, it would accept what exists as a natural morality. This has only been sustainable in strongly Christianized societies where the "secular" morality was *in reality* a laicized Christian morality. This becomes absurd when we speak of the morality of the Marquesans or the Chippewa. Additionally, we have seen the impossibility of establishing continuity between natural morality and Christian morality.[23] The second attempt at conciliation consists of saying: live out the

22. From another point of view, in the perspective of communism itself, the theory of the "common stretch of road" is absolutely reprehensible, as we have tried to demonstrate in the report to the National Synod, 1959. [TN: Ellul is referring to the "Rapport du Synode Nationale ERF, Paris, 27–30 May, 1959." This document contains a nineteen-page treatment of "Christianity and the Great Ideologies, Notably Marxism," which, though it bears the name of Pierre Burgelin (who was charged with reporting to the synod on this topic), is laced throughout with Ellul's thought. For example, when it notes that pushing political opinions to the level of absolute doctrine is a serious plague to church unity, or when it notes on page 140 that Marxism "is a particular form of the search for a rationally ordered universe," we could easily link this to Ellul's theses in *The Political Illusion* and *The Technological Society*. The document finishes with eleven "Theses for an Agenda concerning Marxism," which both refuse churchwide adherence to Marxist doctrine and allow room for individuals within the church to adhere to the (officially atheist) Marxist party. It is helpful to note that Marxism was more widely and welcomingly received in mid-twentieth-century France than, for example, in the United States.]

23. For example, as Häring does, assimilating the heroic death of soldiers with that of the Martyrs (I, 313).

Christian morality and you will see that "in reality society will accept you."²⁴ (Be Christian and you will become rich, you will succeed, etc.) This is a very serious misappropriation of Christian truth, and all we can say is that in this case, there is *no more* Christian life. No value system, no human conduct, no moral mythology can essentially coincide with Christianity. There can only be accidental and temporary coincidences.

Finally, while there can be agreement, this does not mean that Christian morality extends or completes natural morality, but only that the life of faith does not annihilate nature, and that God does not abandon even the most rebellious humanity entrenched in their sin.²⁵ But this in no way confirms the interpretation of the *primus usus legis* [TN: "first use of the law"] (or the *usus civilus*), in which Christian morality is law, functioning as a brake and inspiration for everyone.²⁶ We have already indicated why this interpretation seems impossible. We recall that there is a theological error in this interpretation, for it presents morality as coming from God, who is understood as the supreme Being; to this extent it will be accepted by many. But for the Christian, this implies that morality is not founded in Christ, which is the worst of all betrayals. Now, from the moment that this foundation in Christ is established, it can no longer be heard by non-Christians. Agreement is no longer possible.

Finally, we can consider a humble morality of the world. When K. Barth reckons that it would be possible to agree with an ethic that renounces claims to an absolute scope for its own wisdom, that does not pretend to be "ultimate," nor to be clothed in a Myth, nor to define a "Good," he certainly has a point; but to us, this example seems rather illusory and hypothetical! For let us not forget that an ethic which highlights the limits of the human condition, the precarity of moral judgments, etc., *always* raises this relativism and skepticism to the absolute level!

---

24. We thus return to the effort of the Christian to justify their morality: a validation of Christian morality on the basis of general ethics is impossible. To want to link the former to the latter, or to claim to develop, extend, or enrich the former by the latter, is absolutely out of the question. Nor can there be any question of discussing them on the same level with other parties. Barth, *CD* II.2, 519.

25. Cf. Søe, §10.

26. It seems impossible to accept an identification of the Decalogue with a *lex naturae*, as has been often done, and perhaps by Luther in the *primus usus legis*, for the idea that the Decalogue is called to "uphold discipline among the unsubmitted" implies living in a Christian society, as we have already shown. The Decalogue is a law that was *revealed* to the *Jewish people* as a chosen people. It is not a common law for all, and it does not express what is naturally found in the heart of man—without which we do not understand why it had to be revealed on Mount Sinai amidst thunder and lightning (cf. on this subject Bonhoeffer, "A Theological Position Paper on the *Primus Usus Legis*"; Niebuhr, *Nature and Destiny of Man*, 106).

2. Most of the time, there will be conflict between the two moralities, or ignorance and indifference on the part of the morality of the world toward the Christian morality. This latter case should be that of secularism. The Christian cannot ignore the morality of secular society; as we have been saying, he must take it into account, as with any other morality in the society where he finds himself. But the secular morality might know nothing of the existence of an independent Christian morality, perhaps even by choice. It is not obliged to respect the demands of this other morality. But, in principle, it does not have to oppose them either; it respects . . . thus there is indifference. And consequently, secularism can affirm that there is not and cannot be a conflict since tolerance is the supreme value. If conflict breaks out, it will be the fault of the Christian, who will have manifested their intolerance and thus transgressed the secular morality—this is exact. And a secular person obviously cannot penetrate the rationale in which tolerance is not the ultimate moral value for the Christian, and in which certain concrete consequences of the faith produce intolerant conduct. In this case, the conflict is provoked by the Christian's application of the Christian morality. Conversely, it is possible that the morality of the world would openly contradict the Christian morality. This is the case with the morality of communism (for example, in the idea that there is no personal virtue: belonging to a class makes man good or bad, whatever his personal behavior may be; or again, everything that contributes to the good of the proletariat is good, including lying, betrayal, assassination); the same goes for Nazi morality, or even the morality of increasingly technical society (whose scale of values perfectly contradicts Christianity).[27] In these different cases, from the perspective of the non-Christian the conflict can be resolved in two ways. The first solution is to prohibit Christians from demonstrating their belonging to Jesus Christ in their acts. Of course, they will retain their interior freedom, their beliefs, their spiritual life. But this interior life may not be expressed in behavior; indeed, what concretely disturbs the unity of action in society is divergence of action, not divergence of belief. Already under the Roman Empire, Christians were not reproached for their faith but for their refusal to participate in imperial ceremonies and their refusal to tolerate other worship—that is, for their sociomoral attitudes. As long as the Christian conforms to the same common practices, they are perfectly accepted. If their faith does not translate into unusual acts, if under the communist regime they hold to the slogans of the party, if they work to build up socialism, if they do not publicly testify to their faith, if they do not critique

27. TN: for this latter, Ellul writes *la morale technicienne*, literally *technical morality*. In the context of his analyses on the growth and dominance of technique in society, this latter applies to the West more broadly. See also part II, chapter 6 of the present volume.

the government even for its antireligious politics, all will go well. In other words, there is no problem, provided they do not live like a Christian or obey a Christian ethic. Thus, the first solution is to eliminate the Christian morality entirely. The other solution consists in subordinating the Christian morality to the societal morality, that is, to make use of the Christian morality in service of the conduct required by the non-Christian morality. When, in 1943, the Orthodox Church under communism called upon Christian charity to develop the feeling of solidarity and to get Christians to give exceptional gifts to the state, when the churches in Hungary and Czechoslovakia developed the theme of unconditional obedience to the state as a duty of conscience (arguing from Romans 13), this served communist morality, which happily permitted the call to Christian behavior in this case and for this particular collaboration. In a more general manner, we find the same attitude, for example, among the bourgeoisie and with technical morality: the value of work, dedication in everything we do, sacrifice for the greater good, the spirit of service instead of pleasure—these virtues are eminently useful for the development of technique: consequently, technical morality basically allows Christian morality to the extent that it collaborates in this development (even while it rejects everything that contradicts it in this same morality). The eminent dignity of the poor, the subordination of servants to their masters desired by God, the sacrifice of the temporal to the spiritual—we know very well that the bourgeoisie employed all this in its morality to maintain the situation of the working class. Here, too, certain traits of Christian morality were taken up insofar as they could contribute to the construction of the bourgeois world, and they were integrated into a general system that was foreign to them. In this same Christian morality, all that was opposed to normal behavior in the bourgeois world was certainly not forbidden, but progressively eliminated; it passed into silence, rejected into the shadows. Now, by the very fact of this amputation, what was formerly an authentically Christian virtue ceased to be so when it was integrated into another moral system, diverted from its origin and its end. That is why, though the viewpoint of bourgeois morality is identical with Christian morality on many concrete issues (family virtues, private dignity, charity, etc.), in reality it is a caricature of the Christian life, and fundamentally its worst deformation, since it does not serve the glory of God but the construction of a certain type of society. It is obvious that if Christians accept either of these solutions, the conflict is resolved. If the church in the socialist world conforms to the communist order in all its behavior, the problem is resolved by an exterior constraint. If the church is in the hands of the bourgeoisie, and if the priests and pastors are recruited exclusively from this class, the tension is reduced by conforming the church to society. Now for a

Christian, neither of these solutions is acceptable. On the one hand, he cannot accept that his faith has no concrete consequence and remains purely interior; on the other hand, he cannot accept that Christian virtues would be diverted from their origin and their end. But we must understand that if the Christian upholds this double requirement—first, that his faith must be expressed in specific attitudes, and that the entire problem is one of incarnating the truth; and second, that the Christian life is complete, indivisible, that it has no utilitarian goal and that its only orientation is the glory of God; if he refuses to allow that the Christian life would be made to serve the grandeur of the state or the efficacy of technique, then it is he who, here again, provokes the conflict. We must be very clear on this fact: when there is a conflict, or at least tension between Christian morality and another morality, it is the Christian who provokes this tension, and he alone. The non-Christian is in no way responsible, since he has no reason to admit the demand of faith as valid and of superior validity. But then this also means that there is no tension between the two systems except for and in the Christian. *For the Christian*: there is no tension for the others. We have seen how non-Christian society, groups, and even individuals seek to eliminate tensions that are unbearable, that they can see no reason to maintain. By contrast, the Christian finds himself placed in a tension between the morality of the society where he lives, which he must accomplish, and the will of God.[28] Whether we see a morality of distress opposed to a morality of values (Ricoeur), or a morality of responsibility opposed to a morality of conscience (Weber)—in which the first is a morality that judges acts on their consequences, not their intentions, and the second is a morality of absolute respect of certain values, regardless of the consequences—in both cases (and we could find other qualifications), this signifies that the Christian finds himself caught in an opposition of moralities that he can neither refuse nor eliminate. *In the Christian*: this tension only exists in the very person of the Christian. It is not a conflict in itself, nor an opposition of doctrines, nor an objective difference of a scale of values. It is not a theoretical and intellectual divergence: if it were, the conflict could certainly be resolved.

---

28. The constant effort of Christians in establishing a morality has been to refuse the tension between the commandment of God and the decay of the world, as Søe has indicated (§30). Thus man can either flee the world (for example, in monasticism) or relativize the commandments (the Lutheran *Berufsethik*, for example, which ends in a constant reference to grace, evaporating ethical consequences). Social Christianity also relativizes the will of God by denying the radical opposition between the order of the world and revelation.

When the Commandment of God is known in truth, in Revelation and in Grace, *it unmasks* the lie of our commandments and moralities. *It contests* the human who arbitrarily chooses his good, grants his own permission and approves of himself. *It excludes* the reserve that man would like to secure for himself by obeying God conditionally. *It dispossesses* man of his power of judging good and evil by himself.[29] Consequently, it devalues all human morality. But this is not to say that it eliminates and annihilates it.

In any case, whatever resemblance there may be between the content of the commandment or values of the law of God and human moralities, there is a radical difference of orientation and objective: "In contrast to all other claims, the claim of God is that by which we are claimed as the possession of Jesus Christ . . . Whether this takes place or not, whether we accept it or not, is what decides whether our permission is the permission of the divine command and our obligation its obligation, whether we have to do with the command of God or with some other."[30] In contrast to every other morality, the Command of God can only have one meaning and one goal: to bind us to Jesus Christ.

It is not that there is a theoretical opposition of a system of Christian morality, on the one hand, and whatever system, on the other. We shall see that it is impossible to formulate a system of Christian morality. There can only ever be a question of the Christian life as a consequence of the will of God. This life is lived, or it is not. If it is lived, there is Christian conduct (and thus a Christian moral). If it is not lived, there is nothing. The conflict is thus situated at the level of life, of the incarnation of a truth, of a demand. It is produced in relation to a decision that must be made. There is no problem that could be resolved intellectually. Of course, it is very easy to find responses, solutions and conciliations from a theoretical point of view, but at this level there simply is no meaningful Christian ethic. When we talk about tension, therefore, it is not some intellectual game; it is the very reality of the life of the Christian, and it must stay this way. Properly speaking, this tension is constitutive of the person of the Christian engaged in the world. It cannot be formulated in abstract terms since it only manifests in concrete situations where decisions must be made. And each time that a decision is made, the conflict subsides; there has been a response, but not a solution. And the conflict is renewed instantaneously at another level in the new situation that is created. The entirety of the Christian life thus unfolds in this tension between the two moralities; it can never find an equilibrium, nor arrive at a "satisfying" solution. It is never finished. We are not in the

---

29. On these four points, see Barth, *CD* II.2, 583ff.
30. Barth, *CD* II.2, 608.

presence of a neat dialectical play with continually renewed syntheses, ultimately because one of the contradictory elements—the will of God—never lends itself to a synthesis and can never become an object within our grasp. As before, this tension manifests uniquely in concrete situations and is also renewed with each person. What one individual discovers as a temporary solution to a contradiction cannot help his neighbor or his son. The experience of the contradiction must be renewed by each one. What one person has done can only be a witness and perhaps an example for his neighbor. But this tension, which is inseparable from the Christian life, does not result in neurosis since it is integrated in the circuit of faith and hope. These two powers that bind us to Jesus Christ bring the tension back to the reduced dimensions of our earthly life and prevent it from overwhelming the person, the key to our psychology, in a hopeless negation of all response. Beyond this tension in which he finds himself, the Christian knows that a response has already been given that is incomparably greater than the conflicts which he encounters. And this response is not outside of or alien to his contradiction: it is not a compensatory conviction, nor a response having nothing in common with the anguish that can be born of conflict. In fact, if conflict exists, it is precisely because of this faith and this hope. They precede the tension. It is because Christian faith and hope are manifest in a life that this latter is henceforth plunged into contradiction. There is thus no preexisting conflict between the will of God and the morality of the world, and then a hope that would come to appease the conflict. First, there is the hearing of the Word of God which, in manifesting his Will, produces faith and hope in us, and then the appearance of the conflict that we enter into when we want to obey the will of God. This conflict necessarily arises when the decision of God calls the order of values established by the world into question. We know that Kierkegaard particularly insisted on the fact that the call which God personally addresses to a man produces a suspension of the ethical order in which he normally lives. The vocation that God formulates for this individual might not fit into any moral framework. This does not mean that the order of values is objectively or collectively abolished; this order subsists in this group for these individuals who have not heard the command of God, and the one who has received the call cannot speak of a suppression of this hierarchy and of these conducts. But for him, the intervention of God creates a consummate rupture with all morality, including Christian morality. For this man, there is no longer any good except the good expressed for him in this order of God. For the encounter with God, though it has moral consequences, is not first and foremost the creation of an ethic; above all, it is an encounter of the one who lives in sin with the one who extends grace, of the one who is destined for death with the one who raises the dead, of the one who is determined with the one who liberates him; and by this very fact all morality, all order, and all hierarchies of values are negated.³¹

The Morality of the World is one of the penultimate things that have not been absolutely condemned by the absolute of revelation, nor valorized by a supplement of grace, as Bonhoeffer has shown (*Ethics*, 159): "Christian life neither destroys nor sanctions the penultimate." The Good defined by moralities has nothing to do with the Good, nor with our salvation, but it is still useful in allowing possibilities of living on earth. Niebuhr, too, says that every moral obligation aims to promote harmony and overcome chaos, and consequently it contains an element of validity for faith; but this validity is neither ultimate nor *integrated into* Christian truth or assumed by it.³² Incidentally, perhaps we must distinguish here among these penultimate works: political, economic, or technical works, which are the work of man,³³ can be qualified (as Bonhoeffer does) as a necessary stage moving toward ultimate things. For these penultimate things do not exist "in themselves," but are only so in relation to the ultimate things. But neither are they a path that leads directly to the ultimate things; they must pass through the judgment. From another perspective, the morality of the world, as a revelation of the knowledge of good and evil, is of another order. It is practically useful for the preservation of the world. It in no way prepares the way for the ultimate things. It has a *lesser* validity and excellence than all the other works of man. But the Christian cannot claim to treat it as nothing because of its modest utility for man. And in the same way, in a situation of tension with this morality, Christians have to confront ethical relativisms with the law of love, which serves precisely as the limit, barrier, and opposition to

---

31. We find a curious application of this notion in 1 Cor 5:9-12: Paul forbids the "saints" of the church of Corinth from having any relation with the sexually immoral, thieves, or idolaters. But he makes a distinction: if they are sexually immoral, thieving, or idolatrous non-Christians, then it is perfectly normal to continue to have relations with them. They obey other precepts, another morality; we do not have to judge them, we can encounter them and accept them as they are. Otherwise, Paul says, we would have to leave the world (which is *never* the permanent and ultimate command of God). But by contrast, if these are Christians who behave thus, we must cut off relations with them, not even eat with them and reject them, for they have to live according to another rule of life, the only rule that we have to know as Christians.

32. We will also recall a third essential consequence. The Christian recognizes the relative validity of the morality of the world and knows very well that they cannot escape it.

33. Ellul, "La Théologie de la grande ville" (*Verbum Caro*, 1948—complete study to appear). [TN: In the 2013 edition, the editors note that this essay never appeared in the review *Verbum Caro*; instead, it was incorporated into *Sans feu ni lieu: Signification biblique de la Grande Ville*, written in 1951 but not published until 1975 (available in English as *The Meaning of the City*).]

this relativism—which is legitimate from a natural point of view but which must be put in relation with the affirmation of the Love of God, with all that this entails.

In these conditions, the Christian should not try to resolve the conflict by denying this morality of the world in one way or another. We find here another aspect of the lie that we have already denounced (whether in the form of the synthesis of the two moralities, or in the more or less camouflaged negation of the specificity of the Christian life which aligns itself with one of the ethical systems of the world). How could this elimination of the non-Christian morality come about? Historically, it happens under two forms. First, within Christendom, there has always been the grand attempt to make the Christian morality into a universal morality and impose Christian conduct on everyone. For Christians, this morality is so obvious, so superior, so valid *in itself* that they cannot comprehend those who do not obey it. In a "Christian" society, where the church is officially recognized, where the state protects the Christian religion, there is only one morality, which is decreed by the church, and all who belong to this society must obey it.[34] This leads to a dreadful situation, for as we have been constantly repeating, the Christian life can only be an expression of faith. When we make Christian morality into a universal requirement, we detach this morality from its roots, demanding that men who have no faith live as if they did; that is, we ultimately condemn them to hypocrisy. Of course, this problem was recognized, though perhaps not in terms as blunt as these. There were two responses to it: first, in the Middle Ages, there was the theory of implicit

---

34. Häring is very characteristic of this catholic tendency when, on the basis of the characteristics of Christian morality, he clearly formulates the idea that all morality corresponds to these criteria: thus "the morality of Christ and all authentic human morality is of an essentially religious character" (*La loi du Christ*, 1:29). We see the same abusive assimilation when he writes, "It is a conviction common to all peoples that man hears the voice of God and of the good in his heart" (ibid., 1:188). The entire debate ultimately turns around the question of knowing if the Norm of Morality is written by God in the very being of man, and if there is a coincidence between the natural instinct of the subject and the divine will (ibid., 1:351), which we expressly reject. It seems to us that Scripture is very clear on this subject, and that when Jesus constantly opposes the spontaneous conduct of man with "But I say to you . . . ," there is no coincidence between natural instinct and the commandment of God. Additionally, Häring's viewpoint necessarily leads to the consequence that we condemn: to the extent that all morality must correspond to the Christian schema (since there is a natural morality coming from God), whatever does not correspond to this is not a morality. This allows him to liquidate all modern attempts at moral thought in three lines: "From the outset, let us rule out scientific ethics and moral perspectives which sacrifice the human person to the collectivity . . . these conceptions can in no way establish the seriousness of morality; rather, they undermine it" (ibid., 1:34). The error of his premises leads to the inhumanity of his conclusions!

faith (this man who does not have a personal faith belongs to the church all the same, he participates in the faith of the church, so we must require that he behave as a Christian). Second, in the seventeenth century, for example, the Christian morality was made into a natural morality: obeying it did not require living by faith; it was enough to follow our nature. In both cases, the heresy resulted from considering morality in itself, and not the personal will of the God of Jesus Christ; Christian conduct was reckoned to be of utmost importance, not the relation with Jesus Christ. The action of the Christian and of the church can never consist in creating moral obligations elaborated from the outside, presented as universally valid and undifferentiated. The commandment of God must remain a commandment—that is, a personal word—and must come after the testimony of grace. In effect, knowing the law of God intellectually is not sufficient to convince man of its excellence; it must be received within the work of God accomplished in Jesus Christ, and this can only be received in and by faith. In any case, that is why teaching children the law and "Christian behavior" does not mean very much and will necessarily be put in question when the preaching of the gospel is understood. But there is obviously this constant temptation to replace this preaching with a "religious" moral education, both for children and for the masses, a temptation that rests on the need for security and convenience. It is easier to make somebody live according to the precepts of a morality; doing so yields results that are more certain, more visible, and that we can at least count on. To organize a Christian society, we clearly cannot avoid relying on morality, since it can be a common measure for all, imposed from the outside, without needing to take account of personal differentiations. By contrast, the preaching of the gospel risks all possibilities, because it allows God the freedom to intervene (or not to intervene). No society can be organized on this basis, for God's intervention cannot be counted on and does not happen in a mass and collective manner. And now we come upon a third aspect of this same temptation.

One of the big temptations for Christians and contemporary French theologians is to draw false ethical interpretations from the great theological rediscovery that Christ is Lord of the world. This is expressed in two errors:

1. Many are convinced that because the morality made by the men of the world is *also* under the lordship of Jesus Christ, it is thereby legitimate. But we forget that this lordship is affirmed over a world in revolt, that its rebel powers have not yet been eliminated, and that the fact of the lordship of Christ does not justify all the projects of the world, but only that (*a*) these powers are virtually conquered; (*b*) whatever the projects of men may be, they will ultimately be brought before God

to be judged; and *(c)* the end of history is established, known, and inevitable: it is the reintegration of the whole in Christ.

2. The second error comes from the idea that since the lordship of Christ is exercised in the church *and* in the world (according to the well-known image of the two circles), the difference between these two domains is also only relative. We thus consider that the morality made by men *for the problems of the world* comes from God as well, as long as the Christian faith has nothing in particular to say here. For example, on economic or political problems, we accept that Christianity has nothing specific to say, therefore we must look to the most valid solutions of men. But here again, we forget that the criteria of "validity/invalidity" can never consist in superimposing a Christian morality (or requirements of the Christian faith) on the moralities of the world to find points of agreement. Such an operation treats human morality and the will of God as two grandeurs of the same nature, which not only contradicts biblical Revelation but also evacuates the meaning of the incarnation.

It is obvious that since the lordship of Jesus Christ bears on the entire world and on all men, this means that the Commandment of God goes for everybody. But this commandment can only be heard, *re*-cognized as such, and obeyed in and by faith. Therefore, declaring the commandment of God as such before pagans is meaningless. Now, certain texts of K. Barth could lend themselves to confusion in this sense. We must clear up an ambiguity here. When Barth says, for example, that the Christian ethic claims to be valid for everyone,[35] this is based on the notion of responsibility: "The covenant of grace is the beginning of all the ways and works of God and thus the human existence that it determines is that of every man: it is thus each man that it will consider as a responsible being"—this is obvious. But this absolutely does not mean that the Christian ethic as such is enforceable and recognizable by pagans as the only true ethic, for it can only be discerned as true from within the acceptance of the revelation, and it can only be recognized as binding based on the knowledge of grace. In truth, every man is thus responsible, just as in truth he is under the lordship of Jesus Christ, but the ethic produced by faith cannot be proposed to him as universally applicable.

---

35. Barth, *CD* II.2, 137, 150, etc. [TN: Despite its similarities to certain passages, the citation following this footnote in the sentence above is not verbatim from either of the two pages cited. In the 2013 French edition, the footnote is placed as it is here, before the citation in quotation marks, implying that perhaps it is not a direct citation from the French edition of the *Church Dogmatics* either.]

That the command of God is presented to men at the same time that the gospel is announced to them, that they cannot flee into irresponsibility, and consequently that the law is affirmed as valid for them as well—even though they are not Christians, but because they belong to Christ (even if they don't know it)—all of this is true. But it is no less true that the life in Christ which is the whole reality of this ethic is also and at the same time impossible, incomprehensible, literally insignificant, and unlivable for them.

Therefore, one of the essential rules of the Christian life will be to never demand that a non-Christian behave as a Christian. If grace truly renews the person, if the Christian life is already the witness of the life of the one who is in Christ, if obedience to the Christian ethic is the response of love of the one who has received grace to the one who has manifested his love in extending this grace, how then could we ask that a man who has not received or known that he was under grace behave as if . . . as if his person was renewed, as if he knew the grace that was extended to him, as if he knew himself to be the object of the love of God? This obligation could only be a constraint for him; the morality to which he is subject can only be built on the fear of punishment, and God thus becomes the Great Condemner. In effect, this is what regularly happens in "Christian" societies. The other aspect of the problem in a secular or non-Christian society resides in the same conviction that Christian morality is fundamentally superior, which also implicitly contains the idea that the non-Christian should obey it. But since Christians do not have the means to constrain them, they limit themselves to judging others (including Christians who are firmly committed to laicity, and "open to the world"). It suffices to consider the scandal experienced by Christians when they run up against conduct that is truly inspired by another morality. Certainly, they will often exhibit understanding for an individual, but they are intransigent toward the state, for example. Christians never stop demanding that the non-Christian state renounce the death penalty because human life is sacred before God; that the state establish a special status of conscientious objection because God said "you shall not kill"; and these same Christians rightly demand that the state should be secular—but how can we not see the total contradiction here? Why should the secular state recognize the will of God? Likewise, Christians are scandalized when the state follows a realist political policy, seeking efficiency first and foremost, contradicting principles set forth as Christian, etc. But how could we expect a state that is not Christian (and cannot be) to act in a Christian manner?[36] This state is submitted to necessity, and most often

---

36. Barth, *CD* II.2, demonstrates that the good defended by the state is certainly not the good that it could create on its own or preach, but the fact that this state keeps

obeys it. Christians, alas, can play the fine role of denouncing the state, but only because they do not have to deal with this necessity themselves. When they take on these public functions, they generally make similar political decisions because politics is always an art of the possible which supposes that one acts as a function of necessities. This is certainly not to justify the excess, disobedience, and dishonesty of the state. This is not a declaration of "well, *everything* is permissible for the state." Decidedly, no. But on the one hand this state is submitted to necessities, and when Christians want to ignore this fact, they are hypocrites; on the other hand, this state is called to apply a morality that is not Christian morality. It applies the morality of the world, but it is a morality all the same, and it is within this morality and in relation to it that the Christian is called to judge what the state does. To protest against torture in the name of Jesus Christ before the secular state is absurd. To protest in the name of the Declaration of the Rights of Man,[37] a moral element that the state has fixed for itself, is legitimate. And so, recognizing the relative validity of this morality, Christians must recall it for non-Christians; for it is an element of the preservation of society, an element of life, and it must in some way play the role of watchman. The Christian and the church must take absolutely seriously the declarations, principles, formulae, and values in which moralists, politicians, jurists, and even public opinion express their convictions. And taking them seriously, they must take them up, remember them and confront the action of men with the principles they have given themselves.

Therefore, the Christian does not have to judge this morality as such. He does not have to pit the two moralities against one another and assert one as superior to the other, for they are not in competition in society. He does not have to objectively proclaim the Christian morality as a requirement valid for everybody; in the name of what would this objective superiority be recognized? In the name of Jesus Christ? But precisely, in this

---

an order and a law that allows, that makes externally possible, the preaching and knowledge of the Good willed by God. By safeguarding the common life of men, by avoiding disintegration, this state allows for the possibility of Christian community, and consequently, the possible presence of God in the milieu of men. It is a question of a provisional order that does not contain grace in itself but that permits its expression. Consequently the morality of the world, like the law instituted by the community, must not be neglected and treated as nothing by Christians. Christians cannot become the enemies of what is nevertheless the product of the sin of man, but no more can they content themselves with blessing these inventions of man, in letting them follow their own path and in viewing them as purely and simply expressing the will of God (cf. Niebuhr, *Moral Man and Immoral Society*).

37. TN: The 2013 French editors add "of man" to Ellul's "Declaration of Rights," seeing it as a reference to the foundational French human rights text of 1789.

society, Jesus Christ is not recognized as the Son of God. In the name of the content of the morality? But who will judge the superiority of one content over another? But really, Christians do not behave "better" than others. And anyway, this "better"—by what standard? We are situated in the same dilemma on the public and on the personal levels: why should we demand that an alcoholic give up his vice because of Jesus Christ if he does not believe in Jesus Christ? When we engage in this debate, we realize that there are only two responses: either we appeal to the current common morality that is accepted by everybody—with its extreme weaknesses and its variability—or we witness to Jesus Christ and pray for the conversion of this man, which should translate into new behavior. It is in this same sense that we have to pray for the authorities, who are only humans. But additionally, at another level we must keep a running dialogue with the non-Christian and the secular state. That is, recognizing the validity of the morality that they follow, it is *also* fitting to proclaim the will of God, as a witness, announcing this will as coming from God who is not recognized as such, not as a morality that one could obey without recognizing this God. "The Lord of heaven and earth says that . . ." But in reality, Christians and the church generally do not dare to speak like this. They are afraid of being ridiculous. They have the unfortunate habit of misrepresenting the will of God. They do not behave as ambassadors of this Lord. Instead of accepting the conduct of man which naturally accompanies his morality, and announcing the will of the Lord which calls man to something else, committing a double error, Christians prefer to present a morality that expresses the will of God in the guise of a natural morality. The same goes for the state and collective entities. That is why their judgments and opinions in these domains are so frequently inexistent; either they take a purely sociological moral attitude as the will of God, or they are scandalized in the presence of conduct inspired by necessity. But on the contrary, when a Christian announces the will of God in the presence of the state, the tension that had been his personal affair is introduced into society.[38] He becomes an element of contradiction himself. But this is remarkably fruitful: he thus keeps society "open," he prevents it from crystallizing, from sclerosis. The Christian, when he does not condemn, when he does not seek to eliminate the morality of the world, but when he proclaims the consequences of the lordship of God, plays the most fruitful, positive, and original role imaginable: by introducing tension into society, he keeps it alive. He restores its capacity to evolve. He proposes a truly revolutionary direction for life. And in reality, he is precisely the only

---

38. Søe rightly explains how the Christian ethic ultimately always tries to reduce this tension (instead of introducing it), either by a flight from the world, or by relativizing the commandment. All of social Christianity is marked by this error. Søe, §30.

one capable of fulfilling this role. He sets off a positive, living, and fruitful contradiction at the heart of a society that wants to be unified, that claims to resolve contradictions. The state uses violence—so be it. But let it not pretend that doing so is good, right, or human. Human justice can only exist based on constraint, thanks to punishment and threats—alright! To hope for the contrary is a puerile idealism. But let us not say that this is Justice and the Good. Order is indispensable, authorities can legitimately demand obedience and respect, the mobilization of wealth, hearts and bodies is expressed as moral duty—perhaps. But let us not call this Freedom. Now, Justice, Love, and Freedom are not inventions of Man. These are not platonic values. They are decisions of God. They are unbreakable. But they bear within them a decisive contradiction of the pretensions of man, of society, and of the state. There is no getting around it.[39] On the contrary, this contradiction must be made to break out as strongly as possible—not for opposition's sake, but so that this man might *live*, and this society too, and even this state that we oppose, which would die without this contradiction. The excess of order and of mobilization, of duties and constraints, cannot be curbed from the inside by self-discipline, nor by a juridical organization; they only stop when they encounter an external obstacle. And this latter will be the No of the Christian Demand, formulated at the same time as the Yes to this moral order of society. As Ricoeur rightly says, the Christian must continually choose: either they will obey the will of God, that is, love—in sacrificing human justice—or they will exercise human justice (accepting the moral duty of belonging to society) in sacrificing love. This choice can never be made once and for all; it must be continually remade. Nor can this choice ever be satisfying. We can never say "my conscience is clean" after making this choice. It is too simple to say, "As Christians we must obey

---

39. Consequently, the critique that Niebuhr makes of Luther (*The Nature and Destiny of Man*) seems correct when he considers that Luther's position devalues all ethics of the world because they are all marked by sin, and treats distinctions between them as unimportant. But at times, Niebuhr continues to situate the moralities of the world and the requirement of God as extensions of one another. Luther's error would have been to apply his precise vision of the individual—who is radically sinful, whose justice is only sin—to collective life. Consequently, the progress of knowledge, the search for freedom and social justice all count for nothing. In Niebuhr's eyes, this is Luther's failure in his effort to link life in history and the response to grace. But in truth, Niebuhr's effort to maintain the radically sinful character of man and the possibility of socioethical progress simultaneously seems impossible to concretely uphold, and ultimately very artificial. The point of encounter that he establishes between nature and grace (mutual love and sacrificial love) seems to us to repeat the classic error of creating a coincidence between the work of man and the work of God. For Niebuhr, once more it is a question of saving the works of man by themselves, of demonstrating that they are valid in themselves.

God rather than men." This is true, of course. But this cannot be done by our own justice;[40] for if in obeying God I disobey the state (which God has commanded me to obey), I break solidarity with my neighbor (whom God has commanded me to love), I push the unfaithful far from me in judging them (and I can no longer witness to them). I cannot be so certain that this is the "right path." The only proper position is thus to go from decision to decision, from choice to choice, to maintain the tension between the two demands, in such a manner that the breach remains open in the hearts of the men who surround us and in the society where we live. In the moral wall that man tries to build himself, behind which he wants to take shelter from God, there must be a breach through which God's will can enter. And in this society, the tension lived by the Christian between the two moralities is itself the breach through which God passes, when his Word makes his requirement reverberate in a life in whose eyes the Christian has been a witness, in a society where the Christian has lived, in which he has participated. And when this Word is thus present, living, where the Requirement of the will of God becomes indisputable, then the tension can disappear, for the Word brings its decisive contradiction to the moral order which can only explode, since the choice becomes radical and necessary. Then no more obedience is owed to the order of the world. Holiness is a judgment of this order. The explosion of Revelation annihilates the ethics of the world. Whether in the moral life of the individual, in their decisions and their choices, whether in the moral order of society, its imperatives, ideals and structures, the tension would still be accommodation and treason if it were a lasting solution to the contradiction. But in reality this tension is constantly put in question by the demand of absolute obedience, of undivided faithfulness which makes the word of God reverberate in our lives. The one who lives in the Tension between the two moralities must not believe they are more just than the one who chooses one in sacrificing the other, for precisely to this very one, the prophet's question rings out: "How long will you hobble on two feet?" (1 Kgs 18:21).[41]

---

40. TN: The 2013 French edition corrects a typo here, adding in what I have translated as "our own."

41. [TN: I have translated Ellul's French biblical citation here; the NRSV's less figurative rendering reads, "How long will you go limping with two different opinions?"] This conception of the double morality has nothing to do with Luther's notion of the two kingdoms. (Or at least according to current interpretations of Luther's thought. Of course, this doctrine of Luther must not be confused with the doctrine bearing the same name in medieval Catholicism). There are two kingdoms, obeying different laws and moralities, and the Christian is a citizen of two worlds—one temporal, political, where the state is the master—and a spiritual world. Private life (which is more capable of being shaped by spiritual life) is thus completely separated from social life. The Christian

But let us recall once more that the entire ethical effort of man, all of his seeking, all his constructions are not purely and simply denied and rejected by God. Again, we are talking about a work of man; and though it is a product of sin, it is a work that God saves *with* man, with the works of this man. But he saves it in assuming it himself in the death of his son; he saves it *through* judgment (and not because this work is good of itself!).

Certainly, Niebuhr is right to say that it will be judged by Christ and not the Father, and therefore judged on its possibilities and its sin, not on its finitude. But we must go further: to the extent that this ethic is a product of disobedience, God upholds it only in destroying the evil that it represents. But he only destroys evil in assuming the consequences himself in the atonement; at this moment, and in the heavenly Jerusalem, what man calls Good in the course of history and under various masks will become an integral part of what God himself designates the Good. We can thus say that in this way man participates, by grace, in the very will of God for the heavenly Jerusalem. But we do not have the right to draw any implications

---

obeys a calling but does not have to change the order of the world. The authorities of the state must watch over this order, a function given them by God. The state must be built on the law of God (*primus usus*) to attain and establish *justitia civilis* (see critiques and interpretations of this in Thielicke, Bonhoeffer, Søe, etc.). Once again, this idea of two distinct domains must be considered as one of the fruits of Christendom. For Luther, who lived under Christendom, it goes without saying that secular offices, the state, the civil law, etc., are "Christian," inspired by the Decalogue, and capable of establishing a *justitia civilis* conformed to the will of God. It is thus normal to separate a spiritual realm, where the church has its responsibility, from a temporal realm, where the state is responsible. But the fundamental error is to think that Christendom is a *normal* situation. Luther runs into obstacles such as the Jews, and even more the Turks. Is he ready to hand over the government of the earthly city to the Turks? For us there is no division of two domains or two kingdoms, there is no distinction between public and private life, etc. There is only one world in which we live, with its forms of spirituality, and the domain of the church is very worldly: the church is a sociological body, Christians are submitted to political and economic influences, faith is contaminated by religion, etc. And the church and Christians find themselves within this world. Within the temporal, the bearer of the revelation (not the Spiritual) is found, and this is not the same as *two* domains. Thus, on the one hand, the Christian is called to participate in the activities of the world where he lives; he is called to see them not as justice before God but as relatively useful and normal. It is normal that this world creates its morality. But on the other hand, the Christian is called to live the plenitude of the faith that is given it in all its dimensions, without distinguishing between the temporal and the spiritual, the private and the social, etc. In his life, the Christian faith entails transformations in politics, in profession, etc., which are directly referred to the person of Jesus Christ. In this way Tension is established in *one* world (and not separation), a tension that cannot signify rupture any more than adhesion. It is a dialectical relationship, which simultaneously eliminates the possibility of autonomy for the morality of the world, and of autonomy for the morality of revelation in relation to the world. Incidentally, perhaps Luther conceived of the relation between the two kingdoms as a similarly dialectical relation.

concerning the current and in itself validity of this human morality; neither can we see a continuity between this morality and the declaration of the Good in the kingdom of God.

PART II

Morality of the World

Let us clarify right away that, without conducting an exhaustive study of Morality and Moralities, it seems indispensable to map out several points of orientation with regard to the moralities that exist in the world, precisely within the perspective that recognizes the double morality.[1] We must do this from a realist perspective. Much later, we will have to examine the fact that realism is precisely one of the defining marks of Christian behavior in the world. But for now, we can already conduct a realist analysis of the ethical phenomenon simply in keeping with our project. In effect, we are not formulating an ideal morality valid for all men, nor giving reasons why it should be obeyed. We are not seeking the "if" and the "why" of the authority of a possible morality. As we have said, what must be done, what we must obey—according to the revelation, and as a consequence of faith—is the will of God. Consequently, there is no need for us to formulate ethical resolutions, nor to embellish them with justifications, nor to construct a new system. We simply have to consider what is: the reality of the ethical phenomenon—if possible, including all of its facets, in its current form, in its presence. But we cannot give into any exultation that would make moral-

---

1. This will be neither a philosophy of morality nor a sociological study, properly speaking. For the sociological analysis of the moral life, we refer to the chapter bearing this title in the *Traité de sociologie* (vol. II) edited by Gurvitch. We accept the framework traced by Gurvitch, and his sketch of the genres and forms of moral life, which pose us no difficulty. By contrast, we have reservations regarding the relation that he establishes between these genres and forms, on the one hand, and the types of civilizations, on the other.

ity out to be more than it is, which happens with almost everyone who lives a perfectly worthy life or constructs a satisfying ethical system. We cannot transpose the morality that is a real fact—as much in its expression as in its practice and its authority—into the register of the ideal and absolute. Morality does not transcend man. It is of man.[2] Rejecting idealism obliges us to consider ethics at the level of man, and nowhere else. Nothing in this observation and reflection should lead us to make morality into a divine or mystical affair. This could only be the result of metaphysics. Now, taking this position from the outset keeps us from getting into pointless games. Morality is of man. It is created by him; this is what Genesis teaches. This is also a factual observation available to everyone, provided they do not give in to sentimentalism, a need for justification, or the idealist philosophy of a given moment. Of course, this formulation of morality created by man must not be taken in a simplistic or unilateral sense. It is multiform; it is ambiguous. We must consider its various aspects: is it a product of a group, or of a moral requirement? Does it express intellectual rigor or awareness, etc. But in every case, morality's origin, as well as its authority and its structure, reside in man himself. It is neither a divine gift nor a product of nature which is greater than man.[3] It is not universal. It is linked to the ability to "know good and evil" and decide upon them, which man seized for himself. And in this decision, indeed, man resembles the gods. But the progression is not (as it has so often been described): the gods (or, why not, transcendent reason) formulate a morality, they communicate it to man, and by observing it man transcends the human condition. No, the reality is completely different: man, obsessed with a desire to be like the gods (and of course, this is exactly the same when man denies the existence of God: the obsession of being like God is a distinguishing feature of Sartre, whose entire oeuvre can be explained by this sentiment), decides on good and evil. In so doing, he is effectively like the gods; but then comes the bitter aftertaste of application, practice, and judgment. And then man knows very well that he is not god. In examining this phenomenon, realism is the only attitude that allows us to grasp what it is in its totality and without confusion.[4]

---

2. Saying this does not reduce ethics to one of the various activities of man; ethics remains a field of its own, as Barth has shown (*CD* II.2, 509ff.).

3. Several particularly lucid essays easily come to this conclusion: for example, Murry (*The Free Society*) who shows that history does not have an intrinsic direction but that morality consists in the decision to assign one to it; that the only moral process is that of Trial and Error; and finally, that there is no "free" society, but only a society that wants to be free. Of course, man's decision to name the good is not arbitrary.

4. Cf. the excellent line of reasoning by Weil, "Raison, morale et politique."

Without indulging an academic curiosity, it is not without value to recall that the moral phenomenon is composed of a large number of diverse elements.[5] In whatever frame of reference—whether as aspiration, tradition, virtue, purpose, etc.—ultimately, the object of the moral life is *always* the accomplishment of what man calls good in a given time and place. And that is why we cannot completely agree with Gurvitch when he endeavors to eliminate the term "Good" itself from his analysis. To say that "moral experience is a battle against the obstacles which impede human effort (whether collective or individual) as a worthy manifestation of selfless agreement" is undoubtedly correct, but we are obliged to add that this agreement takes place because there is a consensus on the temporal idea of the Good! It is fallacious to spurn this in a sociological study for fear of entering philosophical debate on the Good!

First of all, an "objective" morality exists. It is a system of values or imperatives, whether formulated or not, but that is presented as having an objectivity which imposes itself on all the men in a group. This morality of principles affirms the superiority of a certain conduct and presents certain ideal objectives to attain. Ultimately, its authority always holds to an assertion of efficacy: there is always an element of success in whatever domain grounds the authority of the objective morality. It might promise happiness, the creation of a more elevated kind of man, reward, the favor of the gods, an equilibrium or security to be obtained, the realization of progress, etc.; in any case, it is the proclamation that applying the moral rule will lead us to a situation that is better than where we currently find ourselves. In this objective morality, we can discern at least three totally heterogeneous elements: first, theoretical morality. It is formulated in an imperative manner as a system, either by a religious authority or a philosopher. It can represent a moral ideal. But it is generally a creation of individuals, of notable personalities. It has a very intellectual character, and the less it is directly felt by its contemporaries, the more its authority is established and affirmed. Next, we encounter sociological morality, which results from a collective need; this need comes from religious or supernatural beliefs, or from a political imperative or economic necessity. In any case, this morality does not express an individual conscience, but a collective conviction that both rests on and yet simultaneously constrains individual convictions. Generally, it is not systematically formulated and constructed; but it represents a very

---

5. On the different elements of morality from a theological point of view, see (among many others) Reiner, "Ethik und Menschenbild," 284.

large ensemble of values and imperatives that are more or less coherent or contradictory. It relates either to the necessity of preservation of the group as such, or to an ideal image that the group has of itself and of man. In any case, this morality goes together with a requirement and an authority.

Finally, there is moral custom. In the ethical domain, the group follows certain customs that are no longer requirements (which differentiates them from the preceding case) but have become conformities. These moral customs deriving from the past—not from anxiety for the future—have an authority that rests on their time-tested character, on tradition (and not on a presently accepted ideal image, like sociological morality). These are not simply habits. For these moral customs too are imperatives, with a regulatory content that must not be dismissed. There is a formal judgment on the one who disobeys. But of course, there is a direct link between habits and these customs: deeply ingrained habit becomes custom. A custom that is attacked, degraded, and contradicted by the moral ideal of the moment will be interpreted as a habit. Likewise, the sanction of this custom is only social (as a judgment of the collectivity), and to a certain extent the same can be said for habits. Whatever they concern, these latter represent the purely concrete aspect. At this level, there is no discord between what is and what should be. Habits are exactly and uniquely the real behavior of men in a group, in whatever domain. They can be in complete disagreement with the theoretical morality, while such disagreement with sociological morality can only be relative and does not happen without difficulty. In this case, over time the contradiction can lead to the formulation of a new sociological morality. But this latter offers resistance, formulating judgments that put the new habits in question, dubbing them "bad habits." The conflict plays out at both the collective and individual levels, but there can never be a complete identification of sociological morality with habits. In effect, the former always formulates an ideal, imperative element, presenting models to which we ought to conform; but this is done precisely because this conformity does not happen naturally—we do not spontaneously live in this way. This sociological morality tends to inform habits. On the contrary, it is certainly possible that there may be complete agreement between moral custom and habits.

Opposed to this objective morality there is a subjective morality. This latter is composed of at least two elements: first, we must give an account of what, at best, we can call the "imperative of conscience." As an imperative within himself, an individual feels that this or that act is good. He must obey. The "voice of conscience" tells him what is good and evil. This is a purely individual phenomenon. In appearance, this is an intuitive knowledge of a transcendent reality. The Good, directly known, is imposed with authority. If we disobey, we will suffer malaise and judgment. If we obey, we enjoy satisfaction and happiness. Whether the origin of this imperative is biological or sociological, whether it is the personalized fruit of an education, an economic situation, or the expression of instincts, complexes, and resentments discovered by depth psychology, etc.—we do not need to answer this here; at present, no explanation seems absolutely decisive.

The other aspect of this moral subjectivity is the choice of decision. Placed before the objective morality in one of its various forms, or again having felt the imperative of conscience, the individual is confronted with a choice (whether conscious or not): to obey or disobey. He must make this decision himself, since he will act himself. At this moment (and only at this moment), properly speaking, there is an ethical "situation." The individual will decide on his own what he will do, he will risk this judgment, he will force himself to accomplish the good. He will choose: this choice can be radical and can "create his existence" (to adopt a currently fashionable phrase), or it can be simply one of many successive, fragmentary, smaller choices that will constitute this ethical existence in practice. We could say that in this way, successively, man chooses himself. Choice transforms the individual into an ethical subject. He may subsequently be led to systematically formulate the reason for his decision. In this case, he constructs an objective theoretical morality.

These are very basic elements. They have no philosophical refinement but are useful in their banality, and we must particularly be sure to never abandon either of them, nor focus only on one. The moral phenomenon is the *ensemble* of these elements. Morality is not *only* the ethical system of Aristotle or Kant; the general temptation of philosophers is to consider only these. No more is it exclusively the sociological imperative and the scale of values of a society or its habits, which are the preoccupations of sociologists who treat the other items as negligible. But neither is it simply personal decision and choice; rejecting the objective morality and focusing only on the importance of choice as constitutive of morality is a frequent mistake of Christians, existentialists, and phenomenologists. These various exclusive attitudes are errors: the elements that we have recalled complement one another.

I

Diversity of Moralities[1]

Imperatives, values, virtues, and ethical systems (whether highly-developed or not) differ widely according to time and place. This obvious fact bears repeating, because even among enlightened intellectuals, the medieval presupposition that Western morality is really a universal morality persists. A morality exists everywhere, in every society, but it is not necessarily the same. Morality has no permanent content.[2] Murder is generally condemned, but this is not always true. Without mentioning our own societies, where

---

1. Obviously we cannot speak here of all attempts at morality, but we refer to the remarkable *Traité de l'action morale* by Georges Bastide, which appeared in 1961. On the problem of the sociology of morality, see particularly Gurvitch in book two of *Traité de sociologie*, and also the articles of Jean Cazaneuve, Pierre Ansart, and Andrée Michel on the social frameworks of moral doctrines in the *Cahiers internationaux de sociologie*, 1963.

2. One of the many merits of Karl Marx is to have shown the contingent character of morality, its relation with economic structures and class relations, and its role in the play of social forces. But on the one hand, his doctrine was considerably deformed by Lenin, and still more afterward (cf. for example "Ethik" in *Petit vocabulaire philosophique* by Rosental and Judin in Russian, 1954; Garaudy, *Le communisme et la morale*, 1945); on the other hand, he falls under the same critique that he himself leveled against moralists, that of transforming the relative values of the proletariat into an absolute, and establishing in his turn an ethics of history, directly opposed to the ethics of philosophy (cf. Berdyaev, *Christianisme et réalité sociale*; Niebuhr, *Interpretation of Christian Ethics*, chapter 1 and page 122; on the contrary, the other critiques presented by Bois, "La crise de la Morale et le Christianisme," 82, seem ineffective, as does his effort to justify the validity of a natural morality in spite of Marxist critiques. He is completely unsuccessful!).

murder is recommended in times of war³ (but this is a collective decision, and we could say that it concerns a hierarchy of values—i.e., the value of the homeland is superior to the value of human life), we must remark that in times of peace, individual murder has been posited as a moral requirement (sometimes directly linked to magic or to religion). It was treated this way among the Assassins, the Sicarii, the Thugs⁴—the religious or magical foundation absolutely does not destroy the ethical character of the decision that must be made by the member of a sect or cult, nor of the demands of the group regarding this individual. Murder was not only a magical act; it was truly of the order of virtue. Nor should it be argued that this was limited to small groups: as soon as there is a group that makes a moral demand, there is a morality.

Among the Incas, for example, there is *no* respect for life; and yet, these are highly civilized societies. Thus we cannot say that respect for life is a universal commandment, the foundation of a natural morality. Finally, we should not argue that these examples are aberrant, exceptional, abnormal, and therefore unimportant, for in the majority of "societies of men" in parahistorical societies, we find requirements of the same order. And incidentally, since Freud we know that what is "abnormal" is very important, that it can give us the key to the rest. When imposed as a moral requirement and value, murder introduces us to a moral phenomenon that is almost universal, that of vengeance. In most societies, vengeance is a moral duty dictated by the solidarity of the tribe, family, or group of men. It always plays an immense role, and certain moralities are developed from this basic concept. The Bible knows it, imposing the principle of an eye for an eye; the same goes for Greek society or Roman society, as it still does with the vendetta in nineteenth-century Corsica, or the "underworld" of pimps and gangsters today. Presented by the group as a duty, experienced by moral conscience as an obligation, linked with concepts of good and evil (—the common judgment is that the one who avenges does good. Biblically, the *Go'el* or

---

3. We recall that for certain moralities, war is a nearly supreme value, and I am not alluding here to a Hitlerian ethic, for example, but to more ancient conceptions. For example, consider this text of Heraclitus, *Fragment* 53/8, 112: "War is father of all and king of all; and some he manifested as gods, some as men; some he made slaves, some free . . . we must know that war is the common condition." (TN: I have taken the first part of this English citation from the Stanford Encyclopedia of Philosophy; cf. https://plato.stanford.edu/entries/heraclitus/ (accessed July 13, 2020).

4. TN: These three terms refer to historical groups that employed personal violence and assassination. *Assassins* refers to the Islamic sect of Nizari Ismailis in the Middle Ages; *Sicarii* refers historically to the first-century Jewish sect who combated Roman rule over Judea; *Thugs* refers to groups of murderers in India suppressed by nineteenth-century British colonial forces.

kinsman-redeemer is the one who avenges. Now, this is the Savior and the Redeemer!)—vengeance is one of the deep roots of moral duties. Values such as honor, solidarity, fidelity, etc., which serve as a justification or valorization, are developed on this basis. Now, this moral notion is commonly rejected today. As soon as state power is organized, practicing revenge is suppressed, and bit by bit, it ceases to be a moral duty as it is entrusted to a third party that handles the problem juridically. And as the mechanisms of the police and tribunals gather enough strength, while the solidarity of small groups weakens, this moral duty slowly fades, until it becomes the object of moral reprobation in our day. Vengeance is considered as evil in pseudo-Christian Western society and in para-Christian communist society, for different reasons. This observation concerning vengeance can be extended to the central values of the moral systems of a given moment. It seems we could say that a society's morality is ordered in relation to a value that is either declared or felt to be essential. Thus there is a sort of moral axis. We can thus speak of an ethics of the *Sippe* [*family* or *clan*] among Germanic peoples: everything is coordinated in function of this essential relation of the individual to the *Sippe*, and the good is defined at its base as whatever is useful for the *Sippe*. We can also speak of an ethic of loyalty in groups constituted around a leader, as among the Gasindi, for example, and later in the feudal group: the good comes down to fealty to the lord, and everything is judged by this imperative and in relation to this engagement. Now, this sort of morality can produce moral obligations that we might consider scandalous today. We have already indicated vengeance, which is not personal (it only becomes personal when an ethic of the human is developed but which is relative to the members of a group or to the lord. Another curious fact is the system of collective witness [Fr. *cojeurer*]. When a member of the *Sippe* or its Elder is under legal accusation, it is a *moral duty* for the other members of the group to come and swear under oath that he is right, that the events happened as their brother (or lord, etc.) says—even if they know nothing and saw nothing. Now, their simple oath can lead to a decision of justice. This latter can thus be founded on a lie, or on affirmations that have no connection to reality. This is an ethical imperative to lie and say anything under oath; lies and false oaths here are moral duties, let us not forget. It is not evil but good to act in the interest of one's brother in the clan or family. But where, then, is the respect for Truth that we consider one of the most universal elements of morality? We recall the basic criticisms of the nineteenth century concerning the Old Testament: the moment we see that biblical authors recorded events or facts that they knew to be inexact, they are no longer reliable in any domain. In reality, the notion of intangible truth and its moral value are linked to a very narrow and determined type

Diversity of Moralities

of society and mentality. Sociologists today speak with a certain pity about the notion of a prelogical mentality, created by Lévy-Bruhl; yet it remains exact to the extent that it reminds us that our values and our ways of thinking these values are neither universal nor constant. We have just seen several examples in which values that we take to be indisputable (respect for life, truth, etc.) are unknown, and in which an ethical system can be created "in the interest of . . ." The supreme value can be the leader, the group, etc., and the entire moral system (including, of course, individual virtue and moral conscience) plays in favor of . . . Now, this is in no way limited to a primitive stage of humanity. In the modern era, we encounter at least three moralities "in the interest of . . ." Nationalism: acts are judged according to their relations with the supreme value of the nation (or the homeland). Racism. Communism. These are veritable moralities, subjective and objective, with hierarchies of values and distinctions between good and evil, virtues and judgments, etc. But the moral criterion is exceedingly simple in these three cases: it is a criterion of interest. Everything that is done in the interest of the nation, the race or the proletariat is good. Everything that is against it is bad. This rule, which at times can be variously unformulated or explicit, justifies behavior and gives a clear vision of moral duty to the individual. A simplistic vision? Of course, when compared to the ethical meditations of philosophers . . . But man needs these simple hierarchies; he lives by them, and not by phenomenological or existentialist theories. Furthermore, these moralities "in the interest of . . ." are not much more superficial than the bourgeois morality of the nineteenth century, for example. But they put in question so-called universal moral values. We are shocked whenever Lenin speaks of the physical liquidation of the bourgeois or of lying as good. We can cite another very significant example: Sparta. Here, educating children led them inevitably toward theft and homosexuality. These two items were considered pedagogical values: theft was a test and demonstration of dexterity, cunning, and ability to act, while homosexuality was a means to create indestructible and total solidarity between two comrades. These two pedagogical tools were destined to prepare youths for war. Theft and homosexuality were not glorified as being good themselves, but the command against stealing and the prohibition of pederasty (this latter was punishable by death in Israel in the same era) were completely unformulated; because it was exclusively social, the entire Lacedemonian ethic came to see as good everything that—through danger and in braving the very morality of the group—could prepare the young man for his role as a fighter. Of course, we can set this against the general denial that these are not moralities.[5] Thus in judging

---

5. This is a constant temptation for all who create morality. Thus in modern times

pagan habits, Saint Augustine showed that there was no pagan morality. But he would first have to stipulate that only Christian morality is really morality. But by what authority could one do this? By virtue of the idea of a universal good, always identical to itself, which only Christian morality would express? We have seen that this is untenable. In reality, for the men of a given society, this is the good, and that is evil. And we are trying to see it from their perspective and not from ours, to accept that there really is a morality here, with all of its elements. We must approach it from the relative point of view of human understanding, not the absolute point of view of metaphysics. This is even more true when we recall that lived morality does not seek principles, values, abstract utterances; it proclaims precise conduct, it formulates imperatives and prohibitions concerning concrete situations, it is always relative to relations between men living in a certain place at a certain time. No living morality commends seeking the "Good" abstractly, or the "Truth"; it specifies acts, intentions, objectives that it qualifies as good or true. Its contents are rigorous. Only theorists have been able to content themselves with abstract terms and have sought to give these terms a universal content. But precisely to the extent that living morality is specific, it is necessarily linked to a historical moment; it necessarily fluctuates according to circumstances. To contest that there really is a morality here, one might say that to the extent that these duties, obligations, and imperatives can be reduced to a purpose, that they have a (pedagogical, etc.) goal, then it is no longer really morality, for this latter is characterized by the unconditional respect of certain values and the disinterested character of virtue. This position seems untenable to us. All morality has a purpose, if only the purpose of accomplishing of the good. The unconditional and disinterested are situated at the level of the subjective situation, not at the level of the objective morality. Now, only this latter has permitted us to say that there is a "morality in view of . . ." or "in the interest of . . ." In fascism[6] and in communism, individual virtue is just as unconditional, just as disinterested as in Stoicism or in Confucianism. The situation is truly ethical for the individual who must respect a given value or choose a given conduct. Let us not say that disrespect is punished in these systems: the one who does not accept the

---

Murry (*The Free Society* [1948]), considering that morality consists of "reasonably desiring freedom for all," declares that the USSR does not accept the principle of morality, and that there is ultimately no morality in communism. And again, this is the habitually catholic attitude (*sic* Häring, I).

6. It is a partisan and not a scientific view that leads Gurvitch to say that in fascist societies there is no true morality, because the system of types of moral life is imposed by force (*Traité de sociologie*, 169). In reality, this is no more correct than for any other authoritarian organization.

racist or proletarian morality is eliminated by the social group, the one who accepts it is rewarded. We recall that it was exactly the same among the people of Israel, in medieval Christianity, in Calvin's Geneva, and in Puritan America. Can we say that because there was a social constraint expressed in all these cases there was no morality?

In reality, if we look at what men live and consider as morality instead of referring ourselves to a preconceived idea of it, we see that it varies tremendously according to time and place.[7]

This diversity of moralities is even more accentuated when, for example, S. de Beauvoir (*Pour une morale de l'ambigüité*) concludes that we cannot respond to the question, "What action is good?"[8] "One does not ask their doctor which hypotheses are true." "Morality does not give us recipes, we can only propose Methods." "In the case where the content of an action contradicts its meaning, we must modify not the meaning but the content," etc. This ultimately leads to a pure morality of efficacy since there will never be an external criterion that allows the discernment of good action. There is no value that we could call universal;[9] there is no sense of the good that is

---

7. To say with Häring that "the following principles are admitted by all peoples: what you would not like done to you, do not do to others; we must leave or give to each one whatever belongs to them" (375) is an obvious error! It is not true that all peoples have recognized private property, and the majority have commended taking such property from foreigners, etc.! Likewise, to claim that monogamy is a moral universal principle runs contrary to the majority of moralities; and, in order to claim this, we know what theological acrobatics were necessary to justify the polygamy of the patriarchs (cf. Innocent III).

Here, we must also insert Gurvitch's analyses on the plurality of *types* [Fr. *genres*] of moral life which only accentuates this diversification. For moralities are not only distinguished by their content, but by their very conception of the structure of moral life, and Gurvitch rightly distinguishes traditional morality, teleological morality, virtue morality, judgments after the fact, symbolic images, the morality of action, imperative morality, and aspiration morality. But we do not see how, in these conditions, he can say that sociological relativism has nothing to do with philosophical relativism. As an aspiration toward an absolute morality, we could understand—but certainly not as a reality!

8. TN: At this point in Hopkin's translation, he adds a note directing the reader to Simone de Beauvoir, *Ethics of Ambiguity*.

9. Niebuhr gives us a good example of this (*The Nature and Destiny of Man*) when he keeps coming back to the affirmation that man attains the concept of justice, and in doing so arrives at a true ethic. And he critiques Karl Barth on this basis, showing that it is untenable to make this realization of justice by man into a sort of mystery of Providence. But in reality, Niebuhr does not account for the prodigious diversity of contents attributed to this word *justice* by various civilizations, nor does he realize that the concept of justice that he calls "Natural" and that he finds satisfactory, as a product of a natural society, is in reality what is understood as justice in Western society, that is, a product of the external Christianization of society. Despite everything that accompanies it, it is a twisted elaboration of Christian thought. And it is this Christian

common to everyone; there is no imperative that could serve as the foundation for the construction of an all-encompassing morality. We thus cannot say that there is a natural morality tied to the nature of man or of things. If there were, there would be a certain unity in morality, a certain coherence despite different geographical or historical perspectives. But there is nothing of the sort.

I know very well that many will object to this observation of the diversity of morality: "You are only looking at the superficial level. You are confusing the content (which varies widely) and the applications (which are multiple) with the (regulative, organizing, inspiring) moral function in itself and its principle. All men experience comparable impulses, similar ends; they have a common moral experience. The objectivity and universality of morality are found at the point of departure, in a sort of common vocation of humanity found in man. The diverse developments that follow this primary similitude are only historical accidents, superstructures that, precisely as superstructures, presuppose a fundamental human moral unity. You believe that the whole ocean is troubled because you see the waves, but these only exist because they rest on the unchanging masses of deeper waters. And the reality clings to this immutability."[10] But to me, this abstraction of a moral phenomenon considered in itself, without content, without concrete reality, without defined rules, seems properly unimaginable. It is a purely intellectual operation, perfectly gratuitous, and at the same time frighteningly simple. Morality only exists in particular kinds, and to want to consider it outside of these particular kinds to declare its fundamental identity is simply to say: morality exists everywhere. We can say that man is a moral animal, but if we are intellectually honest, we absolutely do not have the right to go further, to start sketching the portrait of this fundamental[11]

---

by-product that is adopted in the socialist world, as in Africa today. It is thus no surprise that Niebuhr is able to establish a relation between this invention that he sees as "natural" and Christian faith!

10. To claim that the Ideal in itself transcends living notions of the real like Jean Boisset does (in *Le problème de la Morale chrétienne*, 10) is to trust in a category that is totally empty, that everyone can fill in as they please. There is thus no identity. And again, to say that "the most onerous moral attitudes obey a singular order which is that of obligation" (from which we take the universal foundation of morality) is, on the one hand, to neglect the entire orientation of morality without obligation; on the other hand, it simply displaces the problem, for we must explain the origin and the how of this obligation, and in doing so we perceive that this notion is plural, myriad, and itself highly differentiated according to time and place.

11. Jean-Paul Sartre is perfectly right to write (within the hypothesis that there is no God), "There can no longer be any good *a priori*, since there is no infinite and perfect consciousness to think it. It is nowhere written that 'the good' exists, that one must be

universal morality, to find a content and function, since in doing so, precisely for each particular morality, we begin by saying that the specific traits of this portrait, this content, this function, are only accidents, historical consequences, and that we reject this diversity since it is only superficial. Now, for the same reasons, the portrait, the function, and the content of our universal morality that we are going to determine will also be only so many other accidents, superstructures . . . how could they be otherwise? Furthermore, they will be abstract and theoretical. In the name of what authority, by what truth will I attribute unity and universality to the content and function of a morality, or of morality in general, when nothing in the facts allows me to do so?[12]

Let us return to the situation expressed by the Bible. For all men, there is a good and an evil. There is a moral life, a *necessity* of formulating a morality. But man is charged with formulating it himself; there is no preliminary content that could be given in advance. Nothing outside of man has decided "This is the Good." Now, it is he who will say it. And since he finds himself in prodigiously variable conditions, his ethical decisions vary infinitely. If one refuses this, one must take the path followed by many moralists that is not concerned with what is really accepted as morality in a given time and place, and either by sampling from all moralities, or by performing a phenomenological analysis of the individual, one formulates a morality that is then decreed to be the only just, eternal and universal morality, and all the rest is situated with respect to it. This leads us directly into the theoretical moralities. Unfortunately, there is no more harmony between the diverse theoretical moralities than between lived moralities, which destroys the moralist's claim to universality.[13]

---

honest or must not lie, since we are now upon the plane where there are only men" (*L'existentialisme est un humanisme*).

12. See also Bonhoeffer's fine discussion on the moments where ethics goes without saying, and moments where there is no more ethic at all in society, where it is no more than a "problem" (*Ethics*, 363–87).

13. On the ethical phenomenon as an object of reflection, cf. Bonhoeffer, *Ethics*, 363–87.

2

Theoretical Moralities

Of course, it would be absolutely impossible for us to describe, even briefly, the innumerable theoretical moralities elaborated over time by philosophers, founders of religions, etc. The moralities of Moses, Confucius, Aristotle, Plato, the Stoics, Saint Thomas Aquinas, Erasmus, Kant, Nietzsche, moralities founded on order and harmony of the world from Platonic ideas, on the reasonable nature of man from Aristotelian ideas, on the divine substance of Spinoza, on the objective spirit of Hegel, on Durkheim's collective conscience, all of which recognize a supreme Good—or on the contrary, moralities that are limited to man, linked to his condition of exploiter and exploited in Marx, the morality of libertines formulated by Bussy-Rabutin, the morality of eroticism expressed by Marquis de Sade, the morality of violence in Sorel, phenomenological moralities in Husserl and Scheler, the morality of ambiguity in Sartre and Simone de Beauvoir, the "concrete" morality of Hesnard, the "biological" morality of Chauchard, and how many others—it would be vain to even attempt to describe and critique them. Rather, we will try to understand this phenomenon of theoretical moralities as an ensemble.

With one or two exceptions (of which at least one is noteworthy: Confucius), we must remark that the phenomenon of theoretical moralities, reflection on morality, the intellectual elaboration of an ethic, is essentially a Mediterranean phenomenon; this abstract and general, coherent and systematic interrogation of the conduct of men is a fact that is directly linked to the Judeo-Greek civilization. Incidentally, this fact led Westerners to consider that since there was no intentionally organized ethical system among other civilizations, there was no morality either. On the contrary, we must invert this perspective and observe that among the various civilizations that have all had one or multiple moralities, only (or almost only) the Mediterranean civilization created theoretical morality; in short, the latter is thus a phenomenon that is limited in time and space.

Consider, first of all, that theoretical morality is never "pure"; it can never be extracted from its milieu.[1] It is always an expression of the milieu where it is produced, more or less. For example, it never occurred to Saint Thomas Aquinas to construct a morality outside of the assumptions of Christianity. The common intellectual, philosophical, religious, and scientific climate of a moment very strongly (but not completely) determines the moralist who creates a new ethical system. But this moralist aims to do his job rigorously, to create a system that determines as purely as possible what *should be*, to logically structure an ensemble of precepts; to rationally justify the demands of the moral conscience of the moment—and by virtue of this fact he goes far beyond what actually exists as a morality in the group where he finds himself. Generally, he does so in three ways:[2] either by raising moral precepts to the absolute level, transforming them into ideals; or by the rationality that he introduces into ethics; or by the systematization of that which, spontaneously, remains somewhat incoherent. In any case, this introduces a certain discord between the existing morality and the theoretical morality, a distance, a divergence that can keep growing, and can even lead to an opposition—even if the point of departure and the context are identical. This prompts us to consider the biggest weakness of these theoretical moralities: they are unapplied. Whether they are applicable or not, in fact, they are generally only rarely applied. The men of a city, group, or nation give very little thought to the morality elaborated by one of their own. Other than specialists, who is interested in Kant's ethic?[3] It is a philosopher's affair, and

1. Gurvitch is obviously right (op. cit., 147) to pose the problem of the sociology of moral doctrines. "We could ask ourselves if [they] are not simple dogmatisms and sublimations of the hierarchy of types and forms of existing moral attitudes." "They could be revealed as dogmatic ways of justifying and sublimating a situation of fact in the system of current moral attitudes."

2. Bergson saw very clearly that "heroic" morality too was linked to the milieu, but led to transcend it (*Two Sources*, 34–58). In speaking here of theoretical morality, we include not only intellectual morality but also the heroic morality: that which "must incarnate in a privileged person who becomes an example" (ibid., 34). Their common point is that they always involve a morality that is intentionally created by an individual. "Founders and reformers of religions, mystics and saints, obscure heroes of moral life whom we have met on our way ... They are indeed conquerors: they have broken down natural resistance and raised humanity to a new destiny" (ibid., 50).

3. Cf. the analysis of Niebuhr for an explanation of the failure of the Kantian ethic (*Interpretation of Christian Ethics*, 128).

these philosophers do not model mores. Even when there is a deep sense of community between the group and the moralist, this latter remains a stranger, and their morality remains inapplicable. Despite the relations between Sorel and the milieu of labor unions, his ethical works have generated no response. Almost nobody feels directly concerned with Aristotle's ethics, and still fewer today with the ethics of Husserl. Several intellectuals know them, but we could say that simply because they are intellectuals, the debate is situated much more at this level than at the level of the conduct of life. And nobody seeks to change their life according to the results of quarrels between philosophers specializing in ethics. We might be tempted to deny the importance of theoretical moralities altogether: indeed, what good is an ethic, whose purpose is to furnish rules of conduct for the achievement of a good, when nobody applies it?[4] Given that its only goal is to be applied, we could say that this is a senseless undertaking. Nevertheless, we will see that this extreme judgment is not absolutely fair. But we must remember that in reality these theoretical moralities, which by their expression, coherence, and dexterity make a great impression on intellectuals, are quite secondary in the ensemble of ethical phenomena. Incidentally, we must distinguish between two great tendencies among moral theorists: there are those who, based on principles, try to formulate what *should be*, the ideal rule of life, the process for attaining perfection, holiness, etc. This was primarily the preoccupation of the ancients. They thus created a Morality from scratch. Currently, there is a more prudent trend of trying primarily to give an account of what is. The philosopher analyzes the effective moral process. He does not begin with principles, but with observations of facts. He seeks not so much to formulate an ideal as to translate lived morality; he tries to follow the progression of the constitution of a morality. Psychologists and sociologists limit themselves to compiling observations of what is, and to

---

4. Bergson was well aware of the problem of unapplied morality: "No amount of speculation will create an obligation or anything like it; the theory may be all very fine, I shall always be able to say that I will not accept it; and even if I do accept it, I shall claim to be free and do as I please" (*Two Sources*, 47–48). In particular, he is concerned with the nonapplication of Stoic morality (ibid., 60, 77–78) because it remained a philosophy. And he has shown that a morality built on reason has no chance of ever being accepted and recognized (ibid., 85), any more than a morality that presupposes the idealist axiom that the idea of the Good possesses an intrinsic force (ibid., 87). Finally, "not even the dual preoccupation of maintaining social cohesion and of furthering the progress of humanity" will "impose itself peremptorily as a mere rational proposition" (ibid., 90). We refer back to these excellent demonstrations. See also Niebuhr, *Interpretation of Christian Ethics*, 205. The same idea can be found in Mehl: "To every ethic which claims to be self-sufficient, [we] have the right to oppose an argument . . . to wit, its incapacity to go beyond the critical stage and exhortative stage" ("Ethique et théologie," 43).

furnishing a minimum of explanation. We cannot really speak of moralists here, except in the sense of the technical morality (which we will come back to). But based on these given facts, there is a great temptation to try to develop a morality that, formulating ethical rules and illuminating values, would come not from principles but from observations.[5]

This was also the temptation of Durkheim when, starting from the observation of sociological facts, he claimed to "make a morality"—a theoretical morality with a sociological basis, a morality that would be a translation of social reality and the behavior of man in the group, yet that would be imperative. Gurvitch perfectly demonstrated how in reality this led to a semi-metaphysical morality: it required the determination of an absolute good that would be incarnated in society. It required the establishment of an external criterion of morality: solidarity. "The social being is the supreme Good, and conformity of behavior to this being possesses a moral value." Thus, even founded on the observation of facts, sociological morality does not escape the presuppositions of all the theoretical moralities—particularly the permanence of social nature and the nature of man.[6]

This also applies to the research of Hesnard, for example, who starts with psychological and sociological analysis to define a "socialized Morality of action favorable to man," which would be a morality without constraint, focused on action, without reference to interior life. For us men of the twentieth century, these attempts seem much more valuable than everything that preceded them; but perhaps on our part this is a simple adhesion to what happens in our time. Moralities with a scientific foundation claim to be universal. They will finally accomplish the old dream of all moralists to formulate a rule of conduct that is valid for all men. This derives from the presupposition of the universal character of scientific observations. For Hesnard, a concrete social morality should be met with universal adhesion since it rests on solid psychological analysis. Given that the moral imperative would coincide with psychic tendencies and with psychological needs, it should have no trouble being followed; man should spontaneously go in these directions. But for this to work, we must strip notions of sin,

---

5. This is the temptation of taking the sociology of the moral life as the basis of a moral doctrine, in trying "to know and prescribe at the same time." This was already the project of Auguste Comte and of Herbert Spencer.

On Durkheim, see Gurvitch, "La science des faits moraux et la morale théorique chez Durkheim" (in *Vocation actuelle de la sociologie*, vol. 2).

6. This presupposes the elimination of nonscientific elements (for example, the feeling of sin) with the goal of establishing an objective morality (for example, the morality without sin of Hesnard), or this supposes that morality refers to a bigger framework (e.g., history, and the good is evaluated according to its insertion in history, according to historical efficacy, etc.).

constraint, etc., from morality, and sentiments of guilt and defensiveness from the psyche. We would need to remove the accent on moral preoccupations contrary to action, placing it instead on accomplished acts; emphasis would have to shift from the negative to the positive, from the egocentric position to the "act for man." Incidentally, since this morality would correspond to tendencies that already exist in the individual, it would have no difficulty being applied: in reality, once the old paralyzing vestiges of Christian morality are cleared away from the psyche, there wouldn't even be a choice to act: spontaneously, the individual would go in the direction of the concrete social morality. Dr. Chauchard raises roughly this same concern when he tries to demonstrate a harmony between morality and biology, and the possibility of finding biological foundations for a common morality. This is not a question of deriving a morality from biology, but current knowledge of the brain allows us to assert that the principles of traditional and spiritualist morality are in harmony with the biological activity of the brain. According to the biologist, if man could only activate all the potentialities contained materially in the lobes of his brain, we would find the great moral principles in application; these moral activities would express the activity of the frontal sphere of the brain. Here again, we see that we are led to completely do away with moral choice: the individual does not need to choose this or that conduct. He only has to develop the biological elements of his person and this will lead him automatically to live morally. Unfortunately, the moralities that Hesnard and Chauchard take from different disciplines, though equally scientific, do not coincide in the least! But their project is interesting because it demonstrates awareness of the problem of application of morality. It is easy to theoretically formulate a magnificent moral system. The only real problem is to know who will apply it, and how. Hesnard and Chauchard, among others, try to respond by providing a spontaneous foundation for morality. But if we examine matters carefully, we realize that their systems have no more chance of being applied than do other systems! The preliminary conditions highlighted by Hesnard are prodigiously difficult to put in place (and will they ever exist?). As far as expressing the activity of the frontal sphere, who will convince man to do this? It seems it would be just as complicated as getting them to apply moral precepts purely and simply.

We classify the ethical attempts of existentialism among these theoretical moralities. For despite the claims of existentialism to take the concrete, contingent world as the object of philosophy, and its desire to focus only on the whole of man as he really exists, this philosophy ends in extreme theorizing and (unintentionally) takes into account only concepts that are unrelated to men. The plays and novel of Sartre only confirm the distance between real man and the existential concept of man. We will come back to this in addressing the Morality of Values; for now we will content ourselves with two remarks.

1. The ethical inquiry of existentialism is founded on observations of facts that are undoubtedly exact (anguish, the absurd, etc., and the decisive importance of the presence of the neighbor). But it runs up against what in our opinion is a decisive critique: it rests on postulates that it refuses to question, or even to recognize. We will give two examples:

    a. First of all, the construction relating to the presence of the other: the other represents the demand of an alienation of myself, and the encounter or impossibility of encounter with the other constitutes moral existence. But we should ask ourselves, How do I know that I should abandon myself to the other? Whence this importance of the other? Whence this obligation that is imposed on me to consider this other *in this way*? In existentialism I find no explanation of what is ultimately a presupposition; neither the observation of facts nor a preliminary assumption (since this is ruled out) justifies what remains a pure assertion.

    b. The second example deals with the vocabulary used: there is a constant implicit reference to values or virtues, even though their existence has been denied. When Sartre says that justification can only come from solidarity with the disadvantaged, and that to be free is to feel culpable for all the injustice of the world, etc.—what does he mean by "injustice," if there is nothing to measure it, since justice is perfectly unknown and must be *created*—and who are the "disadvantaged"? At what level are they disadvantaged? Is it those who simply lack the necessary material goods? But are we not thus reduced to total subjectivity? Or perhaps we can apply other criteria according to the anthropology that we adopt, and therefore we can derive no justification from them. Why should taking up the cause of the disadvantaged be "good," etc.? The same goes for S. de Beauvoir: when she speaks of "responsibility," she never specifies what question man is responding to, before whom or in relation to what he is responsible. When she speaks of "defeats" and "victories," again, how do we measure them? "Certain actions can be regarded as good," she says, but who regards them, and in virtue of what are they called good? We never get out of these conundrums. The vocabulary cannot be voided of its preliminary ethical content, but we have acted "as if" it had none.

2. The second remark to be made is to note the direct relation between this existentialist ethic and the sociological structure of the world where it flourished—namely, first in Germany in a period of defeat and misery (1918–29), then France in a period of defeats and troubles (1936–60). An ethic denies preexisting values in a society where there are no more common values; it destroys the objectivity of morality in a society where there is in effect no more established morality; it rejects moral idealism in a society that, by the force of things, is becoming materialist, and ethical individualism in a society that is collectivizing sociologically; it proclaims the absurdity of the world because the society where it is spreading is disintegrating and nations are declining. Finally, it claims that the object of ethics is to give man a justification, precisely in a society where man cannot find any simple and sure justifications. We can therefore say that this existentialist ethic is a pure and simple translation of local and temporary circumstances, a reflection of events. This ethic is unthinkable in the USA or the USSR. The only role played by Sartre, S. de Beauvoir, and others is to raise what is simply the product of circumstances to the level of doctrine, metaphysics and duties. By this very fact, they give a rather beautiful justification to the men of a moment, allowing them to remain as they are and be praised for it.

Most of these ethical theories rest on an idealism. We can never say often enough how much damage idealism has caused, in ethical research as well as in Christianity. On the one hand, idealism established an absolute good, and by the same token, the superiority of morality over religion.[7] On the other hand, it plays on numerous *a priori* beliefs that entirely falsify the moral problematic. For example: conscience is an absolute, individual and universal category, with a definite content, in relation with the Absolute. Likewise: man is good by nature; Christianity is applicable in political and economic domains (and doing so would avoid a revolution), under the form of the law of love translated as cooperation (on this point see the "Buchman Movement" and social Christianity); man can follow Reason, etc.[8] The

---

7. Including for Christianity, which becomes a simple morality: for example, Bois, *Le problème de la morale chrétienne*; Peabody, *Jesus Christ and the Social Question*.

8. TN: Frank Buchman (1878–1961) was an American Protestant evangelist whose

Theoretical Moralities

question is not one of optimism concerning man, but of an idealism that denatures reality and (which is more serious for us) Revelation. The doctrine of the Holy Spirit should eliminate all idealism from Christian thought.

Nevertheless, as we were saying, these moralities are not without interest, even when they remain unapplied. The theoretical moralities come with three lessons. First of all, they are always an image that a man makes of Man at a given moment.[9] And this is not without value. If a man's profound experience is a common heritage, if it expresses the universal in a certain manner, then Socrates' or Kant's formulation of a vision of the just Man, the good Man—even if never accomplished, even if this man does not exist—is an image that can speak to the heart of every man, and can be a call that becomes personal to him. The man who becomes aware of himself can no longer feel like a stranger to the Wise man of Confucius or the Free man of Nietzsche. This image created by a man's will ensures that from now on other men cannot remain indifferent and will not be left unscathed. The heart of humanity cannot close itself to what has thus been placed in it. Today we can no longer speak of moral phenomena as we could fifty years ago, because Husserl and Jaspers and Scheler have passed through here. And this is true even if we have not read them—which is extraordinary: it is as if a certain osmosis occurred at the heart of a group in civilization. But we must take care to note that this is true only for a small group of intellectuals. Nevertheless, if this theoretical morality is sufficiently known and widespread, it becomes not only an image of Man, but the image that a society makes of itself. Marx is wrong when he wants to see morality as nothing but ideological superstructure and a veil over reality. If a society proclaims virtues and values, it does not do so primarily to hypocritically hide its lacunae (which this proclamation can *also* do) but to proclaim a goal and an ideal. This is the role of the theoretical moralities, which always tell us in a certain way how a society views itself, by what standard it judges itself, how it wants to be seen by others. Even when the ideal is not accomplished, it is still formulated *in* this society and is an integral part of its life.

From a second perspective, we will say that theoretical morality is never abstracted from its social context; in reality, it is frequently in direct relation with tendencies, with philosophical or religious currents. But more than that, it can be a center where diffuse beliefs and unconscious

---

widely influential WWII-era program of "Moral Re-Armament" sought to supplant political revolutions with spiritual revolution.

9. On this subject, cf. for example, Reiner, "Ethik und Menschenbild."

aspirations of a given moment crystallize. The moralist thus plays the role of a recorder, a catalyst. They provoke the awareness, formulation, and solidification of what latently exists in the group to which they belong. We are right to remember Kant's puritan origins and milieu. But equally, while Kant strongly expresses the tendencies of this seriously Christianized milieu, he retains nothing from Christianity except its morality, focusing on the foundation of this morality and of the good separated from Jesus Christ. This crystallization can be one of the most legitimate functions of theoretical morality. Thus it is not pure innovation, but it presents a serious foundation; nor is it purely hypothetical. The analysis of Lévy-Bruhl is thus exact when he considers the theoretical morality, the "Metamorality," as a translation of a lived morality into intellectual terms, a process that introduces a rationality, a foundation, a justification. But this is not always exact; it is not true of all Metamoralities! We cannot place all theoretical moralities on equal ground in this respect; some are truly the expression of diffuse tendencies of their time, while others do not accomplish this at all.

Finally, we cannot ignore the fact that in certain cases theoretical morality can, in the long run, have an influence on psychology, and (also in the long run) can disseminate certain commandments, glorify certain virtues and contribute to the formation of a new morality.

Sometimes, theoretical morality can also give a true response to a tragic concrete situation. A society can find itself in such disarray that its lived morality can no longer be applied and heads toward disappearance; collective beliefs are shaken, either consciously or unconsciously; the group or the society is incapable of responding to the challenge raised by an event or by institutions. The moralist can try to respond, can attempt to formulate new values or new combinations of values; they can present possible and effective behavior by which the society, in its members, could get out of its predicament. Thus, this theoretical morality can possibly be accepted, if men experience, feel, and believe that it offers a solution; but this can only happen in a crisis, and in the course of successive adaptations—that is, very slowly. Generally, we acknowledge that theoretical morality can be applied in the long run. That is why we take these moralities so seriously. But in reality, this is not the case; only *rarely*, and only after it has been made palatable or diluted, does it happen that theoretical morality contributes to a lived morality. And this leads us to examine the applied theoretical moralities.

In some cases (quite rarely, in all honesty), theoretical moralities have been effectively applied—thus the morality of Confucius, that of "Moses," that of

Saint Paul, the Stoic morality, and the Marxist morality.[10] As for why these moralities were adopted and not others, this is a serious and difficult question. We would have to analyze each case individually since each is particular. Nevertheless, we can make several general remarks: none of these moralities have been applied in their purity, their integrity, to their very end, but rather in adaptations, in the form of practical rules, according to their consequences and not their source of inspiration, and after numerous adulterations. The passage from the formulation of the requirement to putting it into practice produces a profound change in the very structure and signification of this morality. This is the "crisis" of the second generation of Christians, as well as the second generation of Marxists, and the "rediscovery" of the law of "Moses." Insofar as the doctrine remains absolutely pure, it is not applied. It has been said that the morality of Confucius was applied precisely to the extent that he was betrayed by his disciples. There is a lot of truth in this. Perhaps morality is more likely to be applied when it is more susceptible to such adulterations and interpretations. A system that is too rigorously constructed remains foreign to man, who turns away from its intransigence.

Secondly, most often a group or a society adopts these moralities not as morality, but in addition to something else. This is the result of a religion, a politics, or of a political movement, or a social transformation. We must not forget that the morality of Confucius was only applied in a general fashion from the moment that the Han emperors proclaimed Confucian orthodoxy; the same goes for Christian morality and Marxist morality. We can even see this adoption of a theoretical morality by the state as a rather general historical phenomenon. The state needs a global moral affirmation if it is to truly claim to direct society. Now, it is much easier to adopt a theoretical morality because it is well formulated, clear, precise, and systematic. For there to be a moral orthodoxy useful to the state, there must be a *doxa*. It is even possible that this decision of the state is one of the deciding factors

---

10. We are familiar with Bergson's doctrine explaining the application of these creative moralities. They must be based on an emotion, on a passion (*Two Sources of Morality and Religion*, 40–41), capable of being crystallized in representations (ibid., 46–47), with religious emotion being a privileged example. Then this moral must be incarnated in an exemplary man, "a person admired and venerated"; moreover, "the great moral figures" form an ensemble, a sort of "divine city which they bid us enter" and call out to us (ibid., 68, 98–100). But in any case, the realization of this morality supposes that it enters "in a society whose state of mind was already such as their realization was bound to bring about" (ibid., 74). Thus in all cases, these are vital forces that are in play, and "a system of ethics which imagines it is founding obligation on purely rational considerations, unwittingly reintroduces . . . forces of a different order" once we try to put it into practice (ibid., 89).

as to which moralities will be applied! After all, even Stoicism spread in the Roman Empire via the ruling classes.[11] It will be objected that we are only displacing the moral problem by making it a mass problem—that morality, even if applied by *only one* man (and if it is theoretical, by its founder, for example), is still itself, and in itself—that collective application is not what really counts... And yet, it actually is this common application that counts. Morality supposes a relation between the men of a group, and these men obey a morality in function of one another. Robinson Crusoe did not really know a morality. And the solitary moralist who obeys his own ethic in society does it in *Pro* and *Contra* relations with his group. The problem of collective application is decisive, not because of the number, but because of the very nature of morality.

Incidentally, in addition to state intervention, the application can also arise from a social mutation. We know very well that, for example, the Christian morality was inapplicable among the peoples of Africa or Oceania except to the extent that the social structures collapsed from the shock of conquering Westerners.

Finally, these theoretical moralities also have the best chance of being applied when they are a crystallization of an ambient moral state. This presupposes a sort of preliminary agreement. When an ethical system derives from collective aspirations, it is understandable that it could easily be applied. It is simple to demonstrate how precisely moralities that have been applied, however theoretical they might be, had deep roots in social habits, aspirations and judgments. This has been demonstrated on many occasions for Christianity, for Confucianism, etc. This is why we can say, for example, that among the diverse moral systems that theorists propose today, only the morality of the Normal (which we will discuss later) has a chance to be applied. Only this morality responds to the convictions and needs of contemporary man. And the others—existentialist, phenomenological, etc., which are much more intelligent, more beautiful, and perhaps even more true—have no chance, and will remain in the realm of intellectual games.

---

11. Contrary to the widespread belief that Stoicism expanded among and by slaves, it is in fact in the milieus of intellectuals, jurists and politicians that it had its primary influence.

3

Values

We cannot avoid addressing Values, and must do so precisely at this point in our treatment. The philosophy of values brings the clearly metaphysical character of phenomenology and existentialism to light. From the perspective of morality, it is a theoretical morality (and moreover, a metaphysical morality); the analyses presented in the preceding chapter thus apply here. But on the other hand, this philosophy of values energetically repudiates this metaphysical character; it rejects the domains of morality and duty, claiming to give an account of reality and to be based in experience. It claims only to say and describe what is. Consequently it must serve as an introduction to what we call lived morality. But the essential question to which we will try to respond is obviously, Does this morality of values accomplish what it claims to, does it really give an account of what is? We are right to hesitate between a philosophy of values and a sociology of values—the first focusing primarily on the justification, validity, and authority of values, and the second studying their objective reality, their variations in function of social settings. The masters of this philosophy habitually repudiate the second aspect, considering it superficial and secondary. As a concession, they recognize that values are tied to sociological realities, and above all to culture, which is in effect the background for the communication of values, the means by which men conceive and share the same values. They admit that cultures condition values, but quickly return to the fact that there is no culture but human culture, and that ultimately only the person counts. Oftentimes, they even consider that values determine culture, and that economic and political conflicts are in reality conflicts of values. The sociological reality thus takes a back seat. As for us, we are tempted to put values back in their sociological setting and to accept as real only what can be learned by sociological analysis of values; but first, it is fitting to briefly state just what we are talking about here.

This is not an easy thing, since many phenomenologists and existentialists recoil as soon as we ask them to give a definition of values or value. Value cannot be defined. It is felt, it is sensed, we rely on it, it guides us, but it is so ethereal that it escapes our grasp in even a minimally precise manner. Nevertheless, biased definitions abound.[1]

Value is defined by personal experience in the life of a man as that which allows him to give depth to the world, and it can only be known in action. There is no perception, no preliminary intuition of value; it only appears to man through his presence in the world. One can never deduce the value of Being, it is not a conduct conformed to Being. It is the contrary of a moral principle. It is often compared to an attracting magnet or a pole of orientation, but once again not in a predetermined manner. The value can appear in relation with man and the concrete; it continually provokes man to movement and can never be institutionalized, objectivized. In acting, man chooses his values, actualizing them in his action; and when he chooses the values that make him act, he accomplishes the moral act par excellence. We can thus see that this philosophy presupposes the freedom of the man who chooses his values and who is free in his choice. The value is a motive for making a decision of personal freedom. In his freedom man encounters the value, which fixes a limit for him. The ethical subject is necessarily free since his decision will promote the value and reject the anti-value. Moreover, man's freedom is inscribed in this ensemble of choice which contains an original system of values. We also see that this philosophy of values defines a "situation ethic"; the value is not known in advance, but only by man in a situation. There is no predefined good and evil in themselves that man can grasp. At every moment, he is at an ethical starting point. Taking this to the limit, we could say that every man reconstitutes morality at each moment, for the individual only invokes the value and grasps it anew when he encounters an obstacle. These several lines allow us to grasp certain difficulties and contradictions in the philosophy of values. We should first reflect on the historical moment of this philosophy's appearance. Here is a

---

1. At base, without employing the term, Bergson already expressed the existence of an ethic of values in speaking of "the other source of morality," of a morality of aspiration, call, or impetus (*Two Sources of Morality and Religion*, 34–59), of an open posture of the soul, which demands an effort, an ambition, and which implies an emotion tending toward the accomplishment of a moral value that is a drive, a need for movement, etc.

philosophy that, on the one hand, proclaims that there is no metaphysical good, no rules, no commandments, no imperatives in themselves, instituting an ethic of ambiguity and compromise. On the other hand, here is a philosophy that promotes values, proclaims that the only ethical situation is that of choice, that only value has a revolutionary function, and that man is free. And this philosophy is developed between 1930 and 1950. Situating this philosophy in its historical moment brings to light its double character: it is a "translation of the moment" and a "compensation." At a moment where the man of Western civilization finds himself plunged into complete ambiguity, where there is clearly no more notion of good and evil, or where the good is constantly contradicted, where there is no more sense of duty, where every action stems from compromise, where rules no longer have authority—at this moment the philosophy that ideologically translates this state of fact, that places individual choice above all moral certitude, is dominant. But likewise, at the moment where the freedom of man is pushed back from all sides, where its determinations are the most pressing, where order triumphs and no truly revolutionary movement is possible, where values are in crisis and contested—at this moment philosophy plays its compensatory role, proclaiming the existence of what is disappearing, affirming it louder and louder as the reality exists less and less.

Incidentally, these contradictions appear at the very heart of this philosophy of values. We will take two examples: it claims to reintroduce concern for the concrete into morality; it must start with the concrete man. "I must start with myself, with my existence, with its limitations." These values are situated rigorously in this world, as close as possible to what we are. They are objects of experience, which is decisive (while the moralities of Kant or Durkheim wrongly dispossessed man of his experience); the experience of the value is the experience of a person. The individual is the starting point. Now, this project is realized in practice; each philosopher of value begins with their experience and their person. This is powerfully fascinating. But it concerns the experience of a philosopher, a philosopher by trade no less, which is to say a Western man, from the milieu of the twentieth century, extremely cultivated, specialized in a certain form of reasoning and a certain sibylline language. And by describing his experience of value to us, this man claims to transmit a common experience, valid for the average man, and universal.[2] He claims that what he himself has experienced and recognized

---

2. Bonhoeffer's remark is very fitting when he recalls that man is primarily a living being and not an ethical subject, and that too often moralists forget that life is not a series of great ethical decisions, and ultimately that the ethical phenomenon is a limited case. The "Thou shalt" only appears where the duty is impracticable or forgotten. Bonhoeffer, *Ethics*, 366–67. [TN: Ellul's remark paraphrases the following citation from the

as a value is also real for man in general. Reading these works clearly shows their incompatibility with real men. Other than these philosophers, no man has this kind of experience; no man attains this kind of freedom or lives his life in this perspective. No man is this "ethical subject" which we are talking about. The "concrete" that we pretend to restore is the concrete of the philosopher himself. Another contradiction concerns the notion of situation ethics.[3] This latter claims to restore freedom to the individual, releasing them from predeterminations of good and evil, and to respect the full subjectivity of the individual, making them fully morally responsible. But if we consider man in his reality, placing him "in a situation" is to place him in his concrete situation, which is defined in respect to the economy, society, and family. Now, at this moment—the only moment that matters— the ethics of the situation becomes the most objective and objectifying thing imaginable; the individual in his inner self, his intentions, his sentiments, no longer matters. What counts is the situation and his reaction to it; he belongs to a certain profession, a certain class, suffers a certain alienation; we will hardly take his virtues and vices into account, focusing only on the situation: and whatever he might be in himself, he will never overcome this determination. In effect, the operations performed by the philosopher of values concern a perfectly disincarnate man; choices, freedom, the situation, all this is the result of an intellectual operation. This ethics speaks of a man who belongs to no time and no place. He does not belong to a given society, has no gender, no work, nor does he belong to any group; he is solitary, and under the influence of nothing and no one. When this philosophy speaks of society, it is only to say that society records the desires and aspirations of the person. Despite the incessant reminders of the concrete and real man, of historical situations, etc., reading these studies plunges us right back into the absolute of man in himself. It seems that the differences of professions and

---

cited pages: "The 'ought' only belongs where something is *not*, either because it *cannot* be or because it is not *willed*"; Bonhoeffer's italics.] It is curious that we need to recall these fundamental truths in addressing value ethics and phenomenologists—those who had the precise intention of beginning with man as a living being. Bonhoeffer sees reality clearly when he admits that the phenomenon and ethical moments exist, but that they are borderline cases (*Ethics*, 366).

3. It is currently the custom to affirm the superiority of situational ethics in relation to legal or traditional ethics, but in an article in *Forces nouvelles*, Etienne Borne has perfectly shown that in a situation of war this situational ethic could lead to accepting all behavior; and ultimately, torture in the Algerian War or the attacks that the O.A.S. consider legitimate could be justified in the name of situation ethics. [TN: The O.A.S., or *Organisation Armée Secrète*, was a paramilitary group that used terrorist tactics to prevent Algeria from attaining political independence from France.] What is tragic, he says, is that we do not perceive the substitution of one morality for another, and that a situational morality ultimately permits all immoralities (*Forces nouvelles*, 1961).

intellectual formulation, in the money we earn or the time we do not have, has no influence on the experience of value, on his ethical condition. This abstraction of man is undoubtedly the most serious internal contradiction in this philosophy.

Now we must address the essential question for our subject. Leaving behind the consideration of this philosophy as such, we must ask ourselves if it really accounts for reality. When this philosophy speaks of value, when it reduces ethics to this relation with values, when it shows us that values are decisive for the conduct of man, is what it shows real or is it an intellectual construction of the philosopher? From the outset, one observation prompts us to proceed with great caution: the extraordinary diversity of theories concerning value or values. There is a diversity of definitions, foundations, functions. Values are described as the structure of reality immanent to our action; a manner of qualifying the world; the motor of action; a perspective of engagement; the reason for our behavior; or even the transcendent absolute that determines man from the outside; the value of what is worthy of being sought, or on the contrary, that which is actually sought; the construction of human reality, or an independent grandeur, without antecedent. They have been called the reality by which a person becomes an authority for another; that which gives meaning to an event; that which mutually illuminates the significations of the world; or again "the condition which allows me to keep my dignity as a subject in the world . . . which allows my projects to be realized for the good of the world . . ." and even "the reality which gives us sufficient authority to interrupt temporal determinations . . ." Or, on the contrary: "The value is a relation between the infinite source of all value, which must be called absolute Value, and determinate values which . . . harbor a possible aspect of negativity." Or, completely opposed to these various definitions: the value is the appreciation of a subject in relation to an indefinite sensitivity—and also the product of a relation of things with a collective ideal, with a collective affectivity. We could keep going with this enumeration; but at the very least, we can say that this extreme diversity of concepts cannot reassure us. And we encounter the same problem when we seek the foundation of this value and of its authority: it is built on the existence of the social group; the transcendence of an absolute value; recognition of the person of the other; prolongation of the organic structure of being (satisfaction and dissatisfaction); a collective social ideal; the structure of instincts; it is a creation of God, etc. Faced with these disagreements, we only see that if the value was easily recognizable, a real object of common experience (as all the philosophers of value claim), there should at least be common elements in their expression, and certain identical elements. Our malaise is accentuated when we consider the arguments of each one (they are all convincing—and I must say that I am just as convinced by the theses of Mr. Le Senne as by the contradictory theses of Mr. Gusdorf and Mr. Mehl), and when we take one system in particular, we perceive that the development of the notion of value leads almost inevitably to profound contradictions in the system itself. Finally, we cannot escape the question, By what are values defined and determined? Everyone agrees in saying that there are values, there are anti-values. There are things that are values and others that are not; yet, who decides? This is only clear among those who recognize a transcendence, an absolute value that determines all the others. Everywhere else, we wander about in confusion. One philosopher gives us an exemplary and non-exhaustive enumeration of values: the unconditioned, the absolute, the good, the just, the holy, freedom, love, etc., and tells us that poverty, powerlessness, and sickness are not values because they threaten solitude and the contraction of being into itself, that they are contrary to the expansion that characterizes the action of values . . . But this means that sides are taken from the beginning, and it is not true that man freely chooses values: there are preexisting values that are a function of a preconceived idea of the author, which itself owes nothing to values. Someone who does not share this idea of the other would advance other values, over which there would be disagreement. Another philosopher presents a tableau of values based on instincts: but there is hardly a necessary link between the chosen values and the instinct named. Thus the sexual, maternal, etc. instinct gives values of Love, Friendship, Communication, Solidarity; perhaps, but we might just as well say that it creates the values of Eroticism, Racism, Lying, Resentment, etc. Here, too, the choice of these values really depends on an antecedent presupposition. The question that is not asked is still that of knowing, for each one, in the name of what he decides upon this or that value; and on the other hand, what is the limit of the value? Where does it stop? What could cause it to become an anti-value? The notion of value is ultimately so vague and uncertain (not in a given author, but in this philosophy as a whole) that anyone can make it mean almost anything they want. Of course, this does not mean that the thing does not exist. But perhaps we can conclude at this point that in all cases, value is a notion created by philosophers; as such, it is not an existing reality. But this presents us with a new question: Is this notion created by philosophers a general concept that, in spite of our critiques, abstractly accounts for multiple realities and brings them to a unity, or is it truly an empty word, put forth as a result of a whole philosophical system? It is certain that, if we stop talking about value and instead speak of *values*, we perceive that they actually exist: friendship, work, truth, etc. In all societies, a given act, intention, aspiration, will, organization, or idea plays the role that these philosophers attribute to the value. Incidentally, we must leave behind us the developments linked to nineteenth-century Western civilization and admit that racism, violence, nihilism, prostitution, cannibalism, etc., are also values or rest on values. Thus man experiences a just and an unjust, a true and a false, a pure and an impure, but there is no experience of value. In other words, it seems to us that in society and in the life of man, there are extremely diverse realities, fulfilling diverse functions, with diverse origins—all of which vary greatly—which philosophers group together by calling them Values. They thus establish a common denominator to escape a complete relativism, a nominalism. However, they make a group out of elements that are so diverse that they never manage to establish this true common denominator, nor to supply a usefully synthesized concept. We will say, then, that these realities concern us, but not the elusive and indistinct concept of value. We know very well that this approach will be attacked; it will be said that we are taking the content of the notion of value while abandoning its function, that we hold on to the appearance and reject the deeper reality. But the discord between the appearance that we experience and what the philosopher calls profound reality is too important for us to retain the latter. So, we will speak of these realities which are real in society and for men—freedom, equality, the nation, power, solidarity, the beautiful, luxury, etc.—without forcing them to form a unified whole. And when we employ the word Value because of linguistic convention, this should be heard without reference to the philosophy of values. Lastly, we observe that most functions that this philosophy attributes to values, most of the effects of the presence of values, can be explained without recourse to this concept. Value in no way defines the meaning of our presence in the world, nor provokes my engagement in the world, nor represents the purpose that I pursue in being present to the world. All this is just as much a product of my education, my work, the newspaper I read, the conversations I follow, the order I receive from the state or my superior, or my most material interests. It concerns my relation to the group, the groups to which I belong . . . Of course, some will say: but all this is value too. Well, then Everything is value, and it no longer means anything. To say that value makes the subjectivity of the subject, gives it authority, keeps it in existence—that we cannot eliminate the value of the subject without in the same stroke annihilating its very existence—this attributes to value properties that ultimately belong to God. To think that the divisions between men are due to ruptures of values is to accord very little value to the objective reality of economics and politics. To reckon that value affords man a possibility of becoming that is renewed each instant is to make an abstraction out of the concrete reality of the life of man, which is inscribed in a duration that matters for him because it is his life, nothing more. And we have no need of value to find the direction of history; Marxism, for example, has made every effort to completely evacuate moral values from history—and, at least in the form that Marx gave it, has succeeded. Likewise, we cannot say that a society which does not refer to values will be incapable of uniting itself and of uniting individuals in pacts or treaties, nor that all human rituals refer to values. For this, it suffices to have common beliefs, prejudices, collective sociological presuppositions, a similar education . . . Now, here, simply believing and having such a presupposition totally overwhelms the reality of that which we believe, or the reality of that which truly founds the presupposition. Believing in the same thing effectively unites men, makes them act together, gives them a reason to behave in this manner—even if the thing they believe in absolutely does not exist. We now arrive at an important point in this discussion: the philosophy of values speaks of value as existing, active, objective, etc.; yet no other foundation exists, except for certain patterns, prejudices, beliefs, which have an efficacy. What we are raising here is no minor question of semantics: to deny the existence of the Value as a global reality, on the one hand, and to retain Justice, Liberty, and Love, on the other hand, implies two things. First, these forces, these ideals are part of a given society, a certain civilization; they are included within it, defined by man; they depend on the cultural, intellectual, social, economic context, etc., and they vary with this context—whereas if this value is this active and objective thing "in itself," it encompasses the culture and the civilization, determining them, orienting them, taking on a sort of eternal value, an inexhaustible richness, and provoking man to action. Second, these forces, these ideals have no other "value," no other force, except the reality that this man attributes to them; their very being depends on the belief of man; they have no decisive and exclusive character; while if we give Value a grandeur on its own, it becomes a motivation that in reality excludes all others (since everything that we might invoke on the economic or political level is integrated into the level of values) and is decisive on its own. The simple existence of the value gives sufficient reason to act. These two consequences seem very important to us, and (if we want to maintain a realist perspective) even determining, in our view. Consequently, if we retain the word "value" out of convenience to describe one of the elements that constitute morality, we will use it to signify three elements: first, the belief, the conviction of man that values exist, which give a decisive reason to act and decide. Second, it will refer to man's attribution of value to certain facts, certain measures of greatness: for example, man desires equality, and he attributes a value to it; or again, the nation or labor are facts, and man attributes value to them, transforming them into a value (i.e., the object of a belief, etc.). Finally, I will use value to refer to certain realities that really exist, that are desirable and desired by men, having a grandeur in function of which man acts and decides, but that are independent of all synthesis, of all reference to a coherent objective system, and have no significance in themselves.

If, then, we consider values only in this manner, we can make the exact same observation regarding them as we made for the whole of morality: there is a prodigious diversity among the things to which man attributes value, in which he believes. It is certainly very surprising, when reading the philosophers of values, to see them declare that values are uniform, universal; that their differences are only secondary; that between one society and another they differ only in details; that differentiating elements are only apparent, and the desire for the same things develops everywhere. Likewise, we are told that regardless of their intellectual or moral level, men always know what they are talking about when they designate this or that as a value, that every value can be understood and recognized by any man (from any civilization), that the value is permanent, untouched by the passage of time (and consequently throughout history), etc. All this means that values are similar in all times and places, though this might never be said so bluntly. Now, this rests on two presuppositions: that the value exists in itself, independently of circumstances (even if we affirm that it is bound to history and is not an absolute), and that there is a human nature which is always the same. It really seems that perhaps we have not given enough attention to the realities themselves. Simply saying that if no value is common across historically different civilizations then the past is incomprehensible, is to believe that we can effectively understand past societies. Now, modern historians know very well just how uncertain they are of having effectively understood past societies; they know very well that they do not see these latter in themselves, but through their twentieth-century lenses. To simply say that behind differences of detail in sexual and parental requirements, there is a uniformity of social stylization of the sexual instinct and parental relations, is to believe in an essence of Marriage and the Family. In reality, if we set aside the juridical forms, the taboos, the beliefs, the moral prescriptions that vary tremendously, what is left? The simple fact that the sexual and parental relation is regulated everywhere, it is the object of a morality . . . now, that is rather poor! Only an abuse of words and unending abstractions allow us to say that there is a sort of unity in the values of the human species throughout history, a universality of values. On the contrary, we observe that in fact there is an enormous variety. Not only is it false to say that all societies have one same conception of the true, the just, the beautiful, of freedom, etc.; it is not true that all societies considered these to be values. Love is not seen as a value in China or among the pygmies. To Athens and Rome belongs the merit of having made Justice a value in itself. And Malraux has demonstrated how the Beautiful only became a value in the nineteenth century. Likewise, the economical is a value since the nineteenth century. And in Egypt under the Ptolemies, Incest was perhaps the supreme Value characterizing the king! By what authority do our philosophers of values refuse the title of value for the Race in racism, for Violence, or Prostitution, since in these groups these facts played the exact role that they attribute to value? This is not a difference in simple appearances, nor an affair of exceptions; it is not a matter of seeing it in a different light. There is an unbridgeable distance between systems of values; it is impossible for values to correspond to the same thing across diverse societies. These values are linked to a given society, and even within this society they vary in content: we can see a certain continuity between thirteenth- and nineteenth-century Frenchmen, but the value of freedom is radically different if we examine it in the thirteenth, the sixteenth, and the nineteenth centuries. And values perish along with the society to which they relate. Everything ultimately depends on man's decision regarding what he calls a value; we can only speak of values in a given historical situation. But the history of a society and the decision of man are not limited to shining a light on a preexisting value that was waiting in the shadows; they call something that did not exist out of nothingness, making it exist. That is why this value disappears when this decision changes or when the situation is modified. And the relation between the content of a value and a given social state tragically appears in the collision between two societies where the same word covers fundamentally opposed values—for example, the communist world and the Western world. Men can understand one another not because they refer to the same values, to an objective value, but because of the identity of their patterns, their prejudices, their beliefs, their presuppositions. And these latter give content to the values that these men speak of; because of these elements, they know what they are talking about. And these elements come from the many material, intellectual, and spiritual structures of the society to which they belong.

We are also told that the value always bears an ultimately revolutionary force; that it liberates us from tradition, instructions, and imperatives; that it represents a power of individual opposition to the established order, an external challenge, a drive to transgress limits; or a source of open morality pushing man to the fullest realization of himself. The value is said to initiate scandalous acts, putting the reigning morality in question, establishing distance between the value itself and its determinations; finally, it is supposedly the source of contingency according to which man sees history, politics, and order while refusing their absolute character. And naturally, the value is degraded when it is integrated into the order; when it becomes universally recognized, it no longer demands a personal engagement. At this moment, it ceases to be a value and is nothing but a thing. But this conception already implies the recognition of value as having a distinct being and a specific power. If by contrast we consider the reality in which values are inserted, we will recognize that values are just as valid when integrated into order and duty as when they represent challenge and conquest. Why privilege one over the other? Why deny value to the order, the institution, the organized, or the traditional? This latter is not just an obstacle that prevents the value from manifesting itself; rather, it is a framework without which the value of opposition could not even exist. The value of conquest or self-affirmation only exists strictly insofar as the value of order permits this challenge and this affirmation. If we take Justice, there is just as much value in judicial and democratic organization as there is in the demand for Justice among philosophers and the economic democracy of communists. And it is absurd to say that because organization no longer implies personal commitment, it is therefore not a value. To take an example, what good are the most just institutions without men who participate in these institutions, committing themselves precisely because these institutions express the justice for which they were conceived? On the contrary, everything we call value presents the rigorous and complementary two-faced character of stable organization and external challenge. These two factors are indissociable, yes; but in the former of the two, is the value really just a thing? And why not, if we have renounced the myth of the living character of the value? The value inspires both an order and a will to transgress this order, but neither of them is a value. It is just as inscribed in a closed morality, in a social group's equilibrium which it hopes will endure, as in an open morality, a personal aspiration that breaks barriers and opposes this equilibrium. When the personal aspiration becomes a social movement, when the social movement becomes a sociological structure, when the sociological structure solidifies in institutions, these are successive stages of expression; there is no passage from value to non-value. The proof of this is essentially that the men of a society attribute value precisely to a given institution, commit themselves to defend it, and judge according to a scale of values that most often comes from the sociological structure in which they are integrated. If this is the case, we can say that there is not a distinct domain of Ethics, and then another domain of Value. The relation between the two is complex, according to the philosophers of values: ethics never has a value as its aim, we are told, but values can inspire a certain ethical behavior; they mark off the territory of the moral life, orienting it: "The ground of values offers us the soil of moral existence." All this is correct, but it seems we must go much further, to come to see values as one of the elements that constitute ethics in its various senses, in its diverse applications, and in its full scope. In both cases, it is really man in society, and society by way of man, who create them. They attribute value, just like they define imperatives and distinguish between good and evil. We will see shortly that these ethical determinations that man makes are not arbitrary. The same goes for values: man cannot choose just any value but is bound by precise limits; he is not free to decide, "this is a value." But with the limits and drives that we will study later on, it is nevertheless man and man alone who causes a word, a thing, or a being to take on value. There are no hidden deities that man unveils, no secrets of creation that he simply incarnates.

Now, the opposition between value/revolution and non-value/order led to another opposition, and this is the last point that seems essential for us to examine. The philosophers of value often make an opposition between Value and the Sacred. Already sociologists see that the sacred inspires traditional morality and taboos, while value corresponds to Mana, the power that permits us to transgress the sacred. The sacred establishes the order of social phenomena, organizes relations. Sociological religions, civilizations, a society—all these find their security in the presence of a sacred that is a source of imperatives; while for a value to be made manifest, these beings must be free and express themselves spontaneously, since they must be "subjects" to translate the value. This opposition seems completely unacceptable to us. The link between value and the sacred seems rigorous. It has been perfectly established (Caillois), for example, that if there is a sacred of order, there is an equivalent sacred of transgression that exhibits the same qualities. In primitive society, "value" is thus an integral part of the Sacred. And in all societies, a value only exists through our belief in it.

In reality, saying that we only know the value by acting presupposes belief: we would not act if we did not believe this! Historically, every time that man expresses a value, attributes a value, there is a point of origin or insertion of the sacred. The value only adds value insofar as it sacralizes. It would not be itself if it did not engage us, if it did not provoke respect, if it could be constantly put in question, if it did not divide, if it did not give a meaning to life and motivate to action; now all this is very precisely part of the sacred. The link between the two is much more rigorous than incidental. The "value dons the attributes of the sacred," we are told, but in reality it would be nothing without these attributes; man would not treat it as a value. The justice that is merely the precise definition of philosophers or jurists is in no way a value in the eyes of men. Whether national, social, or metaphysical, it only becomes a value when it contains a power of seduction, of adhesion, of exaltation that draws men into it—when it contains the force of the sacred. Thus, we find that the relation between value and the sacred is in fact a reciprocal relation.

To say that the sacred always evolves towards the status of a thing is to misrecognize the nature of the sacred; of course it can be this, but it is also always other than the thing on which it settles. Incidentally, this would not distinguish it from value, since we have acknowledged that the normal process concerning value is also one of being changed into things, and that it is at once creative of order and destructive of this same order, like the sacred itself.

Incidentally, on this point, we must make a final observation that contains an aspect of value which is often neglected. When man elaborates a value on the basis of a fact, when he transforms a simple fact, an institution, a relation into a value, this generally has a disastrous effect. As long as the fact remains only a fact, it has very little force within itself to ravage man spiritually or even physically. It is only armed and dangerous from the moment that man couples it with value—or, according to the best of these philosophers: reasons of existence and regulation of existence; foundation of the relation of man and the world; creation of an effective structure of the lived universe; obvious goal of instinct; ends that man gives himself, and justification of his acts; significance of the fact; meaning that we find in life; manner of being present to the world, of structuring and signifying the real; limits to a freedom; etc. Now, if we consider not the philosopher but the average man, the diverse functions that we have just listed are fulfilled in the modern world by the Nation, Work, Technique, the Economy, the State, the Party, Progress, etc.; these are facts transformed into values. Now, these facts can be perfectly legitimate and normal as facts, but precisely from the moment that they become values, they take on the power of sacrifice (offered or demanded); they become the reason for the integration of man; they are endowed with a devouring and conquering force; they demand respect and adoration. The fact of being a member of a Nation becomes Nationalism, and the fact of the State produces totalitarian claims. Let us not speak of anti-values here, for it is in this nationalist, statist, productivist, partisan or technical vocation that today's man finds the meaning of his life, the reason for his engagement, the means to express himself and to encounter his neighbor, who shares the same values. But this leads to the exclusion of the Other, who, since he does not share the same value, is Without Value. Modern wars have become absolute, because they are all wars of religion, insofar as Nations and States are Values. Modern Work and economic life are the most overwhelming since they fulfill a religious function that legitimates all sacrifices, insofar as Work and Production are values. The Philosophers of Values tell us that these latter create communion, interpersonal relations, that they are sources of expression and the creation of subjectivity—fine; but let us never forget that a communion that creates itself demands the excommunication of outsiders; and that in the fallen world whose Prince we know, this affirmation of being is always paid for by the sacrifice of this being itself, or the annihilation of the other.

4

Lived Moralities

A lived morality is always situated at the sociological level. This is not only because morality only exists in the relation between individuals (as we have seen), but also because the various elements of the moral phenomenon are direct or indirect products of the social group. Since we are considering the facts, we cannot accept the principle of the "philosophies of essence," which reduce morality to an "action of the essence of the Supreme Good on the subject." But if it appears certain that morality is a creation of man, this in no way implies that we agree with the "philosophies of existence" for whom the subject creates their own values. For the subject has barely any freedom of decision and interpretation; they are part of a social group without which they would not exist. All creation of morality happens in the dialectic between the subject and the group (or groups) to which they belong.[1] This is true on the condition that we do not consider morality as a decision of an individual or a protest against the social order. As we have said, while these are two constitutive elements of the whole of an ethic, they are not its only elements and they are only important in relation to the others. The relation between morality and society is certain. There are three forms of relations between them. First, no society can survive or develop without a morality. We have already indicated that morality is necessary for groups of any kind. Society must provide its members with a criterion of good and evil, a hierarchy of values, an ensemble of imperatives, objectives

---

1. Bergson (*Two Sources of Morality and Religion,* 14) had the merit of showing how moral obligation rests on social pressure, all while not coming from the outside, since each one of us "belongs as much to society as to himself."

to attain that are qualified as "good," a determination of justice and injustice, and prohibitions limiting a field of free action. If these are lacking, society cannot function. If it were founded on pure interest or pure constraint, society would encounter insurmountable psychological obstacles, or would dissolve amidst incessant conflicts. For half a century we have spoken of the Moral Crisis of the Western world. We feel it, we know it; we diagnose the extent to which this crisis of morality endangers the whole of society. This crisis of morality manifests precisely in the fact that society no longer provides individuals with imperatives and values. So everyone seeks for himself; each small group dictates its own morality. There is no more common ground for action, no more sense of civic virtue or willful solidarity. Now, this absence of common morality not only vitiates individual conduct, but also jams political mechanisms and economic organizations.[2] Everyone agrees that institutional reforms are powerless if the moral reform of individuals does not take place. Yet precisely, we do not know how to accomplish this moral reform since it depends entirely on the existence or inexistence of a morality. But it is not in our power to individually create such a morality. The experience of our time demonstrates (and the humanities allow us to understand better and better) that men can only live together and cooperate on the basis of a common moral structure. This latter gives them a reason to accept one another and to decide upon a common goal. This is true for marriage (which has no reason to last if the moral unity of the couple does not come to replace their primitive love) as well as for nations. For example, one of the obvious problems of international order is that the absence of collective morality prevents the formation of an international society. On the one side, the USSR applies a very precise morality to international orders, drawing on Lenin; on the other side, the West applies (rather unconsciously) a traditional pseudo-Christian morality; there is no common point between the two. There thus cannot be any sufficient or lasting juridical agreement between them. There can be no enduring cooperation since the scales of moral values and goals are opposed.

To fulfill its role, the morality necessary for the life of the group must have a double character, which can seem contradictory at first sight.[3] First

---

2. See the excellent critique of the morality of French society in 1930 in Mounier, "Pour un technique des moyens spirituels."

3. The well-known description given by Bergson still applies (*Two Sources*, 18–20, 25): "In the ordinary way we conform to our obligations rather than think of them . . . habit is enough, and in most cases we have only to leave well alone in order to accord to society what it expects from us . . . It is society that draws up for the individual the program of his daily routine . . . we naturally decide on what is in keeping with the rule . . . Duty, in this sense, is almost always done automatically . . . Thus, owing to the interdependence of our duties," these miniscule duties form an ensemble, and "all

of all, this morality must be "individual-psychological." Man must have the conviction that this morality effectively defines good and right. He must not contest it. He must feel it individually as a value, in itself. Either the individual must obey it unconsciously like a discipline (not an external, arbitrary or constraining discipline, but one that is inwardly felt to be just and legitimate)—or the individual must consciously adhere to it because it gives him motivations for conduct that are sufficient and just in his eyes, as well as justification for his acts. Secondly, this morality must be "social-political."[4] The individual phenomenon that we have indicated must be the individual phenomenon of all members of the group. This ethical system will therefore be collective and common, without which it obviously would not fulfill its roles of rallying individuals and generating cooperation. It must institute a common order and *also* (not exclusively or primarily, but *also*) give economic and political structures a reason for being. If one of these two qualities is lacking, society will cease to be tolerable for the individual or durable in itself. Durkheim is certainly right when he discerns three factual elements in morality: the spirit of discipline, attachment to the social group, and autonomy of the will, by which the sociological factor becomes personalized, and thanks to which man can offer both critique and adhesion, which are moral acts.

The second order of relations between morality and society relates to the origin of morality. If we consider the facts, and as we have refused to believe that morality is a gift of the gods or inscribed in the nature of man from the beginning of his existence, we are obliged to say that morality is produced by a social group as it endures and develops. As a condition of its life, the group constitutes morality through a sort of vital reflex. Each group develops the morality that it needs; it might be more or less comprehensive, complex, or obligatory. And "social group" here refers not only to global or national society but also to smaller groups (associations, political parties, the church, family, unions), whether constituted voluntarily or spontaneously (e.g., social classes, one's "milieu"). To the extent that it is a living

---

duties are tinged with the hue taken on exceptionally by one or the other of them." There is an undivided whole of obligation. "Conceive obligation as weighing on the will like a habit, each obligation dragging behind it the accumulated mass of the others, and utilizing thus for the pressure it is exerting the weight of the whole: here you have the totality of obligation for a simple, elementary moral conscience."

4. The reduction of all ethics to individual morality is rather characteristic of the bourgeois period. As Karl Marx as shown, since the bourgeois is part of the ruling class, and since he does not want to recognize himself as belonging to a class or engaged in class struggle, he believes or pretends to believe that social relations are only multiple personal relations, and that consequently we can transpose personal morality into social relations.

entity, each of these groups elaborates a morality that seems imperative to its members. In a global society, there can be several moral systems that are more or less compatible or contradictory. Their relation is established according to a moving hierarchy that does not necessarily correspond to the importance of the group. It seems that we cannot retain Durkheim's idea in which a group's size directly corresponds to the degree of obligation and hierarchical elevation in its morality. It is not exactly correct to say that household ends *must* be subordinated to national ends simply because the homeland is a higher social group. This is sometimes the case, but not necessarily. In a global society, there can be conflict between two moralities that are linked to different groups. Currently, one of the most prevalent conflicts is the conflict between a morality of order, tradition, discipline, command and obligation on the one side, and a morality of revolt against whatever is static, crystallized or established on the other. It is perfectly useless to claim to choose between the two, saying that morality is one and not the other. These are simply two complementary aspects of one phenomenon, linked to two orders of different groups, or again to two successive stages of the evolution of one group. But in any case, neither can we say that the morality of revolt is a purely individual morality: such a morality is an illusion, since it always inadvertently refers to the collective morality. Additionally, it is gratuitous since it can be arbitrarily modified by the solitary individual who decided upon a morality for himself; he is not bound by what he has made himself. Even the morality of revolt is a product of the conviction of a group of men, who feel bound by the imperative or desirable quality of this new morality (in opposition to the old morality). Finally, this collective character is equally true of religious moralities, which are not the direct translation of religious commands, but only exist as moralities insofar as there is a religious group that needs to live its religious ideal together.

Finally, the third order of relations between morality and society derives from the fact that morality is never arbitrary since it is produced by the social group. We cannot analyze the process of development of morality here. We hardly believe in the idea of the collective conscience anymore, an idea that was important for Durkheim. This collective conscience would be a moral conscience of the group which is higher than the individual, and the basis for the obligatory character of morality; only a moral power can make a law for man, and this power is society. If, however, we simultaneously retain the element of duty and the "desirable" element, the imperative character and the character of value, the problem is no longer simply explaining the moral obligation that would be imposed by society; this phenomenon is much more complex. A society recognizes "values"—that is, the men who make up this society recognize them together. To them, these "values" seem worthy, desirable, agreeable, etc., and they are imposed with corresponding authority in relations between men. Norms or imperatives can derive from them, or even sanctions, in cases of resistance. But there is no single, systematic process here. It is probable that the recognition of these values, their desirable character and their authority, and the formulation of norms do not come from a kind of homogeneous collective conscience but from complex mechanisms of human interrelations in the group. And the general sociological characteristics of a group can explain the traits of this morality to a certain extent. But it is not sufficient. For the interrelations of individuals in this group are not indeterminate; they are not interrelations in themselves, but on the occasion of... We must therefore add two clarifying comments: all groups are organized around what we could call a "primary motive." This is obvious for simple and small groups—the family is organized around the love of the couple or the education of children, the church is organized around the adoration of God, etc. But this also applies for a global society. In each society there is an essential motive, a primary center of interest, an undiscussed presupposition, a goal recognized by everyone. As examples of this primary motive, we could name Christianity in the twelfth and thirteenth centuries, proletarian revolution in communist countries, the meaning of the city in Greece in the fifth century BC, and today, technique. This primary motive is always simultaneously ideological and material; it is linked to a certain structure and it translates into a certain aspiration. It is neither simple belief nor a simple fact. It includes the conjunction of the two. The hierarchy of "values" of this group is ordered according to this primary motive; aspirations toward desirable and obligatory imperatives are both established on it. The men of this group experience this moral organization around the primary motive that they unanimously recognize, in a sort of tacit agreement. But this primary motive is always linked to the various structures of the group, and morality is constituted on the basis of these economic, technical, religious, political, cultural, and demographic structures. Morality expresses these structures in terms of an obligation and duty, aiming to preserve and perpetuate them, and to orient man to them; at this level, Marxist analysis is partially correct. Structures appear indispensable for life; it is good that they should be respected and surrounded with a halo of value. The ethic that pertains to them will be respected precisely to the extent that we feel this necessary character of these structures, and insofar as the central motivation of society is itself recognized as desirable. If this analysis is correct, we understand that morality cannot be created arbitrarily. It is not in the power of a man to create a morality (whence the weakness of the theoretical moralities, as we have seen), any more than it is in the power of a state or an authority; that is why the moral crisis cannot be resolved by a decision. This fact accounts for the weakness of the argument of those who claim that man is not the initiator of morality, that he does not determine good and evil himself. "If the existence of the true and the good depended on my choice, this choice would never be made, since there is no reason why I could not destroy it just as quickly myself" (Mehl). It might be correct for Robinson Crusoe, but it is false for the man engaged in a society and in a collective action. The argument is applied to the (perfectly abstract) solitary individual of the philosophers of values; it signifies nothing for the average man. When a society no longer recognizes any central motive, or when its structures are no longer felt as necessary—or again when the stated morality is in discord with the primary motive—no morality can be applied. The moral phenomenon is therefore established in simultaneous relation with the concrete structures of society (and we recall that we include cultural and religious structures among these concrete structures) and with the primary motive of organization and signification recognized by all. This means, therefore, that there is not *one* origin of morality. Discussions as to whether the origin of morality is religious or magic or economic are rather vain. The thesis regarding the historical genesis of morality from religions is very contestable, but that of historical genesis based on the economy is just as contestable. There are certainly multiple origins for the historical appearance of morality, and likewise, these origins for the formation of various moralities certainly vary according to the era, the structures and circumstances. There is no pattern for the creation of a morality that is repeated in all societies. In any case, it seems very clear that the moral process is never a theoretical process of presupposed knowledge of a good, a just, an absolute truth that would then be put in practice. It is in relation with the concrete, in action itself, that the individual knows what is right to do; he acts, and he knows at this moment that his action conforms to a good or a true, or even ends up creating them. In a specific sense, we are thus in agreement with Kant's practical reason, or a certain interpretation of values—accounting for the fact that this does not apply to man in himself, but to a man living in a society, in relation to which he simultaneously performs his action and exercises his judgment.

We have said (following many others) that in lived moralities there are widely varying proportions of imperative and value, of collective pressure and individual choice. Incidentally, we need not make these two pairs equivalent to each other: the imperative does not result uniquely from collective pressure; it is felt as a duty by the individual conscience, which chooses itself by accomplishing this duty. And inversely, the desirable is not only a fact relating to individuals; a spiritualist society,[5] a religious society is completely founded on "value." But two difficulties present themselves here. The first relates to what we call the primitive totality. It is plausible that in the primitive clan, the individual remained indistinct and was not differentiated from the ensemble of the clan. If he acted, it was not for personal motives, following a choice; it was according to a collective will, from which no individual will could extricate itself. The primitive totality was in no way a constraint on the individual; since this latter did not exist yet, there was nothing to be constrained. The child in the belly of its mother is in no way "constrained," since nothing differentiates it from its mother. Differentiation between the two only happens progressively; the individual is separated over the course of history. But can we speak of morality in this primitive totality? Yes, certainly, and in spite of everything. A morality in which there is no individual decision, no choice, no deliberation, no personalized awareness that this is a value, no objectivation of this value, yes—but a perfectly constituted, existing, and complex morality nonetheless. In this morality, the social imperative is so complete that it is not felt as an imperative; it is not distinguished from the collective will. It cannot be questioned; and yet there can be no spirit of refusal, revolt or negation. This imperative is founded essentially on religious structures and is expressed in taboos, prohibitions, etc. We know that such taboos abound, and that sometimes they completely regulate individual activity. This is a veritable ethical order, determining behavior. These taboos come from a collective adhesion leading to the disapproval of the one who transgresses them. Public blame clearly gives a moral aspect to what could be judged as exclusively sacred. Now, this (decisive) indication of the sacred reminds us that primitive morality contains another element. In addition to the imperative, there is the desirable. In effect, the sacred always includes this element of forward projection, of what should be expected, of what is good, just, and holy. The mystique that characterizes the behavior of "primitives" implies this presence of value. But we are still a long way from supposing an individual affirmation. This tension regarding the desirable, this affirmation of value is equally a fact of the totality, of the social group in its undifferentiated state which has a certain tendency, which recognizes a value. Thus, morality certainly exists, even though it is in no way a personal fact, and even though the individual might be perfectly integrated in the group. According to Gurvitch's theses, it is possible that magic was the means of personal differentiation. It is possible

---

5. TN: Fr. *une société communielle*; "communielle" has sociological connotations of religion, magic, and communion.

that, confronted with a collective morality founded on the religious sacred, there was indeed a revolt, an affirmation of the individual by means of magic which would thus express a personalized morality, a "morality of aspiration" opposed to the traditional morality. Perhaps it is equally true that in this use of magic, values are more strongly asserted: in archaic societies, Mana would replace what we call the world of values . . . Perhaps. What matters is that we hold onto the fact that there is still a morality before separation of the person from the primitive totality; and while we reach a new kind of morality through individualization, the old morality does not really disappear. This allows us to see the second difficulty. Currently, it is common to consider traditional morality, imperatives, moral law, etc., to be nothing, and to reduce morality to personal affirmation, only viewing morality in its aspects of decision and choice. A moral situation exists only when man makes a choice between two possibilities. For some, the choice in itself and all that it entails is even the essence of the moral attitude.[6] Where man de-

6. The ethical doctrine of the choice rests on a false conception of freedom (for example, that of Simone de Beauvoir, *Pour une morale de l'ambiguïté*) in an absurd and dislocated world. But this is no longer truly a freedom (cf. the critique in Bonhoeffer, *Ethics*, 306–7). Neither is there a choice when *confronted with* the commandment of God, for this latter is not a proposition offered to us. It is not a "possibility" among several others. It is the word of God or it is nothing. Either we hear it as such or we do not hear it. The freedom that it leaves us is that of obedience, but not of choosing obedience, as one among several possibilities. For the commandment is at once the "You shall" and "You can" and "I promise that it will be so" (cf. Bonhoeffer, *Ethics*, 382–85). All other freedom is an illusion. But at the same time, this freedom must cause the one who wants to act to return to the one who is the source of his action (not a good, but a Person), the one who says, "Apart from me you can *do* nothing" (John 15:5). Ethics thus fulfills its authentic function, because it teaches man this very simple truth that the will of God is *revealed* in order to be *done*. It seems that this should go without saying, but experience shows that Christians continually need to be taught this.

Ever since man seized the power to decide on good and evil, he thinks that he has to choose between a good and an evil. But we must realize that it is only to the extent that man does not recognize the word of God, does not listen to God's voice, that he claims to have and to make this choice. If man listens to the voice of the good shepherd, he no longer has this choice; if he recognizes that the good is the will of God, there is no more choice; disobedience, unbelief have no more reason for being, they have become (according to Barth's formula) "the impossible possibility that evil constitutes for God himself." Disobedience to the word of God is never a choice, it only makes manifest that man is incapable of taking what God says seriously; it is only the proof that man listens to every word except the word of God, it is only the precise proof that man is not free, that precisely he has not chosen. Henceforth, we are in the presence of a radical contradiction: for natural ethics (all moralities), choice is the ethical situation par excellence; choice characterizes ethics. Yet on the contrary, in the presence of God, we are before a concrete decision that is already made. There are not several possibilities, nor interpretations of a general law, there is no proposed choice between a good and an evil: "This supposition is in itself the fruit of our disobedience and unbelief" (Barth, *CD* II.2, 670). The man who claims to exercise ethical choice is simply a liar. In these conditions, there can be no conciliation.

cides on his own, he performs an ethical act. Thus, one's engagement, one's becoming-aware, and the mastery of one's destiny make morality, and not the objective and preliminary determination of a good, a just, a true. We already encountered this affirmation in speaking of values. But we would like to add two remarks here: first, this presupposes that man is free, and that he decides, he chooses, freely and on his own; morality is thus this exercise of freedom. If there is no freedom, then in the act of making decisions, there is no morality either. In fact, when we examine the writings of these moralists, we perceive that everything effectively rests on the presupposition of freedom. This is worthy of careful consideration. At the moment that sociology, biology, and psychology are closing the circle of determinisms around man, affirming his conditioning, describing an ever greater level of conditioning; at the moment when political regimes and economic planning are diminishing the sphere of even apparent and outward freedom with lightning speed; at the moment when psychoanalysis unveils the extraordinary link between our most inward drives—at this very moment, philosophers tacitly adopt Sartre's metaphysic and affirm the possibility of a pure and simple negation of determination! This is an easy way out. And this philosophy's success is explained if we consider it to be a compensation for reality. If we do not presuppose this freedom, we cannot reduce morality to decision and choice. Of course, these exist, but at a very apparent level of freedom, resting on a foundation of determination. They are only part of the moral life.

And here is our second remark: reducing all morality to individual decision is an extreme reduction of ethics. How many times do we really choose in our lives? How many days pass by without a true choice on my part? How many of my acts and my thoughts are products of a conscious and voluntary decision? Most of the time, the average man automatically and involuntarily obeys a moral order resulting from the education of his milieu and his social and psychological setting. He practices the virtues, he is moved by the misery of his contemporaries, he is usually honest, he doesn't murder anyone. He feels shame when he cheats on his wife . . . But all of this is indisputably "moral," and this involves no decision, no choice: habits, reactions, and imitations—these constitute 99 percent of our moral behavior. To want to eliminate all this reduces the moral life to a very tiny domain. Moreover, in an amusing repetition, we can say that it is presented as a "duty" once again. Man becomes moral when he exercises choice. Man must develop his awareness, he must construct his freedom, etc. All this is a "duty," and it is precisely the philosophers that refuse the Morality of Duty who formulate this morality of choice; and in so doing, they simply move from one duty to another! But the morality of choice diminishes the moral life, not only in each one of us, but also throughout the course of history. It presupposes a perfectly individualist society, a society where the individual is considered as a value, where he is separable from structures: in reality, this morality of decision is a romantic idea adopted in the nineteenth century and formulated philosophically in the twentieth century. Of course, choice and decision have a prominent place and great value in lived morality, but they are only one aspect of the moral phenomenon and are always situated in relation to the context of society. Today, we could no longer write what Durkheim wrote: "All actions which we call moral have a common character: they all conform to preestablished rules. To conduct oneself morally is to act according to a norm, determining behavior in a given case before we even need to take part. This domain of morality is the domain of the duty, and the duty is a prescribed action."[7] And yet, it is nevertheless correct! If we regard the facts and not a theory of man and of society, morality is indeed this. But it is not only this. In any case, it is impossible to declare that if morality is limited to determining a duty and separating it from being, it excludes humanity and has nothing in common with it. This is true for theoretical moralities; but in reality, morality actually does determine imperatives, preestablished rules. There is indeed an objective "You shall" in lived morality. It is not only a "doctrine of engaged human activity which from the start must shed light on the meaning and function of the values which orient the human adventure" (Gusdorf); when it is expressed in this form, it is as theoretical as the morality of Kant. To link morality only to the affirmation of man, to make it into a sign of increased human self-creation and progress, the guide and companion of self-realization, and the realized equilibrium of oneself to oneself, is to make it into an extreme rarity that does not concern the average man—that is, to make it into a mystery. To exclude from morality the intervention of any kind of orthodoxy that judges the action of man is to exclude the facts. The only argument put forth, incidentally, is that this morality would provoke the alienation of man . . . and that the success of human life is not situated in alienation, which presupposes that morality is the success of man by himself (which already represents a taking of sides on what morality *should be*) and that man is free . . . We have already said that this is a question of pure belief. Of course, we can declare that those who stop at closed morality, constituted in the social group, with its imperatives and its dreary duties are lazy, weak, cowards—that a "moral

---

7. TN: I have translated Ellul's citation of Durkheim directly. The English citation reads, "There is an aspect common to all behavior that we ordinarily call moral. All such behaviour conforms to pre-established rules. To conduct one's self morally is a matter of abiding by a norm, determining what conduct should obtain in a given instance even before one is required to act. The domain of morality is the domain of duty; duty is prescribed behavior." Durkheim, *Moral Education*, 23.

man," the "authentically living person" refuses this mediocrity, and institutes an open morality, a morality of decision, aspiration, conquest . . . and ultimately devotes himself to the realization of himself: we have heard this before the phenomenologists, particularly in Nietzsche, and even from Hitler. But to us, it seems more serious to refuse neither one nor the other; the morality lived out by the mediocre and the cowardly is the morality lived out by man, just as much as—and even more than—the morality of the hero.

5

The Attitude of Man toward Morality

Moralism and Immoralism

Man adopts a certain stance toward morality—toward all morality, and toward the morality that exists in our society (which is not yet technical morality); in other words, his behavior is never fully in line with the morality of his group.

1. There is always a certain gap between morality and individual behavior. It is very commonplace to distinguish between Morality and Habits, Duty and Being; this is so evident that we will not develop it. But we must note that this opposition between Morality and Habits is becoming less and less exact. There are three reasons for this.

> *a*) To the extent that we currently no longer conceive of morality as an absolute but as relative—varying in content according to time and place, having no religious or natural permanence—morality is no longer totally rigid, a quality that formerly set it apart from habits; it adapts more easily.
>
> *b*) To the extent that morality is a product of the social group, it is therefore obviously a product of *habits*. But on this terrain, there are two remaining elements of opposition between Morality and Habits: first, a gap in Time. Morality necessarily drags behind habits; it evolves less quickly. In reality, it expresses yesterday's habits. Yesterday's habits tend to become today's morality, and today's habits will provoke

tomorrow's morality. A second difference concerns rationality: habits are a spontaneous phenomenon, while morality is always more or less constructed and organized. It is a collective ideological construction. This construction can be more or less conscious and voluntary, but it always exists. Its relation to habit is ambiguous, for it can have two different objectives: it can either be designed to conceal reality, camouflaging behavior and habits, refusing to see what really is, in which case it is an ideological veil; or it can express a veritable will toward the True, the Good, the Just, etc., passing judgment on habits. All morality includes these two factors; it is never completely one or the other. Most of the time, it is a will to reform habits toward the good and a will to camouflage them simultaneously.[1]

c) Finally, a third factor of rapprochement of morality and habits relates to the progressive development of technical morality [*la morale technicienne*]. This latter tends to inform behavior in such a manner that it precisely expresses the good of technique [*le bien technique*]. Thus the opposition between what must be done and what we do is attenuated—but precisely because it concerns "what must be done" in the order of technique. Incidentally, the development of certain (sociological, psychological) techniques tends to modify the relation between Morality and Habits. The perspectives of social psychology and depth psychology lead us to consider that Duty, moral Obligation, and the Meaning of Sin are harmful for man, so the notion of Normal is being progressively substituted for the idea of the Moral. From a sociotechnical point of view, what is Normal expresses the good. Establishing a conflict between the Normal and a moral Imperative is harmful for the individual and for society. Consequently, there are systematic attempts to promote a morality of behavior conforming to social utility (cf. Hesnard, *Morale sans péché* [*Morality without Sin*]), expressing the Normality known via surveys, polls, etc. (the *Kinsey Report*, for example).[2] At this moment, practical behavior in the private domain is presented as Morality, and we confuse what is with what ought to be.

---

1. Marx's analysis of Ideology can be applied here, showing that all moral (or immoral) positions are the result of false consciousness. The spiritual dimension permits man to add an element of conscious deceit to his ignorance of his situation, in seeking to appear loyal toward values or toward himself. This all comes back to the biblical assertion that ethics is the fruit of the rupture with God.

2. TN: The editors of the 2013 French edition include references to the French translations of the 1948 and 1954 editions of the famous Kinsey reports on human sexuality; see the bibliography at the end of the volume.

2. But in our society, there is still a Morality that appears as an imperative. This morality confronts the individual. What, then, is the behavior of man toward this morality, what attitude does he adopt, and what does he make of this morality? In fact, for him it is a matter of resolving the conflict that exists between his life and the morality. No man likes and accepts this conflict. Two paths (and only two) are thus open to man: moralism and immoralism.

Moralism

On the whole, we are concerned here with the operation by which man takes possession of morality in one way or another, making it into an instrument for his benefit. It is not an object that he modifies but one that he takes advantage of; and precisely to the extent that man takes morality seriously, that he seriously confronts it, his attitude will be a Moralism and he will make use of Morality. But what will he use it for?

1. In the hands of the Moralist, morality essentially becomes an instrument of justification. We will not insist on the importance and the mechanism of justification; we should simply note here that this justification includes a double process. Either morality will be constituted in function of our own behavior, and we will end up demonstrating that the Good is what we do—this is direct justification. Or we will bend our action, our attitude, our works to a moral commandment which we accomplish *so that we can* declare ourselves just, *asserting our own justice* (and thus our superiority) over the unjust. As hard, as difficult, as pure as it may be, this system of morality will thus never be anything other than a means and mechanism of justification, since it is only observed in order that we can say, "I am right." In both cases, it is a veritable process of creating a good conscience. When used by man in this way, morality is a means that allows him to discriminate between the good and the bad—with the assumption, of course, that I am on the good side, whether by direct or indirect justification. It is thus a means to avoid putting ourselves in question: since I am on the good side, I have no need to question what I am or the society where I live. But reciprocally, it authorizes the questioning (and ultimately, the destruction) of those on the other side, those condemned by the morality. Very often, this was one of the aspects of the drama of Christian morality, of puritanism: asserting his own justice, the puritan condemned everything that was not him. This specific moralist was rightly accused in *The Crucible*[3] [Fr. *Sorcières de*

---

3. TN: Arthur Miller's celebrated play *The Crucible* employs the historical episode of the Salem witch trials to satirize the destructive and unsubstantiated accusations of

Salem], or even better by A. Chamson (*Le Crime des Justes*) and many other novelists after him.

2. Moralism then makes the Morality into an organization of Convenience. Morality is thus an instrument destined to make relations between humans as simple as possible. Consequently, this moralism flourished in societies of comfort, of convenience (bourgeois society, for example) and of conformity (since conformity is the best guarantee of well-functioning social relations: this is true in the U.S.A. and in the U.S.S.R.). But the convenience that morality bestows on society can present itself in two forms:

a) The first convenience consists in establishing a model behavior that everyone can count on. There is a norm of average social behavior that allows us to know how our neighbor will generally behave. We can expect that he will respect my car, that he won't insult me, etc. I expect certain gestures and certain words from him because the common morality dictates them. And in function of this legitimate expectation, I will establish my own behavior toward him. I presume my neighbor will perform a given act, so I will act in this manner; I will not lock my car, I will offer my hand . . . We can calculate these relations as a result of Morality. And that is why there is a moral scandal when the neighbor does not fulfill my expectations, when he does not behave as we suppose he will. Such, in effect, is the source of the moral scandal itself. We can appreciate that this common obedience to the same morality simplifies relations considerably; they can thus be calculated in advance, expected, and free from suspicion.

b) The second convenience comes from the possibility of ordering and judgment that morality presents. In fact, it is impossible to live in society without making judgments about men, without establishing a ranking of individuals. It is practically superhuman to approach each new individual with new eyes, totally free from prejudice, with complete simplicity of heart. This demands great love and great availability. For convenience's sake, to simplify and speed up relations, man prefers to stick to reliable criteria that allow him to know in which preexisting box to place a given individual. Can we "socialize" with them or not, can we use them, and how far should we trust them? And so on. When it is transformed into moralism, morality allows us to easily respond to all these questions. Moralism allows us to avoid entering into the complexity of other beings, their existence, their motivations . . . If we had to do this for everyone, our work would never end. This

---

communist collaboration leveled against American citizens under the authority of U.S. Senator Joseph McCarthy.

opposition between appearances labeled by moral judgments and the profound reality of beings that requires another judgment has been shown by Faulkner and many modern novelists who all follow Dostoyevsky on this point.

c) The third element of this organization of convenience is the transformation of morality into a screen that allows us to avoid personal human relations. Each one presents his moral façade to the others, allowing him to remain hidden in social and human relations. Only these moral façades confront one another, which allows for simple coexistence without pain or conflicts. Morality allows us to avoid real and direct contact with our neighbor. For we must not forget that in reality, contact between humans is terribly difficult. In this contact, the man who reveals himself to me in his reality becomes my neighbor; this neighbor thus obliges me to reveal myself, to reveal what I am in the depths of my being. Deprived of the protective armor of morality, we are only what we are. And it is always painful to let ourselves be seen *only* as what we are, to publicly confess what we would like to keep for ourselves. Now, only the relation with the neighbor forces me into this manifestation, this revelation, this confession. It is in my relation with the other that I am unpityingly stripped bare. As long as I am with an organization, a crowd, an anonymous interlocutor, or any old visitor, I can take shelter behind a cluster of conventions and pretexts; and the best mask is the morality that allows me to be seen in my best light, as the virtuous and just being that, after all, I would really like to be. A little good will on both sides is enough for both parties to believe (and thus to be satisfied with) the other. But this is only the encounter of two masks and two accomplices; in no way is this an encounter with the neighbor.

3. Finally, Moralism makes Morality into a process of self-determination. In the hands of man, morality becomes a means to declare oneself autonomous and perfectly independent—autonomous both in the eyes of society (which no longer determines me once I have cornered its morality and can thus give *myself* the stamp of justice and virtue that coincides with what society can say about me) and in the eyes of God. Thanks to moralism, I have bound God's will, and I know in advance what he will decide about me (i.e., that I am good). Now, under this aspect of moralism, we can include both the man who limits himself to faithfully transcribing the collective morality, and the one who destroys false gods and the good conscience of a given moment, establishing his own moral criteria and redefining the good for himself. In effect, Moralism is not only a sociological operation;

it is equally a perfectly individualist operation. The individual can claim to cloister himself in his system, from where he can destroy the others, validating his own justice. But to the extent that he determines himself, insofar as he claims to know good and evil on his own (which he defines in function of his own experience, his own spiritual journey, etc.), insofar as he makes himself the judge of the Totality—in reality, this man who creates a moralism (which is certainly higher than preceding moralisms) performs exactly the same operation. More subtle, more intelligent, less useful—systematizing this morality on one's own is nothing other than the permanent assertion of self-determination that man always claims for himself; it necessarily ends with the subject developing the good conscience that he claimed to destroy by eliminating the elements of traditional morality.

4. We can finally give a very summary analysis of moralism. For all men, moralism is certainly the greatest power of destruction of the person. It destroys the person of others through judgment, labeling, the refusal of personal relations, and the refusal to consider individual determinations. But this reverberates just as quickly in the moralizing person. By refusing personal relations, he refuses himself; for we are becoming more and more aware that to a large extent, each person is made up of his system of relations. Indeed, the moralist simultaneously locks himself up in a system of explanations and justifications, then crystallizes. Finally, he transforms himself into a Value (self-determination) and these two facts prevent him henceforth from questioning himself or allowing himself to be put in question. But if we juxtapose these three facts, what do we see? What do we mean by this triple indication?

Simply this: that in reality, the moralist denies himself because he denies his own future. For if he refuses to be put in question, he refuses all serious possibility of evolution, and if he excludes or denies his neighbor, by the same token he eliminates his future; for we only have a future to the extent that we have a neighbor. This neighbor formulates the demand of life and truth for us, and to the extent that he obliges us to reveal ourselves, he is the one who opens up for us (in our reality and not in appearance) all the virtual possibles that are excluded by an attitude of moralism. Concerning Christians, we might add another effect of moralism: it is the power of destruction of faith par excellence, for moralism leads the Christian to integrate God into himself. When this man claims to be *autonomous*, when he attributes the ability to *judge* to himself, when he *determines the Good*, when he *justifies* himself, he performs four operations that are exclusively reserved for God, since God alone is autonomous, the Judge, the one who ordains the Good, and the one who justifies. The Moralist strips God of his being and pretends to attribute it to himself. This usurpation is an exact inversion of faith. Such are the effects of Moralism in outline.

Immoralism

If Moralism is so catastrophic, should we then believe that Immoralism is the solution? In fact, immoralism is no better than moralism. And most often, immoralism comes down to being simply one particular aspect of moralism, leading man to the same consequences. When a man is faced with a moral system that he refuses, he claims to be an Immoralist. What does he mean by this? What does this mean? It seems that we can distinguish three forms of Immoralism.

1. In certain cases, the immoralist is the one who follows his own desires, his own tendencies. Many times, these passions and tendencies are condemned by morality, restrained, repressed. Because he *cannot* repress them and repress himself, the immoralist is thus in opposition with the current morality. He is accused by it. But rather than adopting the attitude of the accused, rather than accepting this condemnation (which is very unpleasant), he will quit the system and refuse this morality. He thus flips the situation around, judging the morality from the lofty position of his own inclinations. "I refuse to be accused, I thus refuse to be bad, I refuse to subdue my instincts or my desires; so, what accuses me is bad, and I in turn accuse that which attacks me; I deny it and I destroy it." We must immediately note that this is an attitude of personal justification, and an attitude that negates all that denudes me (*and thus the very attitude of moralism*). The one who thus denies the morality that puts him in question often claims to be acting in freedom, claiming "to liberate himself" from morality. But this is a lie: this man is in no way free, for only his passions, instincts, and needs are now "liberated"; in doing so, he has demonstrated that he does not control them but is rather completely enslaved to them. The liberated immoralist is a slave of his passions. And the proof of this slavery, the evidence of this non-liberation that this type of moralist always exhibits, is the extraordinary need to explain and justify himself in the eyes of others. Take André Gide or D. H. Lawrence, for example, who spent their whole lives and devoted their entire work to seeking public and social approval for their immoralism (it is remarkable that this was honored with the Nobel Prize: Gide thus succeeded in his search for justification);[4] this

---

4 TN: André Gide (1869–1951), French writer, winner of the 1947 Nobel Prize for literature, whose writings include *The Immoralist* (1902); and D. H. Lawrence (1885–1930), English writer whose novel *Lady Chatterley's Lover* (1928–29) was the subject of a 1960 obscenity lawsuit on account of its explicit sexual description.

very fact demonstrates that they were obeying the same interior process as the Moralist.

2. A second, more common type of Immoralist is the one who limits himself to repudiating yesterday's morality (which is still applied today, though in decline) in favor of current habits, of what is currently normal behavior. This immoralist thus follows the sociological current of the moment and of his milieu. He wants to be fashionable. He seeks to be socially normal. This is pure sociological conformism. Now, the subsisting morality is frequently in discord with these habits. When this discord is latent or weak, we do not perceive it. When it breaks out more strongly, little immoralists sprout up who prefer to follow the habits of their milieu than a moral imperative. Because of its conflict with the group, the morality is liquidated; and the individual proclaims himself to be an "Immoralist" (and if this proclamation is seen as good in the eyes of the group, all members of this society will call themselves immoralists in chorus). Such is the precise situation of the Parisian Existentialists, who limit themselves to following a worthless sociological trend.

Of course, in such a situation, it would take more courage and independence to uphold morality! For example, in the context of French society in 1950, it is more difficult and authentic to defend Catholic morality in its intransigence than it is to attack it; but still, it is a retrograde combat that is lost in advance. What must be highlighted concerning this form of immoralism is that at bottom, it expresses a concern for social ease, for convenience in relations with the other members of the same group; morality would lead to friction between them, and its negation is a means of facilitating simple social relations. In other words, it is exactly the same operation as moralism—responding to the same concern and the same absence of personality; the only difference is that they address different milieus at different moments. In this way, we can find René Bazin and Hervé Bazin, his opposite, united in the same pattern![5]

3. Finally, we will retain a third type of Immoralist. Concerned with the truth, the theoretical amoralist refuses Morality for fundamental reasons (scientific reasons, for example). The two most famous examples are Freud and Marx. But in these cases, two remarks are in order: the first is that these destroyers of Morality are deceived when they think they are destroying Morality in itself, for in reality they only ever attack *one* kind of Morality: for these two examples of Marx and Freud, they are only concerned with the bourgeois morality of the nineteenth century. The other remark is

---

5. TN: René Bazin (1853–1932), French writer and lifelong defender of the monarchy and the values of the church; his sister was the grandmother of left-leaning French writer Hervé Bazin (1911–96), whose novels portray family life as destructive.

that right after these immoralist theorists destroy a moral system, another system of morality immediately comes from their very work, replacing the old morality. Their amoralism is only a transitional phase between two moralities, and they themselves are the creators of the new morality: they cannot escape it. After Freud, a pragmatic moral system of behavior and of the Normal was born. But this is even more striking for Karl Marx. On the one hand, Marxist society in the U.S.S.R. is certainly the most moralist of modern societies; in its foundation and in its expressions, it takes up the old bourgeois morality that Marx thought he had liquidated. This is necessary so that socialist society can live; and if it concerns the morality of the nineteenth century, it is because in its stage of economic progression, the U.S.S.R. is at about the point where Western society was at the end of the nineteenth century. But on the other hand (and much more importantly), we find ourselves in the presence of the creation of a Marxist systematic Morality by Mao Zedong. His most important contribution to Marxism is certainly the transformation of Marxism into morality. The two aspects of this theory are as follows: first, there is a predetermined mold of the ideal socialist man, and everyone must be poured into this mold, must continually pass through it, conforming ever more closely to the ideal model; for no living man can perfectly incarnate the perfect virtue of the socialist man (one might think we are talking about the good old moral manuals of 1830!). Second, there are six criteria of the Good, and in applying these criteria to actions and to men, we can clearly classify them into good and bad. These six criteria are: unite the people, support the construction of socialism, consolidate the dictatorship of the proletariat, consolidate democratic centralism, reinforce the direction of the Communist Party, and support socialist solidarity. Now, when we analyze these criteria, we realize that they are criteria of behavior aimed at facilitating a certain political and social technique. In other words, we are in the presence of a particular form of elaboration of the Morality of Technique [*la Morale Technique*], which we will examine shortly. Thus, the amoralism of Marx leads to the formation of a technical Morality [*une Morale technicienne*]. Concerning immoralism, we can thus conclude that it is always illusory, either as a justifying hypocrisy or as a mystification covering a social conformity or a return to another morality. Amoralism has no value on its own and in no way resolves the problem of the conflict between man and morality.

Now, man absolutely cannot avoid adopting one of these two attitudes. Either he is a moralist, or he is an immoralist. He cannot simply be "Moral." He cannot tolerate an intangible Morality that would be opposed to him, a true expression of the Good and the True, which by this very fact would be a pure demand on him. For him, in this case, this morality would be exclusively an accusation. It would entail a process of putting him in question. Now man cannot accept this accusation, this putting in question, and simply remain there. In order to simply maintain his morality, this man would have to accept being condemned by a morality that he recognizes and accepts as true. Having done the impossible to accomplish the good, this man would say, "This is all nothing according to the absolute truth and good; this truth condemns me." The man who is simply and truly immoral would be in the same situation; he would likewise accept the same condemnation of a morality that he too recognizes and accepts as true, and would say, "I recognize this good and this truth as such, but I refuse to accomplish them." Now, in both cases, this is an intolerable, unacceptable situation. Man wants nothing more than to be justified and to be right. Either he is a moral man, and he is right thanks to morality (and thus he becomes a moralist), or he is an immoral man and he is right in opposition to morality (and he becomes an immoralist). But man cannot accept remaining, living, staying in the situation of the accused. It is an absurd situation that he necessarily seeks to get out of. And what he will not accept from an absolute, religious, etc., morality, he will accept even less from a relative, contingent, limited morality: he will evacuate this latter as soon as it puts up any resistance. This leads us to two incidental remarks: first, Christians must recall that when a so-called Christian morality is elaborated, it leads man into this same impasse; this morality is no different from the others. Second, we could say that to get out of this impasse, man will need a third way: a recourse to an instance that is superior to morality. This is precise, but it involves the intervention of an extrinsic power, which takes us beyond the problematic of autonomous and natural morality.

6

Technical Morality[1]

Lived morality is transforming before our eyes. We are in the middle of transitioning to a new form of morality that we can call technical morality [*la morale technicienne*] because it tends to bring the behavior of man into line with the technical world, to constitute a new scale of values in function of technique, and to create new virtues.

The morality that currently exists in our society (which we usually call bourgeois morality) is composed of two rather different elements: one part is a leftover from the Christian morality produced in the Middle Ages which was transformed in the sixteenth and seventeenth centuries, emphasizing individual virtues and oriented toward charity; the other part is a technical morality, emphasizing collective virtues and oriented toward work. Incidentally, we must recall that these two elements are not contradictory: at least in the form that it took from the sixteenth century onward, Christian morality prepared the way for the development of a morality of technique [*morale technique*]. In effect, at that moment this "Christian" morality corresponded to the development of the bourgeois world. It thus insists on defending property (theft becomes an important motif in this morality); it makes Work into a virtue; it affirms individualism; it insists on the fact that God gave the world over to man so he could exploit it. All this has justified man in

---

1. In this technical morality, we include (among others) the morality developed by "human relations" in the U.S.A. as well as the morality of the U.S.S.R. This latter is much less dominated by Marxist concepts than by technical facts. Cf., for example, Henri Chambre, *Le marxisme en Union soviétique,* chapter 6; Johannes de Graaf, "Marxismus und Moral in der Sowjetrussischen literatur"; E. Delimars, *L'éthique marxiste et son enseignement en U.R.S.S.*

committing himself to the path opened by the bourgeoisie—workaholism, productivity, primacy of the economy, etc. On the other hand, insistence on the desacralization of the world by Jesus Christ since the sixteenth century lent greater justification to the development of technique. The world was no longer a place inhabited by obscure forces, by gods or demons that we must respect; it is material, and man can do what he wants with it. Finally, the Reformation completed this with the clear dichotomy between private life, personal virtues, and salvation, on the one hand, and the on the other hand collective economic or political behavior which eludes the control of the church and situates itself outside of the "spiritual" domain: there was thus a sort of spiritual indifferentism toward sociopolitical questions (while the Catholic Church had always tried to subordinate the sociopolitical to spiritual direction). Thus, this Christian morality was favorable to the flourishing of the moral "values" of Technique. When inserted into morality, these values led to the formation of this particular bourgeois morality (which we will not describe here, since it has been done on many occasions). Incidentally, this morality was rather vigorous, since it tended to impose itself wherever Western society took root (i.e., African countries), and since the U.S.S.R.—who claimed to have eliminated this bourgeois morality—instead brought it back, accentuating its characteristics with a completely new rigor (at least within the U.S.S.R. and in matters concerning privacy). We know of the strict discipline reserved for adultery, and the fight against alcoholism, corruption of the youth, and theft—all very bourgeois ideas.

In reality, this morality was perfectly adapted to the development of a society defined by technique [*la société technique*], at least in what we might call its first phase—which we are still experiencing in the West, which is at its peak in the U.S.S.R., and which is just beginning in Africa and Asia. But in the West, where we are starting to transition to the second phase of the technical society, this morality is no longer perfectly adapted and sufficient. That is why we are witnessing the formation of a new morality, purely technical, in which the elements of the Christian morality contained in bourgeois morality are progressively being eliminated. This technical morality is not yet complete; its constitution is currently in progress, but it is assuredly the morality of tomorrow.[2]

---

2. Niebuhr's analysis of the qualities of the new morality of modern man and its contradiction with the Christian ethic (in *The Nature and Destiny of Man*) is excellent: the conviction of the goodness of man; the search, not for virtue, but for social reorganization or educational program to resolve moral problems; the validity of reason to guide man, faith in Salvation by History (or faith in Progress); suppression of the conception of a fundamental evil by particular evils, etc.—all this is included in what we are calling technical morality.

Technique implies the creation of a new morality. It informs the totality of public, professional and private life. We can no longer act except in relation to ensembles of techniques; we must therefore create new kinds of behavior, new ideas, new virtues. At the same time, man is offered new choices that he is completely unprepared to confront. Now, the more technique becomes precise, demanding, and efficacious, the more it needs someone who is efficacious, precise, and prepared to implement it. And these qualities are not just questions of competence; one must devote oneself to them. This man must know how to use technique, but also how to serve it. His moral qualities must be on par with the new world that technique is unveiling. Some moralists have already caught a glimpse of this problem. But since they are idealists, their resolution points in the opposite direction: technique threatens the life of man, so a new morality must be founded that would allow man to give a new meaning to his life, that would help him rediscover the unity of his life, and that would restore the value of his freedom. Their undertaking is laudable, but inadequate; it is desirable, but inexact, in contradiction with reality. For if it were instituted, the effect of such a morality would be to render man resistant to technique, unavailable for full technical service, reticent in the face of progress, oriented toward another center of interest than technique, placing this latter on the bottom of the scale of values: all these things are unacceptable in a technical society. So, this undertaking (which, again, is desirable) has no chance of success. Most probably, a new morality will be created, devoted to subordinating man to technical values, making him a faithful servant in confidence, loyalty, and in the spirit of willful service of this new master.

Technical morality exhibits two major characteristics: first, it is a morality of behavior, and second, it excludes the moral problematic. It is a morality of behavior—that is, it only concerns the behavior of men. It is not interested in questions of intentions, emotions, ideals, or debates of conscience. However, it only neglects them to the extent that they remain interior affairs. If these interior movements ever purport to express themselves, then this technical morality will enter into conflict with them. For man's behavior must be determined by exterior motives and objectives, presenting him with attitudes that cohere with the technical world in which he must live and act. His behavior must be exact, precise; his acts must be coordinated with the play of the various kinds of techniques that proliferate in our society. And this behavior must be decided not in virtue of moral principles, but as a function of precise technical (psychological, sociological) rules. Only the exterior act matters, and this act must be determined for technical motives. This is one of the most important results of the Human Sciences— all of which, despite their proclamations and declarations, are always impregnated with morality aiming to adapt man to the technical world. We know very well that the optimum usage of any technique is only attainable if the user is psychologically adapted, if he has no moral scruples or moral or physical malaise, if he follows the rhythm of the machine, if he agrees with the operations, if he has sufficient moral motivations, if he has a scale of values that allows him to find satisfaction and dignity in his own eyes in the very use of these techniques . . . This behavior in agreement with techniques, which is required of man so that these techniques can operate at maximum efficiency, must be a morally justified behavior. Thus, it cannot be imposed from outside, mechanical, constraining; man must adhere to it for moral reasons. However, this behavior itself is not chosen for moral reasons! He is determined by organization, by planning. The more an organization (whether work, the state, family life, habitat, circulation, hygiene, distractions, etc.) is perfected, and the more precisely behavior is defined, at the same time, the more planning tends to replace the moral imperative. The old objective morality, duties and imperatives, "closed morality"—all this is progressively eliminated by organization: it is this latter that now dictates the real duties, the true social imperatives, and that attaches a moral value to them (and thus justifies them). But at the same time, this leads us to put in question the entire problematic of the choice between good and evil, individual decision-making, subjective morality, and open morality. There are fewer and fewer choices to be made (I mean *real* choices), since good behavior is the behavior that technique demands, describes, and makes possible. We have already seen that for current moralists, morality is the domain of ambiguity. But when they formulate this, they do so based on their reflections, their wishes, and a traditional society; they in no way address the morality that is useful for a technical society. In this case, technique excludes ambiguity. The good is clear. Acceptable behavior in a universe of technique is terribly unitary; it blatantly imposes itself on the individual. There are not a hundred ways of using a given technique to reach an objective. Technique is itself a way of acting. There is no doubting or discussing the behavior demanded of the individual. At present, man is generally convinced that technique is the good, that it contributes to the good of man and will make him happy. If man ever recoils before a certain aspect of technique, the evidence of the good of this technique is confirmed, reinforced, assured by the means of pressure at the disposal of technical civilization; the evidence of its successes, the weight of necessity of its development, the certitude of progress, the marvelous synchronization of techniques; how could man fail to be inwardly convinced by all this, how could he avoid participating with all his heart in the elaboration of this good? And if there are still any problems, psychological techniques can reach into this heart itself, personalizing the objective reasons for this behavior, using technical procedures to obtain adhesion in good will and even joy itself in the accomplishment of the duty that—like everything else—ceases to be painful and tiring in the comfortable world of techniques.

On the one hand, in the eyes of contemporary man, the progress of technique in itself is the Good, and on the other hand, techniques provide the necessary behavior favorable to this progress. Technique offers man an easy and efficacious realization of the good, justified in advance. Man's decision is obtained by adhesion to the progress of technique. There can no longer be any debate or personal decision; the good is obvious, it coincides with power, and there can be no question of his escaping it. We end up in a conformism more perfect than anything ever attained by morality. In effect, never before has morality been supplied with unassailable authority. Never has the Good been so obvious and indisputable. Never has there been factual confusion between the Good and Happiness. Never has there been an identification of a personal moral decision of the good and social material development: all this is realized and acquired by technique. The Good of technique is irrefutable and cannot be rejected; man is heading toward a situation where he will no longer be able to choose evil. And in a certain sense, we can perceive that this will lead to the end of morality.

In this technical morality, a scale of values is constructed that are really valid for man, and that the individual accepts as such. Undoubtedly, one of the important facts in this domain is the transformation of technique itself into a value. For man today, technique is not only a fact, nor a simple instrument, a means; it is a criterion of good and evil, it gives an orientation to life, it carries a promise, it is a reason to act, and it demands our commitment. "A manner of approaching and qualifying the world in function of our constant or momentary needs." What is this definition defining? Technique, or values? We cannot better demonstrate that technique has become a value than simply by showing the ambiguity of this definition. Now, word for word, it is the definition of value given by one of the contemporary representatives of the philosophy of values (Gusdorf). But it is much more exact at the level of the average man. In various ways, technique is undoubtedly a value for him. I say "in various ways," for the meaning of his life given by technique can be comfort or the possession of a given product, just as much as the liberation of the proletariat thanks to techniques, or humanity's happiness. These are criteria of good and evil, since without any doubt, all men today make technique into a good (or a gift of God, etc.), and they cannot avoid talking like this. And when we object that technique presents several inconveniences, they are quick to justify it (it is not technique, but the fault of man who uses it poorly . . . But if it is true that the evil here is the fault of man, this implicitly means that Technique is the Good). And we present this good as irrefutable (it is not possible to put technique in question). In our society, we can put everything in question (including God), but not technique, which is thus revealed as the decisive value. And as a value, it is desirable. All power ought to be devoted to it; it is worthy of man's self-sacrifice (and we find it normal that there should be Martyrs of Science, which today are actually Martyrs of Technique). We could easily continue and demonstrate that every trait characterizing value retained by the philosophers of value can be applied with precision to modern man's belief in technique, to his judgment, and to his behavior in this regard.

But we must move on to a second value of this technical morality: the Normal. In the technical society, the Normal tends to replace the Moral; we no longer require man to act morally, but to act normally. The Normal is no longer an Imperative of conscience; it is obtained via average behavior, whether this is determined statistically, by psychological evaluation, etc. Everything tends to confirm this predominance of the Normal. More and more often, a criminal is not considered to be a man who has done wrong, but a sick or abnormal personal who must be cured, to bring them back to average behavior. Likewise, the highest virtue required of man today is adaptation. The worst judgment that can be leveled on man today is to say that he is not adapted. (Yet, adapted to what? Very precisely, to the *technical* society: sociologists and psychologists agree that technique is most often the cause of such inadaptations.) The principle goal of teaching and education today is to produce young people who are *adapted* to this society.

The socially unadapted person corresponds exactly to the immoral person of old societies. And the Normal presents precisely the same qualities as the old morality. On the one hand, it is the definition of a good, a norm, a requirement that must imperatively be realized. On the other hand, it is a value that allows us to judge, to assess facts, men and events. It is an individualized personal aspiration: everyone strives to be Normal today. And this Normal suppresses the old notion of virtue, of good—we no longer tolerate moral judgment when faced with the decision of Normality. Once a behavior is deemed Normal, there is no place for censuring it in the name of Morality; it is no longer legitimate to decree that what is recognized as Normal is Good or Evil. This is extremely blatant in the Kinsey report, which in reality refuses traditional sexuality morality—not in the name of scientific objectivity, but in the name of the morality of the Normal. Now, this normal is not exactly the same thing as habits. It consists of one part exact knowledge, one part rational behavior, one part adaptation to the objective conditions of society, and one part confrontation of psychological science and sociological science; for it is always the clinician who ultimately says what is Normal. And thus we see how this value is linked to technique and ultimately subordinated to the Value of Technique: on the one hand, it is that the Normal is established in relation to behavior inscribed in a very precise society, the technical society (and it is not by chance that we are witnessing the substitution of the Normal for the Moral as a corollary to the constitution of technical society); on the other hand, the Normal is (and can only be) observed and elaborated by techniques.

Finally, we must retain a third value that is characteristic of this morality: Success. Good and Evil are ultimately synonyms for success and failure. According to the bourgeois formula (which derives from a certain interpretation of the Bible), Virtue is always endorsed by material Success. But over time, we derive from this (and the temptation to do so was far too great for man to avoid it) a belief that Success is the obvious sign of Virtue, since it is the recompense for this virtue. Virtue is not visible, but Success is. Success therefore allows us to presuppose the existence of Virtue. From there, we need only span the short distance of an abbreviation to say that, in itself, Success is the Good. In this orientation, we will seek to build morality on the foundation of success—whence the demonstration that "crime doesn't pay." If we ought not to be a criminal, it is ultimately because it is not profitable. But if we continue in this direction, we must admit that strength is one of the essential factors of success; consequently, we very quickly come to think that the relation is less one of Good and Evil and more of Strength and Weakness. Whence also the ethical importance of the champion: the champion also necessarily represents the Good. In another perspective, for communists, the expression of this identity of Success and the Good is found in the necessity to stick to the direction of History. At each step, the Direction of History is only revealed afterward, through the success of a given undertaking. If it succeeds, *therefore* it really was in the direction of History. And since History ultimately determines what is good, the direction of History manifests the good in the form of success.[3] In reality, there is a fundamental conviction underlying both bourgeois and communist ethical formulations: you can't argue with results. A successful action necessarily imposes itself and cannot be questioned. Now this is

---

3. TN: For more on the "direction of history," see Ellul, *Autopsy of Revolution*.

essentially linked to the operation of technique [*l'opération technique*], since precisely this latter assures efficacy and results. Of course, the measure of success might vary. In bourgeois society, it is measured in money, awards, titles, climbing the social ladder; in totalitarian regimes, one of the essential signs of success will be entry into the Party. The Party contains the Good in itself and acts as its guardian. To be outside of the Party is to have no participation in the Good. To be against it is Evil. Now, the party is never more than an instrument of political efficacy, of techniques of propaganda and government. Here again, we encounter the link between the process of technique and the determination of the good. And likewise, we return to the primacy of the virtue of sociopolitical action over all other virtues.

But we must not forget that in our society, an instrument of success is always an instrument of technique. And very consciously, we are shown that the final aim of Technique is not only a material result, but the accomplishment of the Good: economic abundance will provide for man's spiritual, moral and cultural development. The socialist regime is preparing a new man who, delivered from alienation and capitalist contradictions, will be good; this will happen thanks to technique. But if this is really the goal of Technique, every success of technique participates in the ultimate Good; and to oppose this development is truly to do Evil, and to be demonic.

Technical morality demands a commitment from man. It demands that he practice virtues. We cannot call these virtues new, for they are really just the valorization and spotlighting of old virtues that, once considered minor, have now become major and exclusive. We can also speak of new virtues to a certain extent; for example, Work. Let us not forget that in traditional societies, in *all* societies, work was scorned and seen as animal labor, disgraceful for man. All moral, social, and spiritual elevation translated into the abandonment of work; at best, it was considered as a necessity, though an unfortunate necessity. And this is not only true of "primitive" peoples, shepherds, nomads, etc., but of all civilizations—just as much for the Incas as the Chinese, the Greeks and the Hindus, Scandinavians as well as Egyptians: all these civilizations scorned work. And Christian society too. Despite the two or three biblical texts that encourage work, we must not forget that the general opinion of theologians has been that work was a mark of condemnation, that it was the sign of the fallen condition, and that consequently it was a necessity which must be accepted; but it is in no way a good or a virtue. This judgment is modified with the theologians of the Reformation, who are the first to begin to present the positive aspect of work. But only in the bourgeois society of the eighteenth and nineteenth centuries does it become a cardinal virtue, the father of all virtues. This is the first time in the history of humanity that work becomes a Good, and Laborer becomes a title of Nobility. Now, let us not forget that this happens at the precise moment where Labor is the foundation of bourgeois power, their path to power. Having become the ruling class, the bourgeoisie promote the source of their authority as a value for the whole society. How fitting, since the inferior classes must all work (as they have never worked before), and we ought to grant them moral satisfaction for the sacrifices demanded of them! "Whoever works, prays! This work, which you are constrained to do for the glory of the bourgeoisie, is a moral and spiritual value. In working, you accomplish the good, and your own salvation." Now, if we have demanded the mobilization of all of society in work, it is ultimately because of the development of technique: technique simultaneously allows for and demands man's devotion to work. Technical work is the type of work that has become the chief virtue. And the virtues that are developed in this morality are all linked to work. So while these virtues are often nothing new, their purpose has been modified.

These are the splendid virtues of discipline, self-control, dedication, loyalty to Work, seriousness in accomplishing tasks, solidarity, sacrifice to one's work, etc. All these virtues are coordinated around the central cardinal virtue of "Doing a Good Job." They are all linked to the exercise of techniques. All the virtues that we see (correctly, by the way) as the glory of Western man are virtues of work. Doing good work is the measure of these virtues; sacrifice and devotion are ultimately a function of the creative work of technique. All the virtues are actually aimed at facilitating the play and application of techniques. This results in three consequences:

a) The progressive elimination of other moral values and other virtues: familial virtues, camaraderie, humor and play, etc.—all this is suppressed and counts for less and less. A man can be despicable toward his comrades, or his wife; as long as he practices the essential virtues of work, all is forgiven. He is even taken as an example. Most of the great heroes of our time—intellectuals, aviators, etc.—follow this model. These virtues are eliminated simply because they no longer count in the eyes of modern man, to the extent that they have nothing to do with the "Central Motive" of our society.

b) It is often said that technique is nothing without man, that the decision is always his, and that he is the master of techniques. But in reality, we forget that this man has been molded for the service of techniques; that the virtues created for him are virtues of work; that the buzzword is adaptation, and that man must be "adapted"; and consequently, that morality subordinates man to techniques.

c) In this technical morality, the standard of conduct is objective. In effect, an organization that is well made technically must function. When it doesn't work, if the technical calculation was correct, it is due to a fault of man, whether laziness, dishonesty, unwillingness—such is evil, captured in one word: sabotage. And of course, objectively there can be sabotage here, whatever the intentions of the individual might have been. What should work does not work; it is man's fault, whatever his motives. Evil belongs to the realm of behavior, and is objectively observable, just like the good. But incidentally, it is also obvious that this behavior, which concerns all of society, must be totally punished; moral sanctions tend to change from being interior and conscience-related, instead becoming political or social.

But there is another very remarkable virtue in this morality: confidence in the future, an ability to look the future in the face, a certainty in hope, which is astonishing in the middle of troubled times. It is the virtue of "Everything is possible," which of course is expressed in large part in the value of the Normal. Everything is possible: not only is there no pre-fixed limit, no moral or spiritual limit to action, but the only recognized barrier is that which is not possible today but will be tomorrow. Nothing is surprising anymore: the disintegration of the atom, Sputnik, all this is completely normal. Tomorrow we will do better. But in reality, above all this virtue expresses a morality of excess, a morality of the unlimited, to which modern man adapts perfectly.

The excess of means and successes of technique condition a morality of gigantism and the unlimited. The *Kolossal*, the *Biggest in the World*[4] are expressions of this morality. Man no longer recognizes any limits to his conquest. When man enters into the process of development of technique, at no moment will he have a reason to stop and say "No." Convinced that Technique will lead to the good, that success is the criteria of the good, and that morality is ultimately linked to technique, man cannot stop at any moment in this forward march (this is the Problem of Oppenheimer and the Atomic scientists).[5] Consequently, "More" becomes a criterion in itself: bigger, higher, stronger—this is sufficient. The new morality automatically justifies anything that is "More." Morality thus closely accompanies technique in its development, justifying it as it goes. The Good thus appears in surpassing limits: what we cannot do today, we will do tomorrow—and this

4. TN: I have kept Ellul's spelling for *Kolossal*; *Biggest in the World* is in English in the original.

5. TN: J. Robert Oppenheimer (1904–67), American theoretical physicist involved in the creation of the first atomic bombs in World War II.

is good. But since this is a morality of the unlimited, we need to develop a rule of conduct to offer man, perfectly adapted to the demands of modern society and coextensive with his professional activity. In doing so, along the way, we again encounter the three characteristics of this morality indicated above: on the whole, this is a morality of Profession, of Doing a Good Job, which becomes a total and global morality for the whole of society. It is a collective Morality, essentially complete, total, and even totalitarian. It is a morality that progressively atrophies private virtues and personal morality and that ends in the disappearance of individual moral sensibility to the very extent that it makes this problematic disappear entirely.[6] Such are the characteristics of this technical morality, whose development is underway, and which ultimately appears as a suppression of morality by completely integrating the individual into the group.

We must conclude all this by considering that a response to the question of the good is not validated by its coherence to a social milieu, or to a human nature, nor by intellectual rigor, nor by a serious consideration of man, but by its foundation. "It is only when it has a solid basis that [morality] can be given with earnestness, weight and decisiveness. It is only when it is grounded in such a way that man cannot take up an attitude of reserve toward it—either by appealing to his freedom, or by appealing to his weakness, or above all finally by understanding himself as this answer, in which case the question of the good is certainly solved but no less certainly extinguished"![7]

---

6. In closing, we can evoke the morality that is born automatically from biological or chemical inventions. We recall Jean Rostand's 1962 speech to the Académie française, where he said, "It is in the direct line of our progress to learn to chemically control the elements of our behavior, just as we do with other phenomena of life. Already by the use of hormones, vitamins, or trace elements, we can augment bravery, will, maternal love; after tranquilizing drugs, there will be moralizing drugs; we are promised that soon there will be drugs which moderate envy, calm ambition; when will there be tablets for devotion, pills of goodwill, capsules for self-denial?" This is nothing but the extension of technical morality, starting from the moment that we seek only to conform individual behavior to the collective behavior deemed as good, irrespective of all individual decisions or responsibilities.

7. Barth, *CD* II.2, 564.

PART III

The Impossibility and Necessity of a Christian Ethic

I

The Impossibility of a Christian Ethic

It might seem paradoxical to assert the impossibility of a Christian ethic.[1] In the eyes of most of our contemporaries, Christianity is essentially a morality. Are not many eras in Christian history characterized by the church's insistence on actions and behavior? And as for ourselves, did we not speak of a double morality in part I, thereby indicating the existence of a Christian morality?[2] Nevertheless, all honest reflection on Christian

---

1. It is important to note that the word "ethic" never appears in the New Testament, even though it was common in the Greek philosophy of the same period. Likewise, the word "duty" is never used in a moral sense in the New Testament, though it is often employed in the juridical sense of monetary debt. When the Bible speaks of morality, it uses words like "the law," "walking according to the will of God," "being," "holding to," and as Crespy notes ("Une morale pour les Chrétiens," 694), these terms are in the domain of action, being, and living, not of speculation; this is not the theoretical construction of a morality. We must additionally note that the moral part of the apostolic letters in the New Testament is always less precise and less constructed than the dogmatic part. We could say that there is a complete dogmatic in Paul's writings, but there is not a complete morality; there are only examples of morality, a description of certain elements of the Christian life, but never an accomplished moral doctrine.

2. Niebuhr has given excellent criticism of the ethic that derives all too simply from an "orthodox" theology: such an ethic can become an authoritarian code which ignores the problems of modern man; or create a rupture between the imperative and the real; can take the form of "irrelevant" precepts; can create a premature identification of the transcendent will of God with a canonic moral code; can suppress the tension between present grace and eschatological promise; can suppress the reality of human history to the benefit of eternity; can be the acceptance of an authoritarian order out of the fear of anarchy that sin provokes; can be complacency toward problematic historical

morality absolutely must begin by recognizing that it is impossible, that no Christian ethic can exist, that the entirety of the Revelation is opposed to it, and that as faithful as it may be, all construction of such a morality is a betrayal of the Revelation of God in Jesus Christ, and ultimately a sham. We must keep this judgment in our hearts and minds throughout our study, or else it will necessarily be misleading. Only by knowing that this search is already perverse, that formulating a Christian ethic is impossible, that describing all Christian behavior is at once vain and sterile, that the pretension expressed therein is detrimental to the freedom of God—only in keeping this judgment ever-present in our mind and in our life can we progress in this pursuit, staying within the grace of God, since we will remain under judgment. The morality thus formulated will itself remain under judgment and not beyond it. It can never be a means to escape the free decision of God, nor a description of a Good or of good conduct situated outside of the dialectic of judgment and grace. It is only because we will have accepted that our undertaking is impossible and sinful (and this acceptance is not theoretical or *a priori*, but must be done in a way that is living, submitted and renewed in every moment)—since it too is inscribed in Adam's pretension to know good and evil, and in the possibility which Satan gives him to realize it—that the grace of God can make it into something possible and authentic, if such is God's will. For we must be sharply aware that our will to define a Christian ethic in no way differs from that of all men who claim to establish Good and Evil in revolt against God.[3] The purity of our intention to serve God in no way justifies our enterprise. There is no justification

---

forms since they are all ultimately sinful; a suppression of the positive character of the commandment of love, which, since it cannot be accomplished, has no more function except to reveal evil, sin, and the incapacity of man, etc. (Niebuhr, *An Interpretation of Christian Ethics*). All these criticisms are just and powerful.

3. As Niebuhr very clearly shows (*The Nature and Destiny of Man*), what is ultimately unacceptable in the multiplicity of moralities is not their diverse contents but their claim to be "ultimate" and absolute, the addition of idolatry and the will to power to the formulation of a duty, the refusal of all relativity and finitude, the claim to moral autonomy; in ethics, all of this is the effort of man to deny the determined and contingent aspect of his existence, and is precisely the reproduction of the very sin of Adam. But this does not change for the Christian. We must therefore be infinitely prudent and realize that this ethic only exists in an encounter and confrontation of our concrete existence with the Commandment of God, which is a decision that is not *in* us but *over* us (Barth, *CD* II.2, 645). All claims to know this norm by ourselves, all attempts to confer on our activity a resemblance with God's activity, are rejections of Jesus Christ, repetitions of the fall into disobedience. The Decalogue and the Sermon on the Mount, too (which are often interpreted as principles of a Christian ethic), are only commandments—that is, relative to a given historical reality; they can never become generalized metaphysical notions. Hillerdal equally shows the contradiction that exists between casuistry and New Testament ethics.

in intentions, but only in Jesus Christ. And thus, the only thing that can legitimate this search and make it possible is the decision of God, which we cannot presuppose, which we can only await in prayer and submission.

The biblical conception of the Good which is the will of God straightaway forbids the formulation of an Ethic.[4] This latter is always ultimately the formulation of a Good in itself. All constructed Ethics claim to determine what is good. Even Sartre, who claims to presuppose nothing, nevertheless gives a model of the only possible and legitimate human conduct (i.e., ultimately of the Good) when he shows us the necessity of existing by means of nihilation [*néantisation*]: such is the Good! All ethics *is a definition* of the Good—which is to say, a *taking possession*: it is man who holds the good, even if he proclaims its transcendence. This equally presupposes that the good is somehow *knowable* in itself (whether beforehand or only in action, by reason, by intuition or commitment) and that man's effort leads him to this knowledge of the good; man is the master of recognizing or misrecognizing this good, which always takes on sufficient objectivity. And if it can be known in this manner, it can also be *analyzed, catalogued*. The relation between being situated in current events and the determination of the good necessarily entails the establishment of models and norms—ultimately, of a catalogue. Finally, it always entails a permanence: man would live in a universe of madness if he could not count on a *permanence* of the good, a coherence between yesterday and today, a more or less enduring identity of value. And this is so true that man can never resist proclaiming the universality of a morality or the permanence of the same values through all history. No constructed ethic can escape these three characteristics. Now precisely, to say that the Good is the will of God itself is to deny the possibility of these three elements for an ethic that claims to be rooted in this will.[5] As we have said, there can be no good superior to the decision of

---

4. We will add, as Hillerdal underlines ("Unter welchen Bedingungen ist evangelische Ethik möglich?," 6), that this opposition is already expressed in the fact that there are *apparently* several ethics, several moral models and systems in the Bible: the ensemble of commandments does not display this beautiful unity that we would like to find in the work of God!

5. Nevertheless, this *hic et nunc* does not exactly correspond to the imminence of the kingdom, to Bultmann's "last hour." The existential present, the renewed encounter with the *kerygma* is undoubtedly precise, but neglects the continuity of the will of God and reduces the whole Christian life to obedience in the instant, which it is not. The kingdom of God is not only the transformation of each instant into a last hour: it is also a grandeur that is really coming; it is there wherever Jesus Christ reigns, and it is the revelation of this reign during an effective last hour.

God, according to which this decision would be made, to which it would conform; but if the will of God defines the good, it is not defined by man. The good cannot be something that is integrated into the construction of an ethic, nor even its starting point. And this ethic would still have the trouble of making the good into an existential value; the problem would be ultimately the same. For this good can be neither known nor lived in a way intrinsic to man, but only extrinsically;[6] at no moment can man grasp the good on his own; he cannot insert it into his existence, nor into his social organization, nor into a system of any kind. This will of God escapes him, and as we have seen he cannot discern it from the inside; he can only experience it as coming from outside himself. If he were capable of living or formulating an ethic of the will of God at all, this would mean that he is superior to God, or that there is a higher Good than God (which amounts to the same thing), and that God is transformed into a thing. Now the Good, the will of God, cannot even be directly known by man, but only through Revelation.[7] And insofar as God is the living God, insofar as his will is living, insofar as his Word is not a dusty record or a closed book, but only exists when God himself speaks it, insofar as "My ways are not your ways," Revelation is an act that is always new. It cannot be systematized or analyzed.[8] It cannot be reduced to a bygone era in which it once lived but which is now past, so that now it would be given over to us, delivered into our hands for us to do with it as we wish; in this case it would be possible to make this past, deadened revelation into part of the system; we could construct whatever

6. "He could not possibly regard as the good that which He had chosen for Himself as such . . . [Before the response of God,] we cannot act as if we had to ask and decide of ourselves what the good is and how we can achieve it." Barth, *CD* II.2, 10.

7. Karl Barth has perfectly shown that "the reality of the form of the divine command, in which it demands as permission and is the Law as Gospel, is something which is in principle incomprehensible. Definition and construction in principle lead inevitably either to *legalism* on the one hand or to *lawlessness* on the other"—that is, either the constitution of a system of duties outside of grace, or the negation of all duty and of all commandments: this, in effect, is what experience shows us, by which we learn of the impossibility of constructing a Christian ethic (Barth, *CD* II.2, 602).

8. In any case, while the commandment of God is always a matter of particular commandments, it never decomposes into a sort of chaotic incoherence of contradictory and special directives addressed to individuals who are always different. In the presence of the commandment of God, man does not disintegrate into a series of situations without common measure or continuity; for the commandment comes from God, who is himself coherent. Moreover, as the decision of the goodness of God, this commandment is not confused and does not create chaos; on the contrary, it is the commandment itself that gives true continuity to the life of man. This fundamental unity of the commandment which Karl Barth often emphasizes forbids making ethics into an ensemble of good prescriptions, a catalogue of moral-religious or economic laws; dismantling the commandment of God in this way destroys the commandment itself.

theologies and ethics we would like. But we are given very clear examples of what happens when God delivers something into our hands: in the hands of Adam, the creation becomes a garden of thorns; in the hands of Israel, the law becomes pharisaical casuistry; in all of our hands, Jesus Christ becomes the crucified one. And in effect, when man sees this revelation as a thing of the past that belongs to him, he turns it into a Lie. —Either the Revelation is a living and present Word, and it cannot be systematized in a morality; or it is nothing but a dead letter, and there is no reason why we should use this text instead of whatever else to fabricate an ethic.

The will of God remains perfectly free. It never becomes an abstract law of the effective presence of the one who formulates it. It never becomes a philosophical principle or morality whose consequences we could freely derive, which would remain at the origin of a Christian reflection or conduct. There are no Christian principles.[9] And in most cases, the birth of heresy is made possible by the transformation of the Word of God into principles.[10]

---

9. In its essence and its origin, the entire Christian life is contained in the gift of grace that it is given, by which God justifies it. Such, then, is the life of this man. Grace is the ultimate reality of his life. There is no method for obtaining it, nor for holding onto it. How presumptuous we must be to believe that we could construct an ethic on this basis or from this point of departure (cf. Bonhoeffer, *Ethics*, 146). Already, "point of departure" is significant, for it implies that we depart. No Christian principle could be derived from it. No commandment could reduce this gift to a formula; an order presupposes the possibility of its accomplishment. Grace is accomplished outside of our possibilities. The problem of the relation between justification and sanctification (to talk like theologians) remains intact. It is false to confuse them with one another. But how to bring them together (other than intellectually and theoretically)? On the impossibility of Christian principles, see our book *Presence in the Modern World*. The commandment of God is neither a general rule, nor a categorical imperative, nor a principle of action (cf. Barth, *CD* II.2, 661ff.).

10. Karl Barth (*CD* II.2, 675) recalls that there can be no principles for a biblical ethic precisely to the extent that it is only ever a question of commandments of God. The characters in biblical history teach us that, in the commandment of God, we are dealing with God himself and his action, and not with principles; or more exactly, the only possible principle of a biblical ethic is the very person of the one who gives the commandment. Crespy ("Une morale pour les Chrétiens II," 827) equally considers that the contents of Christian morality cannot be determined by general principles or axioms, as with moralists such as Spinoza or Kant; such principles, he says, are established through speculation on the concepts of duty or of the good; this path is completely foreign to Christian reflection. For this latter, in effect, the heart of all reality is not the idea, but on the contrary the historical revelation of God; faced with this revelation, principles exhibit only a verbal reality.

But when we say that there are no Christian principles, we certainly do not mean by this that only the "spirit" remains, as opposed to the letter. We are certainly not referring to the *Gesinnungethik* and the theology of Ritschl. But as Bonhoeffer says, the problem of the Christian life is that of incarnating the work of Christ in us. Christ is not a model, nor an ideal, etc., he is the one who is coming in us and who is making us crucified and

And this is also why the Bible never presents itself as a book of Philosophy, but as a History. And when the will of God takes the form of a law, it is always presented as a commandment. "You," it calls to the hearer. There is absolutely no question here of a general rule decreed by a legislator; rather, it is the initiation of a personal dialogue. In this commandment, God addresses himself to a determinate person at a given moment. And either this person will hear it as a current address from God, and will live according to this word by pursuing the dialogue with God; or they will refuse to hear it as personally addressed to them, but in this case they can do nothing at all with this order that begins by "You": they will need to substitute a "One," a "Someone." And this is a lie. And the ethic constructed on this basis has nothing Christian about it. It no longer has anything to do with God. We will have to dig deeper into the signification of the presence of the law later.

The free will of God thus escapes us, and we cannot use it as an object of a construction, nor as a goal to pursue, nor as a reason for existing. Kierkegaard is right when he evokes the extreme case of God asking Abraham to sacrifice Isaac. We are truly in the presence of the excessive, limitless, unpredictable, *a priori* incomprehensible character of this will of God, the presence of that which exceeds all ethical norms. And yet, it was indeed the good that was affirmed in that moment, under appearances that so contradict everything we call or feel to be good that it cannot fail to revolt us. But such was the will of God. In these conditions, we understand the temptation of certain authentic Christians to reject all ethics and refer themselves only to obedience to the current word of God *"hic et nunc."* Yet this attitude is not completely right either. It is partial, and we will see further on that it is impossible to stop there.

For at the same time, let us always remember that "when grace is actualized and revealed, it always means that the Law is established."[11]

Still, we must try to grasp this problem of the suspension of the ethical, not only in the exemplary case of Abraham taken up by Kierkegaard, but in a more general manner. Prunet can write, "John pushes the paradox of

---

resurrected along with him. Jesus Christ allows man to become this man that God has become. There are no Christian principles, since Scripture nowhere tells us that God has become Principle, but that he has become man. It never posits principles or ideas, but God acting in reality—so much so that ethics need not ask the question, "What are Christian principles?" but rather, "How may Christ take form among us?" We can easily see that a formal, global, theoretical response is impossible! Bonhoeffer, *Ethics*, 99–102.

11. Barth, *CD* II.2, 562.

the accomplishment of ethics in the suspension of the ethical to the extreme. Along with the other authors of the New Testament, he enacts the unprecedented revolution of denying natural man the possibility of being an authentic moral subject."[12]

To demonstrate the fact that the will of God can suspend ethical norms, or to show that this will of God is in itself the complete Good, we traditionally refer to the privileged example of the sacrifice of Abraham. But it is too easy to counter that this unique example is not convincing, because it is unique: it is a limited case, and ought to be treated as such; it is in no way illustrative. Yet it seems to us, on the contrary, that we can refer to many other cases: there is the polygamy of the patriarchs, the attitude of Abraham toward Sarah in Egypt, the act of Tamar who seduces her father-in-law Judah, and who is declared just. But above all, there is the terrible demand of the *herem*, the ban. We know that biblically, the ban is presented to us as directly willed by God. "The LORD spoke to Moses, saying, . . . 'Nevertheless no devoted offering that a man may devote to the LORD . . . both man and beast . . . shall be sold or redeemed; every devoted offering is most holy to the LORD. No person under the ban, who may become doomed to destruction among men, shall be redeemed, but shall surely be put to death" (Lev 27:1, 28-29). "Now this is the commandment . . . Hear therefore, O Israel . . . When the LORD your God brings you into the land that you are about to enter and occupy, and he clears away many nations before you . . . then you must utterly destroy them" (Deut 6:1, 3 and 7:1-2). God explicitly orders his people to massacre all the defeated populations; men, women, children—everything must be annihilated, including the animals, and their goods, houses, and crops must also be destroyed. Now, this is not a theoretical command, but was applied; and very frequently, we see the endorsement that God gives to the execution of this ban: Arad and its people are devoted to the *herem*: Israel vows to devote them in this way if God gives them victory, which is what happens (Num 21:1-3) . . . Sihon, king of Hesbon: "The LORD said to me, 'See, I have begun to give Sihon and his land over to you' . . . We utterly destroyed men, women, and children. We left not a single survivor" (Deut 2:31-34). The book of Joshua is packed with these *herem* (6:21; 11:12, 20; etc.). And it is frequently noted that this expresses the will of God: "He devoted them by ban as Moses, the servant of the LORD, had ordained"—"The LORD allowed that these peoples would insist on making war so that Israel would devote them by the ban, without mercy so that they would be destroyed as the LORD had spoken to Moses."[13] And again we

---

12. Prunet, *La morale chrétienne d'après les écrits johanniques*, 51.
13. TN: These are my English renderings of Ellul's citation of Josh 11:12 and 11:20,

know that Samuel, expressing the will of God, orders Saul to consecrate the people of Amalek by the ban (1 Sam 15:3, etc.).

Reciprocally, God manifests his anger on Israel when the ban is not fully applied. We recall the story of Achan (Josh 7) where we are reminded that the prescription of the ban is part of the covenant. And the one who takes from the banned goods will be burned alive. But this also applies to Saul, who spares not only goods, but people (Agag), and he is sternly rebuked for his pity (1 Sam 15). And finally, this applies to Ahab, who lets Ben Hadad live "because the kings of Israel are merciful" (1 Kgs 20:31–43). But there is no mercy to maintain! The prophet comes to announce the will of the Lord to Ahab: "Thus says the LORD, 'Because you have let the man go whom I had devoted to destruction . . .'"[14]

We must look this terrible fact in the face. We must neither forget it (which is generally done in modern thought) nor turn away from it, saying that these are barbaric, primitive customs similar among all peoples, having nothing to do with the Revelation. First, we note that it is not historically exact to say that to a certain extent the *herem* is a custom of all peoples: the absolute nature of the ban seen here is very rarely *affirmed* elsewhere. On the other hand, even if it were a barbaric custom, here it is taken up by God; it is assigned a spiritual value that, precisely, absolutizes it. We can do nothing about it: all of this is found in Scripture, is part of the Revelation, and nothing authorizes us to eliminate this or that text because it does not please us. It is true that this shocks our sensibilities and our conceptions of morality and of the benevolent divinity. But it is dishonest to claim, for these motives, that "it is therefore impossible that God would have willed it." From that moment, our attitude toward the Bible is governed by complete arbitrariness. We must *also* treat these texts seriously. Incidentally, we can see their signification very clearly. First, the ban is a sacrifice, a recognition on Israel's part that everything belongs to God and comes from him; but furthermore, it is a recognition that the chosen people of Israel are holy. They are separate and must remain separate. All contamination by false gods must be avoided as it would modify the truth borne by Israel. Therefore, everything belonging to these false gods, all that bears witness to them, must be destroyed. There can be no half-measures between Truth and Lie. There can be no relation of friendship between the people of God and the world

---

cited from the French Louis Segond Bible.

14. We know very well that these different texts do not have equal historical value, in the sense of modern historical science. But even if some of them are the witnesses of a very ancient custom that was effectively applied, they all demonstrate how Israel, the chosen people, saw this custom. They show that Israel "brings the ban into the domain of Yaweh," and it is precisely for this that they are full of significance.

of sin. There is no mercy for demons. And second, the very attitude of the people of Israel, when they practice the *herem*, unquestionably cuts them off from all the surrounding peoples, who will not seek to contact them. In this manner as well, they truly are a people set apart. But if we can clearly see the meaning of the *herem* in this way, this does not make it any more acceptable for our morality; and yet, it is explicitly described as being the Good! What better illustration could we find of the fact that it is effectively the command of God which *makes* the Good, by which an act that human conscience condemns is *nevertheless* the Good because God commands it? And therefore, that there is a truth of the Good which far surpasses all our judgments, before which we can only bow in humility.

Now, in contrast to all that we have just written, we find the obstacle of casuistry. Practically no morality escapes it, not even that of the existentialists (Simone de Beauvoir falls into casuistry again and again), nor that of Häring (despite his condemnation thereof). And yet, from the perspective of faith, casuistry is unacceptable. Søe[15] indicates two major reasons for this: the Christian ethic is an ethic of life, and life is dynamic; every situation is original, as is every man, while casuistry is necessarily static and never fully accounts for all the elements of a situation. The command of God is not a general rule, nor an assemblage of rules; it is always particular for a man, in this moment, in this situation. The commandment does not need to be interpreted. As Barth says,[16] in such cases, any uncertainty as to the will of God is always on man's side, not God's. That is, in each particular case, the question to clarify is not that of the content of the commandment, but on the contrary that of the situation of man when he is confronted by this commandment. We are thus brought to the level of real life, which excludes all ethical casuistry.

On the other hand, casuistry presupposes the mediating role of the church and restores man's sovereignty before God by establishing just situations and decisions. The Moralist puts himself in the place of God and makes use of God's commandment as if it were his property. And if we hold to Scripture, ethics can neither settle cases nor give just decisions; it cannot erect its precepts as laws; it is often interrupted without clearly resolving its questions. But thus, we are tempted to ask: in these conditions, is it even still an ethic? What good is it? And it is certainly true that there are no ethical

---

15. Søe, *Christliche Ethik*, §16.
16. Barth, *CD* III.4, §52, "Ethics as a Task of the Doctrine of Creation."

problems in the gospel.[17] Casuistry relies on analysis, distinctions, discriminations—ultimately on what Bonhoeffer calls "disunion," or as we have seen earlier, it has the character of the *ethics of the fall*. In the unity rediscovered by grace, in union with God, we are in the presence of a completely different ethical orientation, exactly the inverse. But is it possible to *speak* of this orientation? Perhaps it is only livable in Christ, since interpreting the law of God as a function of circumstances, the conditions of human action, etc., is out of the question. As Barth rightly says:[18] there can be a *practical casuistry* in which a man encounters a case of conscience, and can encounter the other, who helps him resolve this problem; but there can be no casuistic ethic, nor technical method of application of the text to the multiplicity of cases, nor deduction of good and evil on the basis of the truth of the text.

In discussing morality for man, we have said that the Bible asserts man's incapacity to accomplish the good. The natural man can know nothing of the true good; and if he is capable of realizing what *he* calls good, he nevertheless cannot accomplish what God asks of him. There is none who is just, not one. Now this situation is not very different for the forgiven man, the man who has received the revelation of God. This in no way leads us to say that this man—this Christian man, let us say—is henceforth good. Here again we encounter a heresy common among churches: those outside are pagans, are wicked. Now, the entire Bible tells us again and again that nothing is intrinsically, ontologically different in this man who is enlightened by revelation. He is saved—he is justified—he is sanctified. But he is still himself. Called to the resurrection, he will die. Illuminated by the light, he nevertheless lives in darkness. An instrument of the kingdom of heaven, he is nevertheless in the world. Knowing the good, he does evil. "Wretched man that I am," clamors St. Paul, observing this rupture between the law of the Spirit and the law of the flesh in his members. And because he has received the revelation of the will of God, disobedience and evil now take on a much more real vigor and form. And because he has received forgiveness for his sin, for him sin takes on a gravity that it could never have had while he was unaware of the price paid by God for this forgiveness. *Simul peccator et justus*. The Christian has not become more capable of doing good. We observed above that though he knows that the Bible stands for the Word of God, he has not become more capable of elaborating an ethic; now we

---

17. Bonhoeffer, *Ethics*, 309–10.
18. Barth, *CD* III.4, §52.

are obliged to observe that he is no more capable of living this ethic, of accomplishing the necessary works himself. On the contrary, because nothing has changed in his condition as a sinful man, he now knows his inability to "accomplish" his salvation. And that is why the construction of an ethic becomes even more impossible for him; it is also why the Bible is particularly severe toward those who—being chosen by God—construct an ethic. It directly judges all morality made by servants of God, as a means established by man to assure his own salvation. Ultimately, morality becomes a means to protect ourselves against the free decision of God concerning us, against the fact that salvation depends on him and him alone. We set up norms (starting from the Bible, of course) as insurance against God, against the unpredictable wisdom that we call arbitrary. If we could present an indisputable virtue to God—indisputable because emanating from his own revelation—then we could rest easy, and God could not condemn us; we would not be delivered into his hands, subject to his free decision. We still experience Cain's anguish. Both Cain and Abel presented an offering, and God chose one. Why? He rejected the other; why? If we could prove to him that he did not have the right to reject this other offering, to reject us, and if we could prove this from his own word, we would have won.[19] We would have bound God in our system; we would know for certain what is awaiting us, and God would no longer be able to do anything that we did not know in advance, that we were not expecting. Such is always the meaning of Christian (or Jewish) morality as seen in the Bible. Of course, this evil plot is not always clear and conscious in our hearts. But it is there. For we must consider the significance of such an act. On the one hand, it means that we turn the Word of God against God himself—a properly satanic work. We see, in effect, that when Satan tempts Jesus, he employs the very word of God to seduce the son of God. It is similar when we make use of this Word to bind God, to insure ourselves against him. On the other hand, such an undertaking signifies that we suspect God of injustice, of wickedness, of despotism. Every morality constructed before God marks a refusal to submit ourselves to God's free will, thereby defying this will (even and especially when it claims to be the expression of this will), for it is at this moment that we deny God his very divinity, from which we expect nothing good; it is the proof that we do not love God, and that our relation with him is not a relation of love, but one of fear and force, of mutual coercion. And the closer that the morality constructed by man gets to the will of God, the more it is suspect, the more it is proof of the absence of love on the part of

19. As Roux perfectly put it (*Les épîtres pastorales*), "We cannot go beyond the grace of God, we cannot add a law or a science of mores to the gospel of God, nor complete faith with a morality."

this man, the more it will be severely attacked by God.[20] This is why we see Christ's harsh attack on the scribes and the Pharisees in the Gospels. Let us never forget that they were not "hypocrites" . . . in the simplistic sense that we use this word today. They were serious men, concerned with the knowledge and application of the law, truly seeking to accomplish what was revealed to the Fathers as much as possible, and by this fact, to be in good standing with God. They were very authentic men of goodwill. Now, in their intention and their concern to live according to the law, there was certainly a truth; but their will to settle their accounts with God, and consequently to ask nothing of him, as beggars, to owe him nothing—this was the radical evil of their lives. And by this fact, *because they* accomplished the law of God *in order to* owe nothing to God, Jesus Christ thus condemned them much more severely, and on the contrary welcomed those who lacked the pretension to accomplish the law—the pagans, the prostitutes . . . precisely those who are immoral.

There is no Christian life without the action of the Holy Spirit,[21] without his inspiration, without his guidance. Here again, this necessity of the

---

20. Niebuhr shows very well (*Interpretation of Christian Ethics*, 20) how Christianity which takes on a purely historical dimension (for whatever reason—liberalism or a transcendant theology detached from the real) actually depends on corruptions of its own *ethos* and its culture. Morality ultimately plays a corrupting role inside the church.

21. We do not presume to summarize the theological doctrine of the Holy Spirit, whose interpretations are numerous and infinitely nuanced. We will limit ourselves to indicating, under the form of propositions, what we have held on to as elements necessary for comprehending the problem of ethics.

It is not by the ministry of the church that God governs the world or directs the life of Christians but by the action of the Holy Spirit. The church therefore does not have to formulate an ecclesiastical ethic, and still less need she formulate "commandments" (Søe, *Christliche Ethik*, §9).

Sanctification is the work of the Holy Spirit in us (de Quervain, *Ethik*, 1:75) and the Keswick movement was right to powerfully recall this (see, for example, Cruvellier, *La Sanctification par la foi*). We need not cede to any spiritualism, but neither ought we deny the specific action of the Holy Spirit. That is, the Christian life has no other reality than that which the Holy Spirit gives it.

The Holy Spirit never integrates himself into our person or becomes part of us; he performs a work on us. He is never given over to us, there is no method for obtaining him. The good that he makes us know is never an objectivized given. It is important to live a life in conformity with the demand of the commandment of God, and *in this manner* the Holy Spirit can act by means of our life.

In responding to the action of the Holy Spirit, only faith allows us to accept what the Holy Spirit demands (which is madness or uselessness if taken outside of faith) and to grasp the urgent and personal character of this demand. Therefore, no ethic taken

The Impossibility of a Christian Ethic   197

intervention of God to guide our life puts an end to our own pretension to construct a Christian morality, shows us the impossibility of this morality. In effect, we can try as much as we would like to clarify the commandment of God, but if the Holy Spirit does not act in us, our knowledge is vain, and we will never be able to carry it out. Now, this Spirit blows where he wills. He is unpredictable, in his intervention as in his results. He cannot be bound; he cannot be detained. He comes and goes. When we walk in his light, we cannot be sure that this light will not abruptly disappear; when we think

---

from the commandment could be received outside of the faith. In this sense, we must say that a Christian ethic is necessarily an ethic of faith. But faith itself remains a gift of God (de Quervain, *Ethik*, 1:82).

The Good is never our personal work; it is always the work of the Holy Spirit in us (Søe, *Christliche Ethik*, §20). It is the Holy Spirit who makes us know the good, who makes us recognize a good in an event, who gives his positive qualification to a decision, and who renders the commandment of God living and present for us. Therefore, no *independent* morality is possible. In the Bible, no virtue is described as having intrinsic value; all virtue only has value in its relation to Jesus Christ thanks to the action of the Holy Spirit.

The Holy Spirit can bring about a "suspension of the ethical." As Prunet says precisely, "John pushes the paradox of the accomplishment of ethics in the suspension of the ethical to the extreme" (see the entire paragraph on the Holy Spirit in *La morale chrétienne d'après les écrits johanniques*).

But the preceding propositions imply neither that one's personal conduct is directly inspired by the Holy Spirit at every moment, nor an ethical incoherence which is sometimes upheld based on the text "the Spirit blows where he wills" [TN: Ellul's paraphrase]. In this vein, Barth critiques Søe, who cedes a bit too much to inspiration *hic et nunc* (CD III.4, §52), and Hillerdal rightly recalls the kerygmatic character of Ethics (ZEE 1, 1957).

The Holy Spirit is not a complete mystery. We know that he is the spirit of justice, the spirit of truth, the spirit of love (cf. Prunet, *La morale chrétienne d'après les écrits johanniques*), that the only truth he addresses to man is the truth of Jesus Christ himself, and that in human conduct he exercises no autonomy in relation to the Trinity.

The Holy Spirit only speaks to man by the word of Jesus Christ. He brings this word to life for each one; he makes the gospel present and allows this gospel to be perceived in the law itself. He opens our ears so that God's commandment can be received for what it is. He thus refers himself to a permanence, an objectivity, an event, to which he constantly points us (Barth, CD III.4, §52).

The action of the Holy Spirit does not eliminate the personal decision, the independence, nor the ethical responsibility of man. Man is respected in his independence by God, and God always expects a free decision of voluntary obedience in love from him. God in no way mechanizes man through a dominating intervention of the Holy Spirit. Sanctification thus cannot be heard as a play of spiritual automations, nor as a series of acts that are "holy" because they were ordered by the Holy Spirit. Rather, sanctification concerns a regeneration of the being through the appropriation of the work of Christ, by the intermediary of the Holy Spirit; but this transformation supposes an expression in our personal and free decisions. Henceforth, as Barth says, the task of ethics consists rather in following the history of the relation of God and man, a history in which the ethical event is produced.

we have grasped his reality, we find ourselves suddenly in the presence of the void. Consequently, we can construct nothing coherent, continuous or predictable, neither in our work, nor in our conduct, nor in our projects of moral asceticism, spiritual ascension, or mystical progression; for in the first place, only this intervention of the Holy Spirit renders us capable of hearing and obeying the commandment of God. The Holy Spirit alone causes us to hear the Commandment as actually personally addressed to us, and in so doing, gives us the strength and ability to carry it out. Before the Spirit's light illuminates a given word of God or a given command for us, we have no intrinsic strength in ourselves, no preexisting aptitude to accomplish it, which would be set in motion when this knowledge is given to us. The intervention of the Holy Spirit is not restricted to personalizing the word; it also creates in us the ability to carry it out, *in continenti*.[22] And if we put it off until tomorrow, if we take the knowledge of the Word that has been illuminated and keep it in a jar hidden in our heart, perhaps we will still understand it tomorrow; but in any case, we will no longer be able to do it, for this power is linked to the very presence of the Holy Spirit. God creates in us To Will & To Do. But much more, the intervention of the Holy Spirit can push us to act precisely outside of rules and norms; it can incite us to novelty, to innovation. And there must be no intervening moral judgment at this moment. We do not have the right to construct a morality whose goal would be to prevent the intervention of the Holy Spirit (and in a sense, this is the meaning of Dostoevsky's Story of the Grand Inquisitor), or which would place man in a conflict between Christian morality and the command of the Holy Spirit. Consequently, what good is it to try to formulate this ethic?[23] Why bother, since it is nothing without the Holy Spirit, and since this latter can contradict it—transforming us into enemies of God despite our good intentions? There again, the Bible shows us that, even if we are scrupulous and faithful, accomplishing what the law and the gospel stipulate by our own strength, in a movement of our own, it would be nothing, and would be worth nothing, if not done in the guidance of the Holy Spirit. What Paul says of our prayers

---

22. TN: Latin legal term meaning "immediately," "without interruption."

23. According to Barth's powerful formula, "[The] subject [of theological ethics] is not the Word of God as it is claimed by man, but the Word of God as it claims man" (*CD*, II.2, 546). And this shows better than anything else the impossibility of calling a morality "Christian." It cannot even be a commentary on the Bible! And likewise, we must remember here (Barth, *CD* II.2, 653ff) that the divine decision is the norm of our actions. Now, this decision is not an idea, a principal, a system: it is truly a decision, established in the covenant, made in Jesus Christ. Thus, it cannot be elaborated for us but can only be, in its turn, a source of our decisions. "Ethical reflection will thus be the knowledge that accompanies each of our decisions, in relation to those which preceded them or those which they follow": but nothing more!

is even more true of our works. If the Holy Spirit must interpret our poor prayers, our stammerings, to God, how much more must he be the one who renders our undeserving works worthy, who takes them up before God![24] And the same acts, the same deliberations, the same decisions, which in factual objectivity are identical and, ethically speaking, are equivalent—in reality before God, they have neither the same value nor the same meaning, depending on whether or not they were inspired by the Holy Spirit. Thus, this accounts for the complete vanity of the Christian ethic. What good is it to describe conduct, to indicate works to be done, virtues to promote, if, after having completed all of it, it is exactly the same as if nothing had been accomplished? And in fact, since everything has been accomplished by Jesus Christ, we accomplish nothing when we carry out our moral prescriptions. Our morality thus never attains the objective that it had set for itself.

The Revelation proclaims that being in covenant with God is much less a matter of doing something than of being someone, and really, of living by the grace of God. Action, accomplishing the good, and carrying out any moral law whatsoever (even the moral law of creating oneself, of fulfilling one's potential and acting as a subject—all this belongs to precisely the same order as moral imperatives) have no value in themselves. It is a matter of living. It involves pursuing a certain kind of life, day after day, filling up a particular part of reality with the presence of the truth. Of course, insofar as it concerns living, this life will express itself in a certain conduct, an action. But the action only matters to the extent that it expresses a certain life. This is also what is meant by the notion of responsibility. Insofar as every Christian ethic can only be a sort of formulation of the question, "To what extent am I the partner of God?," it is obvious that it literally cannot exist in the form of a constructed ethic. Since man does not exist in the void, since he is necessarily (because of Jesus Christ) confronted by God, objectively measured against this standard, since everything that he is, does, and wills, is constantly and objectively called into question by God, and because such

---

24. To a certain extent, we again encounter the contradiction between infinite Demand and the finite commandment that Ricoeur highlights (*Symbolism of Evil*, 54–63). And it seems to me that what he describes as the dialectic of the Jewish ethic is inevitable for a Christian ethic as well. The commandment, value, cannot be saved except through constant reference to the demand of the most holy God, and this demand can only be expressed in an ethic; but this latter constantly betrays that which it must express.

is the content of Christian ethics—this latter cannot be a code or an ensemble of objective facts.[25]

In Scripture, morality does not consist in rules, but in a certain manner of living defined by the situation of being the people of God, of being a predestined people. This is indicated by the frequent use of the adverbial phrase "worthy of": it involves living in a manner worthy of the gospel, worthy of the Lord, worthy of God. Now, this is nothing other than the expression of the faith.[26] Faith is the birth and the life of the new man, the one who is allowed to do—and who will do—what is good and acceptable in the eyes of God. For this consists of comprehending and accepting divine justification. This new man can only do good works—but how then can we define what could be considered a good work beforehand in an ethic? The situation is further complicated (and its impossibility confirmed) by the conclusion that Old Testament specialists are reaching, that the concepts and commandments that we find in the Old Testament ultimately do not have a moral content, strictly speaking. The law is not a moral law, and the commandments that constitute it have a completely different orientation and signification. They serve the creation of a certain relation, the demarcation of a certain domain, the opening of a possibility of a certain autonomy, an orientation toward life or toward death; but all of this is not morality. Likewise, "justice" is not morally qualified; it is a force, a demonstration of salvation, a gift, etc., but without moral content.[27] At any rate, seizing or appropriating these commandments and this law as the foundation or content of a moral law is ruled out, for in reality we insert our own concept of morality here; we are the ones who interpret this law through the prism of our human morality.

And yet, despite what we have just said, despite this primacy of life over acts (or perhaps because of it!), and contrary to what is constantly and repeatedly attempted, there can be no question of an ethic of "Models." We will take up the problem of the imitation of Jesus Christ elsewhere, but what concerns us here is the impossibility of creating an ethic oriented around models to imitate. The "saints" are not constitutive of the Christian ethic. This ethic does not conform to the categories formulated (for example) by Bergson and many others—open ethics, ethics of creation, of values, etc.—since grace is the ultimate reality of the life of each one spoken of in the Bible or the church. Retracing the steps of Peter or Paul, of Luther or Calvin, is strictly impossible. The characters in the Bible and the saints can in no

---

25. Barth, *CD* II.2, 641ff.
26. Barth, *CD* II.2, 781.
27. On all of these points, see von Rad, *Théologie de l'Ancien Testament*.

way be models for us because the whole of what they are resides in the word that God spoke over them.[28] Action signifies nothing when it is detached from the person who performs it. We thus cannot consider an action, judge this act, for example, and then trace it back to the person, and judge this person by their act. God alone can do this. We must follow precisely the reverse path: only the knowledge of the person is decisive. And the act must be considered as the act of a given person: and because it is this person who does it, this act is therefore worthy of consideration or rejection. The act is only a signal of something deeper. It has no existence, no content on its own, whatever might be our opinion in this regard. The acts of the Pharisees, however "good," were condemned by Jesus Christ because the "interior" was corrupt. There can be a complete discord between a person and their acts. And in this moment, we only know it by starting with the person. But again, this is something that only God, who reserves judgment for himself, can do. Judging according to morality or any other criteria whatsoever is not our business. We have only tried to bring to light this impossibility of moral judgment by highlighting the absence of a possible objectivity in this undertaking, since an act can never be considered in its objectivity, but only in its relation with the person who does it. According to the will of God, it is therefore not a matter of doing the good, but of incarnating the faith, which is fundamentally different. We are not told to perform works but to "bear fruit." The question of fruit is really a question of the tree that bears it. Consequently, it is pointless to define a morality, to describe acts that must be accomplished, or even to propose a pattern for a "Christian life." All we can do in this vein is still necessarily beyond man, who effectively finds himself in one of two possible situations: either he has not received the revelation, he has not known the grace given to him, and thus how could he understand the significance of the requirement of the will of God? Why should he take the importance of this kind of life seriously? In whose name would he do these acts, these works that we will prescribe or ask of him? Or he has known the love of God and the salvation granted him—in which case, what good is it to impose something on him, to propose a certain type of life? Why then, St. Paul asks, do you still impose commandments—"Do not handle"—"Do not taste"—"Do not touch"? "All these regulations refer to things that perish with use; they are simply human commands and teachings."[29] The one who lives by faith in covenant with his Lord has no

28. Bonhoeffer, *Ethics*, 146.

29. TN: An English rendering more comparable to the French translation of Col 2:22 cited by Ellul would read, "precepts that all become pernicious by abuse, and that are only founded on the ordinances and doctrines of men?" In Ellul's French citation the precept is the focus, rather than the things that perish.

more need of these orders, these descriptions of the Christian life; he knows what he has to do, he knows where he is going and who is leading him. He must choose his path and his works of himself and by his own strength, as one responsible for himself. In both cases, the Christian ethic is thus perfectly vain and useless. We can even say that it is far more vain and useless than any other ethic. For again, any morality can be legitimated in the eyes of men on the basis of something common and valuable to everyone, such as reason, solidarity, existence, instinct, etc., and by this very fact, it has a value of its own. And even if it is not lived by anyone, even if it remains an isolated monument to human effort, it does so as a witness of man, and perhaps as an accusation of those who did not decide to follow it. Yet this is not the case for Christian morality: *either* it is not lived, and thus it is nothing. It has no objectivity and no authority in itself, because it is not a Word of God. If it is not borne by men, integrated into their lives, it lacks even the value of Witness and Judgment that we have acknowledged in human morality, for the only testimony accepted by God is that of living man, and the only judgment is that of the Word[30]—*or* it is lived, but in this case it does not exist as a morality. For the one who lives it lives *by* it; he does not follow commandments or accomplish objectives; he lives by the very Word of God, which nourishes, leads, and carries him. And when his acts conform to the Christian morality constructed by a theologian—well, good for this morality! This life is the justification of the work of the theologian without further ado. For by virtue of the action of the Holy Spirit, the work of each one is perfectly personalized, and his life as well. He is no longer an average man; the one who has been seized by grace is no longer part of the mass of men.[31] He is a person; there is no other foundation, no other reason for the person than the one that is seized by the personal act of God who says "You . . ." But this personalization means that each life becomes singular. There is not one Christian life; there are as many Christian lives as there are Christians. There are not certain works that are Christian; there are as many Christian works as there are decisions of men driven by the Holy Spirit to be carried out in holiness. We thus live in a universe that constantly unfolds in paths which are not marked out in advance, but only open up as we follow them step by step. We live a life of constantly surprising newness. Of course, this

---

30. Bonhoeffer forecefully recalls this (*Ethics*, 326): the Christian ethic demands to be lived, or it is nothing. The law of God demands to be carried out and not interpreted. It is applied or it is forgotten (Jas 1:25). Man can only hold on to the revelation if he lives it. The Word of God is only grasped in the action performed to execute it.

31. It is obvious that all of this is inscribed in the doctrine of the determination of man by election, which nevertheless does not hinder this man's self-determination (on all this, see Barth, *CD* II.2, 510).

does not imply an absence of continuity or a rupture between yesterday and today, but only that the innovation of today could not have been logically or reasonably deduced from the decision of yesterday. For it does not obey a human logic or the reasonable conduct of existence; it follows a deeper logic, a more secret truth that unites yesterday and today but that does not allow us to predict what will be tomorrow.[32]

To the extent that the Christian life is a life of obedience, in which it follows that the only possible norm of one's moral action comes from elsewhere, from one's future, from God, this implies that the Christian must forsake all objective moral systems constructed in advance; for the resurrected life that is a gift from God at each moment is not at his disposal. This is all the more true since the gospel never gives us the means to carry out the will of God—as in Bultmann's comment, for example, that the gospel does not tell us how to love but that we must love. The "how" belongs to our freedom, which God grants us precisely to express true love; but this love is determined by the indication of its addressee, in a commandment that is addressed to us by God.

Because the Christian lives in newness of life, he must express this in his inventiveness; and if the newness bears on the question of how to live, on what should be lived, it is because there is a power at work and not the application of a norm.[33] The innovation of faith is a constant invention of new ethical forms. A Christian morality can thus have a terribly dangerous effect when it prescribes, predicts, channels, outlines. It can exhaust the invention of faith. It can mire the action of the Holy Spirit. It can be the lazy man's pillow, which leads a seriously Christian man to say, "Here is the complete ethical expression conforming to the Word of God, correctly deduced and described in detail. When I fulfill that . . . why should I go looking elsewhere? Why risk getting lost in new paths? Our present paths are guaranteed by the tradition of the church or the intelligence of theologians; this suffices." And so the model furnished by ethics can divert faith in Jesus Christ from its creative power and remove its most precious and necessary element, without which the church falls asleep and the Christian life finds itself outmoded in relation to the world which continues to evolve. For the ethical innovation of faith is not situated in the heavens, but very precisely on the earth, in this place where I am situated. To a certain extent, it is the response given by man to the confrontation of the Holy Spirit's command and the concrete situation where he finds himself. The command of the

---

32. On this importance of inventiveness, see among others Crespy, "Une morale pour les Chrétiens II," 832.

33. Hillerdal, ZEE 1, 6.

Holy Spirit is immutable and eternal, if you will, but only in the kingdom of God will it be realized in its fullness without adaptation by man. Presently, it can only be incarnated very partially, very rudimentarily and according to changing forms, because man changes, and so do the situations where he finds himself. And the responsibility of this man, the work that is personally required of him, is precisely to devise how the eternal demand of the Holy Spirit can be incarnated in the world of today (not the world of yesterday), in the events and disputes of the present time. And because times change and conditions are never the same, the works of the past can be of very little help to us. It is not proper to extend or reproduce them. Neither must we expect the Holy Spirit to dictate the forms of incarnation or the "how" for us; it is sufficient for us that the Holy Spirit render present the full authority and truth of the Word of God, that he clothe us in strength and assure us of the presence of Jesus Christ—beyond that, it is our affair, our responsibility. And alas!, it is precisely this newness, this presence of man that a too well-constructed Christian ethic can suppress.

Certainly, according to the Bible the Christian life externalizes itself in a series of decisions, and already this is opposed to the construction of an ethic. But this particular impossibility is even more visible when we understand what sorts of decisions we are talking about here.[34] These decisions usually lead to an opposition to the world, with the values, principles, and decisions of the world (as we are taught to know it by John and Paul). Now, this opposition can neither be solidified, nor codified, nor outlined. If it is the consequence of an ethical decision taken in faith, if it leads to persecution, then "Blessed are you when people revile you and persecute you . . ." But if it results from an ethic *a priori*, from positions taken on principles, then "Woe to you hypocrites . . ." In the second place, these decisions are opposed to the global, general, macrocosmic perspectives to which, alas! we have grown accustomed in theology; rather, these are prosaic decisions, microscopic adjustments that (precisely because of this character) cannot be the object of any specification, any decision made in advance, or else we would fall back into casuistry. Finally, these decisions are contrary to the spontaneity, the drives, the necessities of the natural man. The entire Sermon on the Mount is there to attest to this. The demands placed before us by Jesus are not justified by any ethical reason. These are not *moral* decisions. And precisely, we thus cannot establish any formal ethic based upon them.

---

34. Barth, *CD* III.4, §52; Niebuhr, *Interpretation of Christian Ethics*, 45, 105, 166, 187.

We cannot formulate an ethic of systematic contradiction of nature, which would simply be another asceticism, a new deformation of Christian morality. As Karl Barth has said, what men must do or not do is not described by the Decalogue or the Sermon on the Mount; it comes from a personal order of God that they must hear.

Finally, in prolonging the preceding lines of thought, the intervention of eschatology ought to show us just how impossible a Christian ethic truly is. We have said that the *ethos* of the New Testament is of a piece with the promise of the inbreaking of the kingdom of God in this world.[35] This presence of the *eschaton* means that we are free in relation to the world and engaged in the kingdom of heaven. The life of the Christian is necessarily a life "at the end of time." He is already situated at a critical distance from this world. This insertion in the kingdom leads to a "de-worldization" (Bultmann). But it is quite obviously impossible to construct the ethic of a life lived in function of ultimate events, just as it is impossible to transcribe the already-present presence of what will only be reality at the end of time in an ethical formula. Here we will limit ourselves to pointing out this problem, which we will examine later.

But faced with the impossibility and inutility of the Christian ethic, we must also recall the danger of this ethic. For from the moment that the Christian life and the revelation concerning this life are elaborated into a system, it is obvious that it can give rise to a good conscience, as the entirety of pharisaism has shown; it is obvious that from the moment where we know in advance what is good and virtuous, the temptation of judgment (and consequently the transgression of charity) becomes more or less constant. We have already indicated this problem; we must examine it more closely here. In this perspective, let us recall the importance of the commandment to not judge others, and particularly the verses from the epistle of James (4:11–12) that take up the line of teaching concerning this judgment. Not only does the author remind us that such judgment is a lack of charity, a claim to put oneself in the place of God since only God can judge, but he adds a very important element that directly concerns us here: to judge a brother, he says, is to judge the law; that is, in the name of a constructed ethic that allows us to formulate a judgment on our neighbor, we judge the very revelation of

---

35. Hillerdal, *ZEE* 1.

God. How can this be? The thought of James seems to be the following: the one who converts to the Lord has received in his life, in his heart, the commandment of the Lord; his heart of stone has become a heart of flesh, he has in himself the very law of Jesus Christ, which he represents. Now, as James says in chapter 1 of his epistle, this law is the law of liberty; that is, because he is freed in Christ, our neighbor is subject to the very liberty of Christ, and consequently his conduct does not concern us. You absolutely cannot judge him; if you claim to judge your brother, it is the law itself that you judge since the law and the commandment of God now live in this brother. Now, if you judge the law, you do not observe the law; therefore, in the act of judging, you become a transgressor of the law yourself. To judge others is to prove that we ourselves are ignorant of freedom in Christ. Now, as we were saying, the creation of a Christian ethic almost inevitably bears this danger of judgment; and we can say this at the spiritual level as well as at the level of historical experience. Every time that Christians or the church have been led to formulate a precise and objective ethic, every time that theologians have taken the concrete consequences from theological facts, we have seen a very quick move to judgments leveled in function of the actions of one group or another, and consequently to dividing men into the good and the wicked, and finally, to forsaking all evangelization since it was preceded by this judgment. It is in this sense that ethics presents a permanent danger for the church.

If, therefore, we consider all the obstacles that the truth of Jesus Christ himself presents to the possibility of formulating a Christian ethic, if on the other hand we think of the judgment that the Word of God brings on all morality, we can thus say that at bottom, Christianity is an "antimorality." Not only can it not give birth to any morality that would faithfully express revealed truth, but even more, it destroys all morality. Whether it be Christian or not, morality necessarily collides with the decision of God accomplished in Jesus Christ, which situates the life and the truth of man beyond all that man can formulate, know or live. As soon as any morality is instituted, whether Christian or not, it comes up against this obstacle and is broken. Of course, it can ignore it or deny it, or act as if this were not the case. But this attitude which is normal for the pagan is impossible for the Christian, who consequently finds that he is situated in a permanent contradiction. He must never forget that the revealed truth is an antimorality and that as soon as a Christian morality is elaborated, it is just as soon put in question, and quickly destroyed by this living revelation itself which it had taken as a point of departure, as a point of reference, and as reason.[36]

---

36. Beyond the intrinsic impossibility of a Christian ethic, we must also think of the

particular problem constituted by the extreme diversity, plurality, and incoherence of the ethical systems found in Protestantism alone: this should make us think. A *morality of repression* of sin (invincible sin, which persists, which can be at best repressed, from which man will only be delivered in the kingdom), *Pelagianism* (our natural capacities are sufficient for complete obedience to the law), *Perfectionism*, with its diverse forms (Roman Catholic, Arminian, liberal... Baptism or conversion or the message of Christ is a seed from which obedience to God develops... It is no longer the law [which is diminished] nor the result of an action that count, but the current work and progression). *The thesis of suppression of sin, of its eradication* (Wesley). *The thesis of ethical relativism* and indifference toward works, or of the distinction between levels of perfection, etc. Of course, we will not continue with the systematic description and critique of these diverse systems, for we are not claiming to present a treatise on ethics here. We will only make one remark. Just as the diversity of theologies can be ultimately explained by the fact that we stray in one way or another from *sola et tota scriptura*, the diversity of Christian ethics can be explained by the fact that we claim to separate the problem of ethics from theology and put ethics in the foreground. The desire to consider the fact, phenomenon, problem, and value of ethics *in itself* and *preferentially* leads to all these errors; ethics must obviously be brought back to its humble place, constantly starting from Christ and his work: Christ is the entirety of the moral life of the Christian. The law of the Christian is nothing other than Christ in his person. It is in him that we are given life, and consequently the law of our life as well. This diversity is not of the same order as the normal diversity that we will discuss later on. In effect, it is normal that ethics for Christians would change according to time, place and cultures. We are not arguing against this ethic. But we are pointing out here the deleterious existence of a diversity of moralities springing from the seduction of morality itself, which takes man out of his relation of faith in God and situates him in relation with morality, outside of the domain of ethics.

2

Historical Creation of Christian Moralities

If there are diverse lay and pagan moralities, there are also multiple Christian moralities, following the changing times as we were saying above, but also according to variations in theological perspectives. For each theological change, Christians have felt the need to formulate a new ethic.[1] But our goal here is not a retrospective of different Christian moralities, nor their history. Still less could we hope to construct a morality by making use of materials taken from ancient Christian moralists; these are resolutely outmoded. Our situation is totally different from dogmatics. It is normal and right for dogmatics to refer to ancient theologians and to understand their own expression of the Revelation of God. On the contrary, for moralists, their work is no longer meaningful for us.[2] But this is not because they were poor theologians, nor because their work was less "valid"; it is because if they really created a true ethic, it was necessarily elaborated in relation with a certain social, political, and economic situation that is no longer our own. Their conclusions (if not their point of departure and their method) are completely out of date. We therefore cannot think to look in Augustine or Ambrose or Calvin or Luther for resources for a Christian ethic for today.

---

1. We could not avoid the "ethical question" defined by Karl Barth: "The ethical question is the question as to the basis and possibility of the fact that in the multitude and multiplicity of human actions there are certain modes of action, i.e., certain constants, certain laws, rules, usages or continuities" (*CD* II.2, 513).

2. TN: The editors of the 2013 French edition change Ellul's "leur oeuvre ne signifie plus pour nous" to "leur oeuvre ne signifie plus rien pour nous."

If we pose the historical question here, it is in a completely different perspective and with a different intention. We firmly believe that a Christian ethic is definitively impossible to construct. How then were Christians and the church led to put one together? How did this necessity progressively impose itself at the beginning of the life of the church, and how and why did it grow? How did Christians themselves come to consider that this problem of conduct and works was ultimately the most important thing—so much so that on the one hand, it ended up overrunning theology itself, leading to a theology of works and the Roman heresy; and on the other hand, of all the elements that constitute Christianity, non-Christians have come to no longer consider or retain anything except its morality? We must recognize that this problem really is quite serious!

The epistles of Paul and the letter to the Hebrews testify that the moral problem was concretely posed already among first- and second-generation Christians. The non-canonical writings make this even more obvious.

We must obviously remember that from the beginning, Christians— Jews who recognized Jesus Christ as the Messiah—found themselves the heirs of the immense work accomplished in Judaism concerning the knowledge and recognition of the will of God as specified in the commandments. Already morality was caught in this tension between unlimited demand and finite commandment (Ricoeur), and particularly in the work of the Pharisees. The curses pronounced on these latter by Jesus and the rupture that he manifested were not sufficient to liquidate this heritage. For this heritage represented the highest ethical experience that man had ever had. Despite the will to oppose law and grace, could one simply eliminate this research, this construction that from the human point of view represented the highest possible approximation of the application of the will of God from an ethical perspective? This was all the more difficult since, even beginning with the unique fact that is salvation by grace, it was no less true that we must live according to the will of God (sanctification), and on this point we encountered precisely what the Pharisees had attempted: "to realize the ethics of the Prophets in an ethics of *detail*," "to stake daily existence without reserve upon the statutes of God . . . Such thoroughgoingness transforms heteronomy into an obedience accepted and willed unconditionally."[3] We must ask ourselves: what else could they do? For the exact question which the Christians would run into concerning the conduct of their lives was

---

3. TN: These citations are from Ricoeur, *Symbolism of Evil*, 123.

exactly the question which the Pharisees had encountered, and they applied themselves more seriously than anyone else to giving a response. It is far too superficial to reduce the Pharisees to literalism and legalism. Their goal is to *live* the law (thus in the present) and to unite a religion of the law as the will of God with a religion of the soul (Herford) and a practice. The temptation to take up the principal implications of pharisaism—scruples of conscience, a concern for accomplishing the commandments, the quest for moral holiness, separation from a corrupt milieu, and of course merit—arises very quickly. The temptation which the Pharisee represents continually crops up in Christianity, and Paul's critique regarding the justice which comes from the law, as fundamental as it is, is not sufficient to put Christians constantly on guard against this ethical possibility which is at once the most difficult in practice and the most tempting for a scrupulous conscience.[4]

From the outset, we encounter two essential questions. First of all, we note that according to Paul (in the two epistles to the Corinthians and the epistle to the Galatians), the first generation of Christians were not morally irreproachable. Drunkenness, lewdness, lies, slander, jealousy, magic, etc.; how can it be that Christians, who ought to live under the guidance of the Holy Spirit, behave so badly in reality? These Christians need to be taught concerning the conduct that they should generally exhibit, and in certain cases reprimanded; it must be made clear that their acts could not have been inspired by the Holy Spirit. It is necessary to fight against an idea that was certainly widespread at the time and that has reappeared again and again throughout the course of church history: "The Holy Spirit guides me, *therefore*, everything that I do is good and legitimate before God." Finally, they must be reminded that in reality they are behaving exactly like the others, like the pagans, and that their faith is not so clearly visible in their human reality. Incidentally, while opposing their scandals and their moral errors, Paul must respond to the ethical questions that are posed to him. The examples taken from the epistles to the Corinthians show very well that from the beginning of the church, it was customary to pose questions to the theologians and to the "Pillars of the Church." The most serious Christians know very well that they cannot claim to resolve all the problems that are posed to them (which are ultimately moral problems) without the counsel of those greater than themselves. Ethical consultations—which will only multiply later on, in the Middle Ages, which will give birth to casuistry and the institution of the Director of Conscience—thus start off very seriously already. And in these two ways, Paul thus finds himself led to develop a morality for Christians. He gives counsel, and sometimes even orders, though

---

4. Among others, see the excellent analysis of Ricoeur, *Symbolism of Evil*, 118–39.

he remains very prudent in this matter. And he does so by ceaselessly going back to the only authority, constantly founding his teaching on the person of Jesus Christ. But whatever the precautions taken, nothing less than a morality begins to construct itself—most notably when we think of those who receive this teaching and who conceive it as an ethical order. Certainly, if Paul is so insistent on the opposition between law and grace, it is not only (according to the traditional and obvious interpretation) to mark the opposition between the ministry of Moses and that of Jesus Christ, between the old and the new covenants. In the epistles, we can also see the concern to fight against the moralism that has been a recurring challenge since the first generation of Christians—even against a moralism founded on Jesus Christ. For they are concerned with their conduct, and they need clarity. They are also worried about the conduct of others . . . In these communities, they could not help judging others, judging one another mutually. Here again the epistles inform us of this misuse: the commendation to not judge recurs constantly (Rom 2:1; 14:3-4; 1 Cor 4:5; James 2:4; 4:11, etc.). Now, this judgment is obviously related to the conduct of others: therefore, the moralizing temptation was already very strong, and all the stronger as they had to fight against those who claimed to be Christians and who behaved poorly, and probably also against the debauched morals of Hellenistic society of this era. They had to separate themselves from the surrounding milieu, to become the saints that they were by the grace of God.

The second question posed was, How can a man who is born again, who has received the baptism of the Spirit, fall again under the power of sin? How can it happen that he who was freed by Jesus Christ could still be the slave of Satan? The epistle to the Hebrews echoes these serious discussions: can a man who has sinned still be considered as a Christian? Does a man who does evil still have faith? Hebrews 10:26-27: "For if we willfully persist in sin after having received the knowledge of the truth, there no longer remains a sacrifice for sins, but a fearful prospect of judgment, and a fury of fire that will consume the adversaries." We know that this discussion is taken up again concerning the martyrs: are those who have ceded to suffering and denied Jesus Christ still Christians? The theologians are divided on this matter. But the problem evoked by the epistle to the Hebrews is murkier still, for we find here a conception of sin that is not exactly the same as that of Paul. It does involve moral failings, and more individually, the transgression of a sort of ethic; but this presupposes clear, exact knowledge of what the Christian should do, of how they should behave—that there is a code by which one could decide who has transgressed it, and therefore sinned—and who is therefore excluded. The orientation of the Epistle to the Hebrews really is pointing in this direction, even though writings that came very shortly afterward, highlighting the moralizing sense of Christianity at the beginning of the second century, were never canonized. Consequently, we can recognize here a certain defiance of the churches and their leaders, a certain suspicion toward moral inquiries. The writings on morality were certainly admitted and collected, they were seen as edifying and pious studies, but they were never canonized. This is very telling.

Now, in the following century this led to the posing of general moral problems, and the ecclesial authorities, the bishops, were led to make decisions in these areas.[5] Questions of divorce, remarriage, usury, the use of money, oaths to the emperor, prohibiting of certain professions, a prohibition to become soldiers or magistrates, prohibitions from attending public spectacles, etc. These are not just purely private questions that are being raised; they concern social and political conduct as well. The authorities give counsel, discipline, and reprimands. Thus, a sort of moral framework is constructed in a customary manner, a sort of current within which the Christian is inserted over time.[6] In line with all of this, penitence is instituted in the second century, which resolves the problems posed by the epistle to the Hebrews: the one who commits a moral fault after baptism must submit himself to penitence (involving avowal of the faults committed; expiation, which can be public; sacramental confession), and afterward the penitent one is reconciled with God. This is not aimed only at moral failings, but it covers these *as well*. In the second century, this is not yet an institution, and still less is there a universally true moral doctrine. Things will change in the third century. On the one hand, the "edict of Callistus" officially institutes penitence, precisely for moral failings (adultery and fornication) and attributes the power of absolution of sins and reintegration in communion not only to the bishops, but perhaps also to confessors of the faith. This will trigger what we call the "penitential question." At the same time, theologians started to become directly interested in Christian morality and brought the problems and teachings of Greek philosophers into Christianity. Until this point, we could say that only Marcion had constructed an ethic (which, incidentally, was an ascesis—the body is an enemy, fasting, abstinence, prohibition of all sexual relations, etc.) which was fully integrated in his heresy. And shortly afterward another heretic, Montanus, formulates precepts of a complete ascetic morality. We highlight

---

5. The concern for classification appears clearly in the *Didache* with its distinction of two paths, the path of the Good and the path of Perdition, with the teaching of virtues and the catalogue of vices.

6. It seems that with Clement of Alexandria we see the first appearance of the idea that wherever we encounter a true morality, this means that Christ is at work; the moral objective becomes the criteria and sign of God.

again that Tertullian will be progressively drawn toward heresy by the moral problem. The moral laxity of Christians and the edict of Callistus seem scandalous to him. The Christian life must be a pure life. He constructs an ethic in turn, but does not manage to vanquish the sluggishness of the church; he who had so fiercely fought the heretics fell in his turn into the Montanist heresy through agreement on the ethical problem.

Among the apologists who borrow part of their doctrine from the Stoics (and it is among them that a moral teaching largely develops), redemption essentially consists in knowledge of a correct morality from a philosophical perspective. The philosophers are placed on equal footing with the prophets. Morality is thus foregrounded; of course, it is constructed from "Christian virtues" and summarizes the rules of the Christian life. The apologists hope that it will convince the pagans, since this morality is very close to the Stoic morality that many pagans respect; the Christian virtues are thus the very same ones that were preached by the philosophers. On this point, the apologists too were openly heretical; and it is not without interest to highlight that at the beginning, Christian morality elaborated as a system was formulated exclusively by heretics, linked to very grave theological errors. The influence of the philosophers will be further accentuated in the third century. And thus things change: until this point, the first Christian ethics aimed to be specifically Christian, with morality scrupulously taken from biblical texts, and this tradition will be carried forward by anchorites and hermits. But in the church and among the theologians, following the apologists, morality will now be principally founded on a philosophy.

And consequently, Christian morality will be built upon the works of these theologians and on the decisions of the councils and the popes, very often influenced by the patterns of the world, of politics, etc. In particular, while from the first century the tradition was hostile to Christians entering military service, the Council of Arles, which followed shortly after Constantine's recognition of the church, decided to excommunicate Christians who refused military service!

It goes without saying that the very signification and origin of Christian morality are thus modified, for it will receive its form and authority from an external doctrinal authority, that of the pope. Consequently, we witness the creation of a good decided *erga omnes* by the ecclesial authority; and from that moment on, the objectivation of the ethical situation cuts off the relation between faith and works.

From these beginnings, the role of ethics does not cease to grow in the following centuries. It is no longer necessary to cite names and follow works. There is no more theological problem that has not been treated from an ethical angle, no more dogma whose moral consequences are not investigated. This magnitude taken on by moral systematization (both in casuistry and in philosophy) can be explained by three motives. The first is undoubtedly a motive of counseling and spiritual direction. The priest continually encounters the question posed at the very beginning of the church on the day of Pentecost after Peter's testimony: "What should we do?" I believe in Jesus Christ, but what must I do to live this faith? And of course, this is linked to the unspoken question: "Am I sure that I am saved? I do believe, but after all, I behave so badly . . . By faith I am saved, but by conduct I deserve to be damned." It is a question of morality. To the first question, faith responds by situating man before his responsibility and his individual decisions. There can be no other response than that of Peter: "Repent . . . be baptized . . . you will receive the gift of the Holy Spirit . . . Save yourselves from this corrupt generation," which thus leaves each one with a personal and irreplaceable decision to make in the presence of this proclamation.

To the second question, faith responds by referring to the free grace of God. He can save you in spite of everything. There is no work that can assure you of this decision, but the love of God manifested in Jesus Christ assures you of his good will toward you and extends far beyond all your moral failings; faith in this is the only condition of your salvation. But this faith consists of delivering yourself with your hands and feet bound into the hands of God, and awaiting his decision in humility, confidence, hope and love, and accepting it in advance, whatever it may be, knowing that it is just and good. Now, these two responses are hardly satisfying for the natural man. He needs to be reassured, he needs guidance, clear certainty, and to be relieved of his responsibilities. The last thing he wants is to live his whole life in the presence of these two continually renewed questions. He does not want to start from zero for every decision he must make, to begin again with the fundamentals of the faith and assume all his responsibility. He does not want to remain uncertain about this salvation that he desires to possess. He wants to be definitively assured of his destiny, so he demands that we tell him his duty plainly. He wants to know his duties and obligations precisely, the "conditions" of salvation—since being surrendered to the pure grace of God seems scary to him. Such was the demand of the crowds in the church. As long as the number of Christians was low, it was possible to repress these questions, to remain in the exact line of individual responsibility. But with growing numbers, the problems multiplied. Priests had hundreds of moral "cases" to counsel; they needed guidelines.[7] The demand for ready-made solutions and prepared responses grows with the numbers of the faithful. And this grows inordinately when men enter the church without a true conversion, when the state gets involved, and when, persecuting pagans, the state obliges them to declare themselves Christians. At this moment, the problem becomes that of a general conduct. We can no longer look for the spiritual meaning of acts and works for each one; we can no longer defer to the individual's decision of faith, since they have no faith. What could be expected of these men who formally call themselves Christians because they want to escape death, ignorant of all Christian doctrine, having had no spiritual experience of grace, holding on to their attachments to pagan gods in their hearts, and to ancestral customs and beliefs in their morality? If the first movement of formulation of a Christian ethic corresponded to a pastoral concern to reassure troubled souls, the second movement corresponded to the necessity to settle upon stereotyped conduct declared to be Christian, according to which individuals could be judged and kept under control, since it was impossible to control their conscience. Incidentally, we very quickly came to the conviction that we could progress from the exterior to the interior, from morality to religion, and that by forcing man to act, speak, and behave in a given manner, a "Christian" manner, we would lead him to adopt a moral conscience through habit and external training, which would then become Christian, and to accept inner, religious motivations for the outer conduct imposed on him.

Now, this leads us to the second reason that pushed the church to formulate a morality. The adhesion of the state, the entry of the pagan masses into the church ended in the creation of a Christian society, of Christendom. Consequently, Christianity is no longer an individual affair; it is collective. Christianity is no longer lived in a church that is itself inserted in a hostile or indifferent society; church and society overlap one another. All societal institutions must be Christian. And since we cannot modify all the institutions—deducing them from theology, creating them from scratch based on the Revelation (which the church attempted, to a certain extent)—very often, we limit ourselves to Christianizing existing institutions, and sometimes in a purely formal way. It was so for the knighthood, fraternities, societies of peace, the monarchy, etc.; but this presented immense ethical problems. In the church, which was being constituted as a society bit by bit, it was also

---

7. Morality in the most restricted sense becomes rigid under the influence of the penitentials (from the sixth to ninth centuries) in Ireland, then in France and Germany. These are directives given to confessors to impose penitence according to the sins committed. Detailed lists of all sins and their penalties are compiled. Casuistry, which had been in place since Ambrose, finds its point of crystallization here.

necessary to create institutions and a morality. But a certain equilibrium was retained between Institution and Event, between the action of the Holy Spirit and moral or juridical rules; this equilibrium is no longer possible on the level of an entire society. In fact, the reactions of Christendom were similar to those of any other society. We have said that all groups demand a morality and institute one progressively. This society that formed between the eighth and eleventh centuries could not escape this sociological law. Under the severity of the Merovingian and Carolingian eras, all moralities collapsed, including Roman and Germanic. Nothing remained, and since new institutions were appearing, a new morality was also required. People living together in society cannot avoid making a morality. But since these men call themselves Christians, since the church directly coincided with society, since the center of interest of this society (provoked by the very eminent action of the church, by the intervention of the state, by the teaching of the monks) was Christianity—the morality that was instituted on very diverse and dubious sources was called Christian. Organized around this central value which was Christianity, the morality of society, this necessary and human morality, was called Christian. A synthesis was thus attempted between these two contradictory moralities, the sociological morality and the morality deriving from the impulse of the Holy Spirit. The entire moral work of the scholastics bears the imprint of this will to synthesize the two.

The third and final reason for the organization of morality (which derives from the second) is the church's will—which was indisputably affirmed, even if not constantly—to expressly (and perhaps even unilaterally) direct all of society. This will to direct, which expressed itself particularly in the areas of economics and politics, had repercussions on ethics. Ethics became a very effective means to direct men. Imposing increasingly rigorous and precise behavior and works, controlling the execution of religious and moral duties with an ever greater rigor (and the Inquisition was this too, not just a form of the fight against heresy), ethics was the means of assuring the authority of the church and maintaining uniformity in society. Society could not be integrated into the system of the church as long as men could exhibit diverse behavior or give themselves over to their moral impulses. Since it encompassed very diverse peoples, an ethic was all the more necessary to create a Christian conduct that would be the same everywhere, on top of the particularities of local habits and behavior, over the diversity (which declined over time) of the institutions of the world. By controlling acts in this way, the church could claim to control the people's hearts. But this presupposed an enormous doctrinal elaboration, and the formation of a systematic Christian ethic.⁸

This evolution of the church authority's mastery over behavior and intentions had very grave consequences. The formation of a totalitarian and authoritarian Christian ethic, an imposed ethic that provides for all individual problems in advance, did not remain an external fact, an epiphenomenon; it modified the entire life of the church and the lives of Christians. First, we must note that this morality—which was created for reasons that are ultimately sociological, and according to a process that is identical for all other moralities—was effectively a sociological morality. It is one morality among others; it ranks among the moralities of the world and can be analyzed as one of them. Of course, we will try to distinguish it by its content, highlighting that chastity, love of one's neighbor, etc., are particular to the Christian morality—which is easily countered by observing that this is simply not the case, that many others have known these values, and that this Christian morality has nothing particular about it. And this is perfectly accurate concerning the line followed by the church. It is perfectly true that the morality constituted in this way between the fourth and thirteenth centuries is a morality of society, that it must be examined like any other human morality, and that its fundamental elements do not necessarily indicate an intervention of the Holy Spirit. Now, this is always more or less the case. We must always remember that no matter our fidelity, our concern to stay linked to the will of God, to respect the freedom of the Holy Spirit—as soon as we formulate a Christian ethic, as soon as we systematize it (and we cannot do otherwise), the moment we bring it to bear (and here again, we cannot do otherwise)—we nevertheless put in place a work that depends on psychological and sociological conditions and that is consequently open to human analysis, to being treated as one morality on the same terrain as other moralities. Just as, from a certain point of view, Christianity is one religion among others, even though it is the opposite of all Religion—in the same way from a certain point of view, Christian morality is one morality

---

8. The discussions of the seventeenth century on probabilism and probabiliorism are characteristic of this attempt, representing the extreme point of the inevitable casuistry. And far from resolving the problem, Alphonse de Liguori only pushes the church deeper into this situation. Even Häring is obliged to recognize that "one has the impression that true religious morality has lost much of its lifeblood in these sterile discussions" (*La loi du Christ*, 1:78). But we must highlight that these discussions are inevitable from the moment that we seek a "Christian morality" that could be applied to all.

among other human moralities, even though Christianity is an antimorality. The most faithful of Christian ethics, as far as it might be from moralities, nevertheless is still *also* a morality. The serious issue is that the ethic elaborated by the church was *above all* a morality. On all points, it followed the formative process of all moralities, obeyed sociological laws, ceded to philosophical temptations; it could not distance itself, could not translate the exclusivity of the Revelation. It was thus a morality like the others, and we would have nothing to say about it if not for the farcical addition of the adjective "Christian." That Christians and the church might complain of a lack in this area, that they might say: we are unable to translate the demand of faith into ethical terms—this is normal, and possible. That they might resolve to follow a morality of the world in whatever manner—this may be awful, but it is understandable. But that they should develop a morality for the same reasons as the world, in the conditions of the world, and following the impulse of the world, and baptize this morality as Christian—this is an imposture. It was called thus because we could not bear the conflict, the contradiction between Morality and Faith, or between the sociological need for morality and the demand of incarnation of the faith. Appending the adjective "Christian" to the predicate "Morality" was a simple but deceptive solution, apparently resolving the tension.

Thus constituted, Christian morality completely ceased to be what Scripture shows us to be the life of the Christian man. From the fifth and sixth centuries onward, it was no longer a question of the action of God for man and with man in his history. Ethics was no longer based directly on the Bible, no longer placed in an indissoluble relation with theology; other foundations and sources were sought. And thus, beginning in the ninth century, we find two main types of works on morality: on the one hand, essays of Christian morality founded on principles; on the other hand, a moral typology of exemplary models. For the first, the movement is more philosophical; for the second, more "historical." The first begins with a kind of consideration of theology that approximates philosophy. Based on Scripture, certainly (but in departing and detaching from it), theological systems are created that obey a sort of internal logic; principles are taken from biblical texts, then the consequences of these principles are deduced and organized in a system. These principles can be explicitly biblical in appearance and can even directly translate biblical formulae. But the error consisted in transforming the Word into a fixed formula, the living and present Act of God into a principle; from this moment onward, no matter how precise the formulation, it becomes a lie and the power of death. Now, if we can conceive of a theology that respects the Word and the Act, it is almost impossible to conceive an ethic in this way. Ethics constantly comes down to

Historical Creation of Christian Moralities 219

the demand for principles; responding to ethical needs has often motivated the formulation of "Christian principles," from the Middle Ages onward. But once principles of conduct have been laid down, we can immediately observe that the conduct derived from them is completely different from the total and living movement that constitutes life in Christ according to Scripture. Whatever the case, we must observe the fact that Christian morality is instituted on and starts from principles that have been both intermediaries and screens between Scripture and the life of the Christian. Above all, these Christian moralities employing principles have responded to the intellectual need and necessity of having clear commandments.

At the same time, another type of Christian morality was created alongside this morality, responding more to the need of piety: the morality of models and exemplary men—that is, the martyrs and the saints. We find ourselves confronted with moralities of a historical character, that is, moralities that retain the biblical idea that what matters is the life of man and his history. But while Scripture shows us the action of God in this life and this history, and that it is this which concretely translates into a remarkable behavior, now, in the morality of models, this behavior belongs to man; it is this man who is remarkable, and since *he* referred himself to God, if we imitate his behavior, then we can find the will of God. This moral approach is founded on the past of Christians and claims to relate to real events; history becomes didactic. Man must be presented both with his own image and the image of the Christian in the description of the past. Just as the morality of principles took its cues from ancient philosophies, the morality of models took its cues from certain historians. It is obvious that the Greeks, or most often the Romans, exhibited this pedagogical concern in writing history—if not explicitly to instate a morality (like Chinese historians from the third century BC), then at least to furnish moral examples. This tendency is accentuated from the third century AD onward, and hagiographers are inscribed in the same line. So, with the morality of principles, we turn aside from the will of God by eliminating history; with the morality of models, we turn aside in reducing history to man—that is, in inscribing this "Christian" morality in the order of the fall and necessity. It is not enough to have rediscovered history to be in the truth!

Incidentally, while this ethic was under development, it irrepressibly tended to become autonomous. We know how the separation between ethics and dogmatics began already with Melanchthon; but it is not until the eighteenth century with the age of the Enlighteners and pietism that ethics is constituted as a separate domain, with either the natural moral conscience or the psychology of man born anew for its object of study. We must note that this autonomy is the more or less inevitable consequence of the constitution of a Christian ethic. Kant only takes what was there from the beginning and pushes it to the extreme. In effect, it was never possible to constitute a Christian ethic without the influx of some foreign element: Stoicism, Aristotelianism, rationalism, and today, quite simply Marxism (creating the famous Christian social ethic). But this had catastrophic consequences from all points of view: it reduced Christianity to this morality in the eyes of men, furnished a morality that was particularly adapted to a certain class (which meant that this "Christian" morality became the "bourgeois" morality), and solidified theological heresies. We will limit ourselves to insisting on this last point. It is obviously very difficult to know which of these elements is the origin for the others. On several occasions, Paul shows that theological errors entail false and erroneous moral behavior.[9] It can happen that in formulating Christian morality, heresy plays a determining role, as we have pointed out above. But additionally, it seems that the existence and development of an ethic influenced theologians, leading them to take objectively good behavior into account in their understanding of the Revelation. A very important first aspect of this theological influence is certainly the transformation from personal to impersonal. The relation with God is a personal relation, which supposes dialogue; it supposes that God constitutes us as persons so that we can become able both to respond to him and to do what he asks of us. But this personal relation is both frightening

9. Without discussing the problem of the relation between ethics and dogmatics, we must at least highlight the ineluctable relation between truth and ethics. We have already seen that heresy and erroneous conduct are frequently put in relation to one another in the epistles; likewise, Roux, *Les épîtres pastorales*, 44, highlights that it is impossible to teach men to live otherwise than according to the truth that is in Jesus (Eph 4). In other words, the Christian notion of truth is not only a dogmatic notion; it also grounds ethics. The one who has received the revelation of the truth is called to remain in the things they have been taught, which are normative for them, and that is why in the epistles, the different aspects of ethics are attached to different aspects of the revelation. For example, Roux indicates that the ethical exhortation of the first epistle to Timothy is envisaged according to the doctrine of the incarnation; the second epistle to Timothy presents an ethics of service founded on the lordship of the risen Christ; finally, the ethic indicated in the epistle to Titus is a baptismal catechesis founded on the doctrine of justification. Incidentally, we know very well that all throughout his dogmatics, Barth shows the ethical implications of each theological proposition that he develops. [TN: Ellul treats the relation between ethics and dogmatics in volume 2 of the present work.]

Elsewhere, Roux (*Les épîtres pastorales*, 194) highlights another relation between heresy and the choice of an ethic. He says that in the church, all discussion of ethical questions that are not posed on the proper footing—that of grace and the freedom of the new man—should be ruled out. Heresy is precisely at the origin of a moral or dogmatic choice that engenders division. Failure to recognize the ethical consequences of justification by faith in Jesus Christ can only end in an erroneous doctrine of the moral life and of sanctification.

for the individual and dangerous for church order, with its possibilities of excess and the troubles it can bring. Thus, we transform this relation into a system of predetermined relations established by the theologian, who determines the norms and signification of the Man-God relationship. And the encounter with an individual is no longer necessary; it becomes the encounter of Man in himself with this divinity. Once the will of God is codified in a moral order, from the moment that it is sufficient to carry out this order to accomplish this will, which no longer needs to be personally expressed or received, this impersonal systematization is possible. Thus, we can do without the encounter with God and the troubles that result from it. In so doing, we simplify the task of the Christian educator, since the process of conversion is no longer necessary; it is enough to insert the child in the moral order, which systematizes the relation with God so that this soul's future can become predictable. But from the point of view of our very conception of God, this entails a very serious transformation: by this move we suppress the freedom of God and claim to have intrinsic knowledge of his will. If, in effect, we formulate a good that is our own, a good that permanently expresses the will of God, this implies that God is an object whose will is not living, but fixed once and for all, immutably, eternally, and that we know this will. It thus involves an opposition between God and his will, subordinating God to the Good, in a way: once again, an objective good existing as a law binds God and prevents him from acting other than according to our decisions. *Our* decisions, for even the most faithful ethical expression is still our work, and it is according to this work that we purport to demand God to act and judge. At this moment, God can enter our system of thought, our theology, as an inert object. And he must be this inert object upon which and by which we reason, or else the whole system of ethics becomes impossible!

Incidentally, this conception of morality reciprocally contains within it the refusal to put oneself in question. Once the good has been defined, described, once we know exactly what we must do, when there is no decision, when we are no longer responsible for making decisions, but only for following what the church authorities propose, certifying themselves that this is the commandment of God—well, if we do it, how could we accept the destruction of this assurance, open ourselves to be put in question by the revelation? If man has done all that he must do, how can he recognize himself to be a sinner? How can he recognize his poverty if he can put his good works and virtues on display? But if he no longer recognizes his poverty or sinfulness, what need could he have of salvation in Jesus Christ or of grace? Such is ultimately the most serious theological question provoked by this creation of ecclesiastical morality; we are necessarily led to a theology of salvation by works, to oppose salvation by grace. Once the ethical system is constituted and applied, we cannot get out of this dilemma: either works are necessary—but in this case salvation is not tied to pure grace, but to works (whatever theological formulae of cooperation, divine presence, etc., we might adopt); or salvation is granted by grace—but in this case works accomplish nothing. Now, *for the life of Christendom*, the accomplishment of works is absolutely and rigorously necessary. This provokes a reduction of the importance of the death and resurrection of Jesus Christ. If works are indispensable for salvation, the death of Jesus Christ is rendered vain, since man can accomplish the will of God on his own (he is only "helped"), and this will is reduced to morality (while the whole Bible says that nobody is capable of doing this work . . . except for Jesus Christ), and if man is called to *accomplish* his salvation by his works, then obedience to Jesus Christ and redemption no longer mean anything. We can see thus that in reality, nothing is left of Christianity.[10]

We will not insist on these specifically theological problems. It is enough for us to have rapidly indicated how the development of Christian morality was associated to the particular development of a heresy. Could this situation have evolved differently? We cannot say. Nevertheless, it is rather important to remember that when the biblical affirmation of salvation by grace by means of faith was again put forth and proclaimed, by this very fact the entire moral system of the ancient church was attacked: this was the principle of unity of the morals of Christendom, of the direction of conscience. The form of the reformation of the church was modified. For we must not forget that there were reformations of the church before Luther. At least three times, there were huge transformations and adjustments; but the chosen path was always moral and institutional, never theological and spiritual. The importance that morality took on in the church is in effect visible by the very type of reforms undertaken in Christendom from the eleventh to the sixteenth centuries. There were considerable and even successful attempts at reformation. But this reformation was conceived as an amelioration of the moral life of Christians (and above all the clergy), and as bringing the institutions of the church to perfection. The immense effort of the Gregorian attempt at reformation is typical. This leads us once more to highlight the reversal that was due to the influence of morality: we must begin from the outside, from acts and behavior, to reach the interior and change the heart. But exterior modification presupposes growth in authority, a better organization, that is, a juridical structure and a juridical morality. In this manner, we have always attacked that which we wanted

---

10. This is what Niebuhr (*Interpretation of Christian Ethics*, 9) rightly attacks when he speaks of orthodox Christianity's identification of the transcendent will of God and a canonical moral code.

to change in the church through juridical means. And from the moment when behavior and society were the essential things, it could not have been otherwise. Private morality and social morality—these were the obsessions of the Middle Ages in a time where habits had an admittedly immoral vigor that posed singular problems to the church. It seemed that starting over from the beginning by addressing theology, counseling, and spiritual teaching, was a far too long and uncertain path to carry out the reformation of this huge body that was the church and Christendom. The other path was much quicker, more efficacious, and apparently better suited for the desired result. What was new with Luther was not the idea of reformation, but the style: the will to reform the church by starting from the center—that is, its *spiritual* life, its theology, considering that morality would follow from this. However, this is a serious question: while the Reformers reaffirmed the authentic content of the Revelation, despite appearances, they did not develop an ethic corresponding to their theology.[11]

---

11. The Protestant theology of the nineteenth century followed the orientation given by St. Thomas, in constructing a "speculative ethic" (cf. de Quervain, *Ethik*, 1:28) emancipated from Scripture and with no relation to the lordship of Jesus Christ. Incidentally, this represented the continuation of the legalist doctrine of the seventeenth century.

3

The Necessity of a Christian Ethic[1]

And yet, a Christian ethic is nevertheless indispensable.[2] And not only at the level of individual conduct, in the life of each person; the very formulation of the ethic is necessary. In effect, what happens when no morality is formulated? We have an example of this with the Reformers, who seem to me to have failed in the enterprise of formulating an ethic. They left the path wide open: precisely because no Christian morality was constructed by theologians, the faithful and their pastors referred directly to the Bible, to the law and the moral texts of the Old Testament and the parenetic texts of the Epistles, and they apply (or try to apply) all of it directly, holding to the letter of the text. Undoubtedly this was all well and good; but it led to deplorable consequences. Insofar as each of these biblical words was directly conceived as the Word of God and obeyed in itself as such, we ended

---

1. Here we will only address the fundamental and permanent necessity of a Christian ethic, and not its necessity for our times. It is true that there is an immense lacuna in our society which is indeed that of the Christian ethic. We are referring, for example, to what Bonhoeffer said in the first sections of his *Ethics*, or again to Piper ("Die Mittelbarkeit der christlichen Ethik," 125), and to Cornelis Dippel ("Christliche Existenz in der modernen wissenschaftlichen und technischen Welt," 129), among many other studies. And incidentally, this lacuna is more evident in French Protestantism than elsewhere.

2. Crespy ("Une morale pour les Chrétiens," 691) rightly highlights that the problem of a Christian morality is not only posed by the existence of other moralities, but by the very character of the Christian faith. This latter, he says, irresistibly falls into metaphysical idealism if we remove its ethical consequences. Neither Luther nor Calvin separates the law from faith. Morality must be conformed to the content of preaching; it is ultimately this logical and reasonable worship that Paul describes in Romans 12.

up with a perfectly fixed ethic, maintained in itself against all the concrete conditions of human life and of the evolution of society. It translated into an attitude of contortion to an unchangeable situation, and a refusal of all that might change it. The superhuman and impossible attempt of the Puritans was to establish a truly monastic behavior in the world; but this thus presupposed that the world no longer evolves, and that once fixed, the situation remains the same. Thus, the theological formulae concerning the truth of the Revelation in its lasting reliability were confused with the moral commandment, and the two were no longer distinguished from each other. The ethical structure once adopted became as inviolable as the theological proposition. It hardened over time, becoming more and more negative and prohibiting. Now, this happened in this way precisely because this morality was "unconscious," because there was no reflection on morality, and because it was thought that one could directly inscribe the commandment of God in life, as a law (which thus marks the highest product of a theology of grace!). The formulation of an ethic in the church is indispensable, precisely to maintain its relative character.

We must essentially highlight the very important fact that the permanent reference to grace or the Holy Spirit (as in the Lutheran *Berufsethik*),[3] that a purely transcendent theology can leave man perfectly disarmed in the milieu of the world, and lead him to a certain moral indifferentism in which everything becomes equally possible, with three potential orientations or justifications:

- the spiritual pietism that claims to place man under the direct, immediate, and permanent guidance of the Holy Spirit;
- indifferentism to the problems of the world, since what is relative is unimportant;
- excessive interest in the problems of the world, about which it is thought that Christianity has nothing to say directly, and where Christians must therefore involve themselves according to the modes of action, options, and solutions established by other men on moral or political levels, etc.

These three heresies, which tend to break the continuity between a life renewed by Christ and its manifestations in action, demonstrate the extent to which a Christian ethic is indispensable. When one of the faithful in the church or an assembly proposes an ethical conduct, whether concerning a concrete problem or deriving from the Revelation, it leads to questioning,

---

3. TN: *Berufsethik* translates as "ethics of vocation."

debate, dialogue (that is, in a certain sense, to a truly ethical situation). And on such an occasion, whatever solution is adopted, we know that it is relative, that it can be put in question, that it only seeks its justification from God, and that this conduct is not situated under the sign of our own justice, but only in the hope of a blessing. Every ethic formulated in the church conveys by this very fact its own relativity and a demand for constant renewal, for we are well aware that it results from a human undertaking; by contrast, an ethic that claims to be the unmediated application of the commandment will claim to be immutable because it is directly inspired by God. Now, an ethic always relates to concrete circumstances of life (and is therefore always changing; we will study this further on); it must respond to these circumstances, or it is not an ethic. Thus, the first eminent service provided to the church and to Christians by the clear and precise formulation of an ethic is to remind them of the relative and continually moving character of morality.[4] This task can only be carried out from the moment that the ethic is expressed as such, and it is impossible as long as the ethic is only implicit. Incidentally, we must think the corollary of what we have just pointed out. At the other end of the spectrum from the Puritan attitude and the Christian moralism that followed it in the nineteenth century, we have since witnessed a crude theological reduction: "Christianity has been reduced to a morality; now, morality is nothing, we must return to the center, to the evangelical kernel, the theological Truth. Let us stop preaching morality; we will only preach Jesus Christ, and Jesus Christ crucified." This too is all very well and good; but Christians are thus led to lose sight of the importance of incarnating the faith and putting it in practice. For good theology is not enough; it must also lead to good action, which does not happen automatically. In this way, theology can become ever more rigorous and intransigent (and incidentally, in so doing, can forge strong personalities), and yet never be inserted in any concrete situation. Thus, once again, the faithful are precisely left to themselves, and in most cases, they will conform to what is normal for those who surround them, obeying the urges of their group and milieu. In reality, despite their very conscious Christian commitment, they are defenseless. Pastors are in this situation themselves! In France since 1930, for example, along with the theological renewal and the seriousness of preaching, this fact explains the incoherence

---

4. On this subject, Hillerdal (ZEE 1, 1957, 6) is right to recall that the necessity of a Christian ethic rests on the two following observations: biblical commandments are not always very clear, and above all do not form an obvious ensemble; there are significant ambiguities. On the other hand, it is not easy to find objective criteria for applying the promises, values, and commandments of the Bible to concrete and present situations. See also Søe, §18.

and absurdity of political and economic positions adopted since 1945. In reality, by adopting this stance, we limit ourselves to following sociological currents, totally powerless to critique, supersede, or to free ourselves from them. We must not think that a faithful theology is sufficient to make the hearer ready for life in the world. That is where ethics enters as a sort of preparation. It does not have the right to furnish solutions in the face of each problem, or to impose them with authority. It can only be a reminder that the specific conduct of the Christian is the indispensable consequence of the faith. It must be an instrument of reflection put at the disposition of the faithful, and at the same time offer them clarification about themselves and about their concrete problems. Finally, ethics will recall that the seriousness of theological engagement must be inscribed in the seriousness of an engagement in the world, and for the particular time that it addresses, it will lay down the conditions and limits of this engagement. But it cannot go beyond this. This preparatory work is modest, but indispensable.

On this subject, Karl Barth has offered this striking formula: the task of ethics cannot be to decide on the content of the commandment of God, nor to judge the action of man, but to circumscribe the limits of the commandment of God and of the corresponding action of man.[5] We are effectively confronted with one of the major functions of this ethic, which can neither formulate the imperative addressed to a man, nor crystallize the will of God for eternity; but in showing the continuity of the Revelation, it can remind man *where* the commandment given *hic et nunc* intervenes. And this presupposes that we place ourselves in the practical and historical situation of the faithful and of the church. Of course, the devotees of the absolute will say that we must not take these weaknesses into account, that we must have confidence in the power of the Holy Spirit. But this is not a lack of faith; it is only to point out that we are not in the kingdom of God, that the church is *also* a human society, submitted by this very fact to sociological laws, and that the Christian is inserted in history, and that in this history he must not only preach the gospel by his words, but must testify to his faith by his life. If we hold on to these two facts, we can derive the following consequences: the church is a human society. Therefore, according to what we have recognized above, this society, even if it does not want to, will provoke, produce, or secrete a morality. The church cannot avoid regulating relations among its members with an ethic—not because it is Christian, but because it is a society. And the faithful will provoke ethical situations among themselves (the novels on the church have shown this a hundred times over!), will guide themselves in ethical subjects—sometimes in ways that are not

---

5. Barth, *CD* III.4, 30.

very Christian. Now, it is always much more dangerous for the church to follow an unknown and spontaneous morality. This is what we pointed out earlier. Because it is a society, it needs a morality. Because it is a Christian society, it needs not a Christian morality (we have seen the impossibility of this term), but a conscious morality—one that knows itself to be relative, humble, under condemnation, at the service of the faithful and not imposing itself on them; these four characteristics of this morality are the mark that ultimately testifies to its Christian authenticity. What will be astonishing here, therefore, is that the major preoccupation of all traditional ethics (defining the good) is excluded. Ethics for Christians cannot begin with the search for the good, "for the question of good and evil has been decided and settled once and for all in the decree of God, by the cross and resurrection of Jesus Christ. Now that this decision has been made, theological ethics cannot go back on it. It can only *accept* it as a decision that has been made . . ."[6] We have equally said that the believer is inserted in history, and that it is in thinking of him as one inserted in history that we should formulate an ethic. But this means that this ethic will continually evolve. Morality must express our way of being present to the world. It thus must be modified when the world changes. To take the Christian morality of the thirteenth century and claim that Christians must live according to its precepts today is an absurdity. Morality can only be made in the current situation.

Bonhoeffer and Barth insist on the fact that it is precisely in this situation of being a Christian inserted in history that ethics becomes both necessary and possible. It is in this sense, for example, that Bonhoeffer shows that ethics is not a declaration of pious desires, but a "Mit-leben," linked to specific persons and to the unfolding of their lives.[7] And Barth shows that ethics consists in following the history of the relation of God and man in redemption.[8]

But this also implies that ethics necessarily includes a relation with the facts of the world. Niebuhr is right to criticize the classical orthodox ethic, which, because it is exclusively biblical, never encounters present reality anywhere. But where and how can this relation happen, without thereby altering the truth, or without the revelation becoming an immanent possibility of a historical process? The accommodation to secular culture in France is particularly noticeable, and this leads us to abandon the truth. It seems impossible to avoid either one or the other error in this research, and Niebuhr's attempt is not convincing! In reality, this work is only possible

---

6. Barth, *CD* II.2, 536 [Ellul's italics].
7. Bonhoeffer, *Ethics*, 370. TN: "Mit-leben" means "to live with."
8. Barth, *CD* III.4, 26.

to the extent that the ethic is conscious, known, voluntary and expressed; and to the extent that it relates to a society that we know in its concrete reality, in relation to which we situate ourselves, and not a society where we merely live our day-to-day lives without control or self-determination. In other words, an ethic must be formulated for the faithful so that they can be present to this world in which they live, and not to a world in the past or an unreal world. To formulate it, we must already have a true and concrete knowledge of this world, a diagnosis of its situation. And this cannot be performed outside of ethical research. It is in these conditions that ethics is one of the constitutive elements of the response that man is called to give to God. God speaks to man, in his holiness, in his absolute character, God reveals himself as the God who saves and the God who commands, and he makes man capable of speaking, of responding. He makes him responsible. The dialogue initiated by God must be pursued. But just as the Word of God is action, man likewise cannot be content to respond to the Eternal one by words that are only words. His word is that of a responsible man. It is commitment. It supposes the giving of one's life in this response. Faith is the response, but faith immediately implies a living attitude that transforms all behavior. Häring very precisely says, "Man's response must be expressed in his particular situation in creation."[9] Thus ethics appears as an indispensable consequence of our situation as those challenged by God. We cannot avoid our condition of responsibility; we can only assume it as we advance in our moral quest.

In any case, when a man wants to live according to the Word of God, or incarnate his faith, it is a matter of lived conduct, of the accomplishment of certain works. Whether we like it or not, when we talk about ways of living, decisions concerning this life, of acts to be accomplished or projects to be implemented, we are talking about ethics. This latter can be either as rigid (as in the commandment) or as supple and indeterminate as we like (as in self-affirmation, recognition of the other); it is morality all the same.

Of course, we will see that the Christian life is not morality. But the Christian life must be described, and in this sense it is an object of morality. But can't we simply live this Christian life? It is true that the spontaneity of faith is essential. Nevertheless we must be attentive, once again, to the concrete situation of the Christian. Experience shows that on the one hand, faith is not spontaneously expressed in works in all circumstances; the

---

9. Häring, *La loi du Christ*, 1:41.

parenetic texts of Paul's epistles and the letter of James are very explicit on this subject. It must be invited, incited. It is not a question of proposing ready-made works in which faith automatically incarnates. This laying out of works to accomplish is strictly the work of the Lord, who has prepared works in advance . . . But the role of ethics here is to present itself as a call, a demand, a goad. It has a possibility, a chance of being heard because it addresses itself to faith. And this resolves a constant problem in morality: how can a morality have authority? How can a morality be heard by the one to whom it is addressed? There are multiple responses in the world to these questions—the weight of society, reason, the authority of the witness, etc. But in the case of the Christian life, the response is simple. This morality has authority insofar as it comes from faith and refers to the Revelation of God. But this authority only exists for the one who recognizes that in effect it is a testimony of the faith of the other, and that in truth it refers to the revelation—that is, for the one who lives in this faith himself.

In these conditions, Christian morality can only be indicative and not imperative, hortatory and not dogmatic. It will consist in applying the demands and promises of faith in Jesus Christ concerning behavior, the new man's manner of acting and living, to the particular and concrete situations of Christians. In effect, this new man must learn to always live simultaneously in the freedom of faith and in the human condition where he finds himself.[10] This morality has a possibility of being heard and taken seriously because it addresses this man's faith; it will be true precisely insofar as it calls this faith to become reality. It will cease to be a vain word because it will have responded to the expectation of this faith, which was lacking a dialogue in the church, and a clarification, an impetus to engage in action. Consequently, the proclamation of the demand of this ethic can be heard and accomplished, for it will have been taken seriously by a man because of his faith; and because the Holy Spirit, responding to this faith, will have granted him sufficient strength to live it.

But even beyond the incitation that it must be, the ethic must also compensate for the lack of initiative and invention among Christians. We were saying that the Christian life must be a continual renewal, a creation of superabundant newness expressing the richness of the Holy Spirit. Now, here again experience teaches us that the most serious Christians lack imagination; they do not know how to personally and spontaneously manifest their faith in a renewed fashion. They fall very easily into their ruts, their habits. Their fathers' Christian ways of living are sufficient for them. The works and the association that were the fruit of faith a generation ago will

---

10. Roux, *Les épîtres pastorales*, 80.

be piously upheld. The political attitude adopted twenty-five years ago as a living expression of a Christian decision will be steadfastly extended and reaffirmed. The path that we opened at the moment of our conversion or in our adolescence still seems right, all mapped out, and we are content to follow it. Now, all this reflects neither the renewed freshness of the inspiration of the Holy Spirit nor the changed circumstances—both of which would require our faith to discover an absolutely new response. The ethic certainly cannot take the place of individual decisions; it cannot put itself in the place of the Christian, nor be a screen between the Christian and God, but it can offer basic elements to counter the lack of invention. It can propose "models," not in the sense of examples to imitate, but in the economic sense of the word: models that will be examples of possible forms of expression of the faith (and not ready-made solutions), from which we can reason and effectively invent something else. Here, then, the ethic will be a boon to the weakness of our faith. In these conditions, ethics seems to us to bear a critical function of decisive importance; in effect, it must continually bring us to ask ourselves if we have really been emancipated from the reign of the law. We do not have the right to consider that we are automatically freed from the demands of the law on the pretext that we believe in Jesus Christ. Now, we quite readily accept all the developments of Paul and the gospels, which affirm that once we are in faith we are no longer under the law; this is certain, but what certitude do we have that we are effectively in faith? This cannot result from a purely subjective conviction, nor from intellectual knowledge. One of the critical elements resides precisely in our confrontation with the ethical demand. In effect, the ethical demand is posed before us to continually teach us that the life in faith is not incarnated on the near side of the law, but on the far side. The example that Jesus Christ gives us in the Sermon on the Mount—"you have heard it said; but I say to you . . ."—is not an example of absolutization or spiritualization of the law; it is an example of the passage from a life under the law to the life in faith. Now, it is never a question here of doing less than the law required, but of going infinitely further. Ethics cannot describe the entirety of this "further" for us, which in effect is left to the spontaneity of life; but ethics must continually recall the lower limit short of which we are effectively under the law, which means that the problem of faith is constantly posed by the critical operation of ethics. Faith does not liberate us from the law to allow us not to accomplish it: a very simple example of this is the tithe. The tithe was one of the demands of the law; life in faith frees us from this demand, but not so that we can avoid paying the tithe—on the contrary! It places us before the problem of the complete consecration of all our goods to God, which must effectively translate into giving much more than the tithe. Ethics, in reminding us of the simple requirement of the law (and of course, ethics is never simply reducible to the law), must bring us to ask ourselves if we are living in faith when our verbal declarations that our goods belong to God actually translate into minimal giving, much less than the law required. This critique enacted by ethics on our Christian life obliges us to ask ourselves if perhaps we are not still living under the law, and if in our own lives we still need to walk the entire path that the law showed to the Hebrews, as a pedagogue. But this critique, this call to incessant invention, does not suppress all continuity or permanence—on the contrary.

Crespy rightly highlights that the Christian ethic is simultaneously invention and custom. This importance of ethics as continuity is not contrary to what we have just said on the importance of invention in the Christian life. If this life were nothing but an invention, if there were no habits, no customs, it would be a disorder—the same disorder that reappears in all spiritualist and illuminist movements. Now we have seen that there really is a continuity in the work and will of God. But reciprocally, morality cannot be only a custom; it must be constantly invigorated, transformed and renewed by the invention coming from the Holy Spirit. This permanence, this continuity, this custom that ethics must guarantee leads us to meditate on another meaning of ethics: it is a support for faith. It is too easy to say that the Christian must live according to the present commandment of God. This is true. But we must not neglect the fact of the silence of God, which is well known in the spiritual life. And if we mention this topic, it is not just in the name of the spiritual experience of man (which is not negligible), but it is also because Scripture itself speaks of this silence. How many times do we see the prophets lamenting that God is far from them, and how many times do we find this declaration in the Old Testament: "The word of the Lord was rare in those days." And Jesus himself knew this silence on the cross. Thus it is too simple to say, "It is sufficient to live according to the commandment that God addresses *hic et nunc*." And when God does not address this commandment? When God is silent? When we go through this dryness, this aridity, where nothing has meaning anymore and where God seems infinitely distant? When we are only aware of this unilateral face of the truth that God is in heaven and I am on earth? For all that, do we stop being "Christians"? Do we stop living as Christians? Do we stop living altogether? Certainly, however, we must try to live even in such conditions. Well then? Well, we need the support of our neighbor and the church. We still need our neighbor to attest to this very grace of God; we still need the church to attest to this very truth of God. And this will happen through counseling and by the Confession of Faith. And this too will be an intervention of God. But what about our lived conduct? What about the decisions that we must make—which, even in these circumstances, must still be decisions of faith? Indeed!—the ethic presented by the church, the morality lived together by Christians will undoubtedly be a help, an example, an open path that can simply be followed during this period of absence and interrogation. Ethics will thus fulfill a sort of substitutionary function, but without going beyond this role: that is, it will never claim to impose itself when the faithful has been seized by the immediate truth of the Word; it will never enter into competition with the living Word.

At this moment, ethics is part of the great movement of memory described in the Bible. When he finds himself in the silence of God, man remembers. Among many relevant texts, let us take those from the Lamentations of Jeremiah (3:21, 24). God no longer speaks to his prophet, so this latter says, "I want to remember," for the acts of God in the past are not effaced, the history of the acts of God is the truth; just because God spoke yesterday, his word is no less true today. Just because I no longer feel God, that does not mean that God has changed; just because God is not acting, his love has not wavered. Jeremiah wants to remember, and he does! He affirms that the Lord continues to be good, despite all his current experiences, because of this word of God that he heard in the past; moreover, Jeremiah's affirmation "I will hope" is not only oriented toward the past, but also toward the future; he hopes against all hope, he wagers that God is constant and that he does not change, and based on this decision, on this "I will," everything becomes good for Jeremiah, even the very silence of God, the yoke, humiliation, solitude—all this now appears as situated inside the love of God. This example can help us understand part of the role of the Christian ethic, which will help man to sustain himself even when it seems to him that God no longer speaks, because in spite of everything, this ethic contains an echo of the truth spoken by the Lord to his church in the past.

It seems to us that at the junction of these preceding indications, we can discover yet another authentic role for morality: it is there to remind us that the Christian must act without waiting for the clear and express orders of the Holy Spirit. In Acts, we see that Peter and Paul make their decisions, establish their plans of action, and engage in travel or "evangelization campaigns," all without the Holy Spirit clearly dictating what they must do. On the contrary, Paul highlights that once they had decided to go to Asia, the Holy Spirit prevented them and led them to Macedonia (Acts 16:1–10). The attitude that consists in saying that we can *only* act on the prompting of the Holy Spirit (and this means a clear and conscious impulsion, of which we have explicit knowledge) is a dangerous attitude, for it can easily lead to doing nothing under the pretext that the Holy Spirit is not speaking. And it can also lead us to accomplish our own desires, since the word of the Holy

Spirit addresses us in a manner so secret that it cannot be submitted to any control by the brothers of the church: but how, then, are we able to discern that it is truly the Holy Spirit and not our subconscious? Saint Paul commends us to submit the exercise of the gifts of the Holy Spirit to the control and service of the church community. Morality is precisely a means of this control. At the same time, it is a call to the necessity of action, of the possibility of putting it in practice, and of the legitimacy of this incarnation even when we are not consciously obeying the order of the Holy Spirit; for we are often reminded that this latter works in us secretly, without our knowing it. And certainly, we cannot live this morality—that is, make it exist—except insofar as the Holy Spirit makes it both necessary and possible for us. If we accomplish what seems today to be the truest application of the command of God, we can be assured that this happens by the power and light of the Holy Spirit, even if we do not explicitly know that he is present and directs our acts.

This ethic, then, can never go beyond the simple reminder that "man's action should *become and be always* that of those who *accept* God's action as right." But this conformity can never imply equality; that is, our action—which ethics must call for or incite—can only ever attest to or confirm the action of God, but never *continue* or *reproduce* it.[11]

This is particularly important at a time when we are witnessing a multiplication of ethical positions claiming to reproduce the act of God in the Reformed Church of France. "These demands obviously do not mean that man is invited to usurp the prerogative of God and to meddle in His affairs . . . Neither for himself nor for others can he or will he do what Jesus Christ did."[12] Ethics is thus the place of critique: far from being the science of the will of God, at each instant it is the interrogation, the putting in question of all that we have already tried to accomplish as Christians, of all that we have already done in response to God.[13] Thus there cannot be a response given in advance. Ethics must contain this prohibition of an *a priori* response—and allow complete freedom for our response today to differ from our response yesterday (which does not mean that yesterday's response was bad). This is what Karl Barth calls the law of repetition and renewal in ethics, which corresponds to the constancy and perseverance of God. But this manifests just how impossible it is to develop a constructed Christian ethic.

We have been saying that insofar as the Christian life is expressed in decisions, it cannot be schematized or codified, and therefore ethics

---

11. Barth, *CD* II.2, 575.
12. Barth, *CD* II.2, 578.
13. Barth, *CD* II.2, 645.

is impossible. But we must consider the other aspect of this same phenomenon: these decisions are ultimately the work of God. They are not incoherent. The commandment of God is not a series of isolated, absurd revelations, for the one who commands is the eternal God, who is one. Each prescription is linked to the other prescriptions because they are all part of the divine order, and they cannot be isolated: each prescription is linked to the others by a hidden relation that is the plan of God. And in the same manner, though human action might be enacted in isolated decisions, nevertheless it is not divided or dissolved. The decisions made by man are inserted in the continuity of the work of God. This permanence makes ethics possible. But furthermore, it makes it necessary, for from this point of view the role of ethics will be double. First, it will point out the path of the ethical event, it will prepare us for this event; now, this work is indispensable for man.[14] Next, if the Holy Spirit guides us by precise orders, if he does not give us any intrinsic knowledge to which it would be enough to refer, a trace of this knowledge "after the Holy Spirit has passed" still persists in us. There is an experience that is not effaced or negligible. There is a memory of this guidance of the Holy Spirit. This memory, as Søe says exactly,[15] has a positive value (when he speaks to us again, the Holy Spirit does not find a *tabula rasa*) and a negative value (this "knowledge" can engender pride and laziness). But this knowledge must be rightly developed, recognized for what it is, formulated in the continuity of the plan of God and held as true until the moment where God has us penetrate further into the knowledge of his will. If we do not apply ourselves to this effort of discernment and development, we thus signify that we do not take the continuity of the plan of God seriously.

The Christian ethic also fulfills the function of restoring importance back to the relativity of the world. It is a temptation for all Christians to minimize or evacuate this relativity, considering that the revealed absolute is all that ultimately matters. Kierkegaard, who perfectly demonstrated how the absolute commandment of God produces an alienation of the world in relation to us, at one time even came to think that this human reality is of little importance. New birth changes us, and this is true even if it is not expressed outwardly. The world thus becomes a child's game, lacking all seriousness. Kierkegaard later recognizes that this is not totally correct

---

14. Barth, *CD* III.4, 15ff.
15. Søe, *Christliche Ethik*, §17.

(after 1846), and that the revelation leads us to a new relation with the world, to another love that cannot be passive, and consequently that must be incarnated in ethical forms, without which the entire incarnation is brought into question. As Niebuhr says, the revelation demands an impossible absolute from us, which leads us to neglect human means, leaving the "construction of the routes to reach the summits" to those who have not realized the total dimension of what must be done. Ethics is precisely there to take the demand of the absolute that the Christian experiences within himself and bring it down to the proportions of concrete problems, to oblige him to take the relativity of human situations seriously. For "the concrete responsibility in which the revelation places us forbids us from being disinterested towards the World."[16]

Finally, ethics fulfills a decisive, inevitable role in recalling the necessary character of the incarnation and of action in the Christian revelation. If we carefully analyze the well-known parable of the houses built on the rock and on the sand, we perceive that the essential difference concerns "putting into practice." Practice, action, is decisive. The admirable developments of Bonhoeffer[17] show the extent to which action in the legalist sense is different from action in the sense of Christian ethics. In the "pharisaical" sense, it expresses "disunion," discord within one's being, the opposition of living to acting, the ever-refined distinction between a good and an evil, the "either . . . or . . ." and finally, Judgment. For Jesus (and for the one who is in Christ), there is precisely no disunion, but a perfect unity of the being, a simplicity of the World and of man reintegrated in God. Thus there is no choice between a good and an evil: choice is only exercised in the knowledge of good and evil which *is* sin itself. (And we see here that a Christian absolutely cannot accept the formula according to which the situation of choice is the only ethical situation.) Neither is there any "judgment" (Bonhoeffer perfectly explains how judgment is sin because it presupposes this knowledge of good and evil). There is only *action*, an action that proceeds from the very roots of the being, that accords with the unity of the being. "Jesus acts; he does not judge." The knowledge of Jesus always ends in action. Christian action is a "pure" action, uncalculated, undeliberated, and not directed to a given end. It happens without "knowledge" (let your left hand not know . . .). It is the fruit of dovelike innocence, and *at the same time* it is prudence. Ethics is there to constantly recall that a Christian life is the response to the permanent contradiction of innocence and prudence, of engagement and knowledge.

16. Bonhoeffer, *Ethics*, 261.
17. Bonhoeffer, *Ethics*, 307–8, 326.

The Necessity of a Christian Ethic

Incidentally, in the presence of this necessity, this urgency for an ethic for Christians, we are led to better understand that which was an impossibility.

Such an ethic can (and should) make the conflict between the will of God and what the world calls morality stand out clearly. There thus can be a conflict of duties, if man finds himself so imbued with human morality that he cannot help considering it as ultimate. But there is no conflict if it is put in its proper place. On the other hand, the role of ethics for Christians cannot be to claim to resolve apparent conflicts in "Christian duties"; we would fall right back into casuistry. And incidentally, there can be no *true* conflict for the Christian. For there is no contradiction in the will of God. This will is one and perfect. But it is neither obvious nor systematic. Seeking it requires an effort beginning with new birth. One must become aware of diverse possibilities, but this does not create a conflict of conscience. For whatever choices we might make, we must give ourselves to the grace and love of Jesus Christ. In any case, there is no right solution that would allow us to avoid this abandon to grace. And precisely this confident abandon removes any tragic weight from the choices that we can make among the possibilities opened up for us by the will of God.[18] If the choice we have made leads to unfortunate consequences, it is ultimately God who assumes them (which, obviously, does not mean that we can do whatever we want). In any case, it is a question of serious, honest seeking of the will of God, in prayer and in studying the Scriptures.

We have insisted on the freedom of the Holy Spirit and on the freedom of the God who reveals himself, of the Will and the Word of the Lord. This is completely true. But we absolutely cannot interpret the word "freedom" in the sense of incoherence, of arbitrariness or absurdity.[19] Without a doubt, God can will and decide whatever he wants. He can change his action at his discretion. But he does not do so. Precisely, the very revelation that he grants us manifests a remarkable continuity in his decisions. It is thus that we can very exactly speak of a plan of the action of God. He has drawn up this plan himself, and he holds to it, exactly as he holds to his promises once he has made them. In the action of God, there are no decisions that are contradictory and successive without relation to one another. On the

---

18. Bonhoeffer, *Ethics*, 269, 323.

19. "When God wills something from and for man, when man's will is claimed by God, there can be no question of an arbitrary and purposeless control which God can exercise just because He is God and therefore superior to man. On the contrary, what God wills from and for man stands or falls with, and is revealed only in, what the same God will do and has already done for us and in us." Barth, *CD* II.2, 562.

On ethics as an expression of man's belonging to God, see de Quervain, *Ethik*, 1:9.

contrary, they fit together with one another remarkably well, and if they seem surprising to us at a given moment, it is only because we do not understand them. There are no contradictions in successive periods of the Revelation. God is himself today, yesterday, and eternally. At no moment does he deceive us concerning himself. What he revealed yesterday is still completely valid. Consequently, we can count on a constancy, a continuity on God's side of things. We are in no way delivered to a despot who plays tricks on us. From the moment that the center of God's Revelation about himself is Love, we know that this is impossible. This implies that he is not making fun of us, that he is not deceiving us, that he guides us in a way that is right and reasonable for him and for us, and not arbitrary or capricious. And consequently, when we refer to his revealed Word, the objective witness of the living revelation that occurred once contained in the Bible, there is no contradiction—when we try to understand the will of God in this time on the basis of Scripture, we are not performing a work that infringes on the freedom of God, since he has submitted his will to the limitation of this objectified word so that we could understand him.[20] It is thus legitimate (and we are even commanded) to take advantage of this past revelation, and to look in it for an ethical teaching today.[21] And because of this, we must be persuaded that there is no contradiction between the objective revelation and the revelation *hic et nunc*, between Scripture and the Holy Spirit, between the permanent will of God and his will *hic et nunc* for every one of us. The Holy Spirit clarifies and makes present, current, that which he formerly taught to the prophets and apostles. He has no "other thing" to add or to say to us. Consequently, all alleged revelation in the present must be submitted to the control of the revealed Word in the Bible, and inversely all interpretation of this latter must be submitted to the *hic et nunc* revelation of the Holy Spirit; otherwise, contradictions could arise. Thus, within this limit, we can certainly enunciate an ethic on the basis of the Word of God. This latter is an eternal word, given in the Bible, objective,

---

20. Bonhoeffer is undoubtedly right when he says that the authority and the possibility of ethical discourse derive from the fact that God himself has formulated his will in the form of a commandment. But it does not seem clear if this concerns Christian ethics exclusively, or if it is true for all ethical research, as the first paragraph seems to indicate. Bonhoeffer, *Ethics*, 366–89.

21. "So then, in face of our situation, we have to ask what is appropriate to us because it is pleasing to the Lord who is the Judge of goodness, righteousness and truth ... This enquiry cannot be replaced by even the most penetrating systematic or intuitive analysis of the situation as such." Barth, *CD* II.2, 639–40. This reminds us that ethics cannot be predetermined, and on the other hand that to think this ethic, we must *begin* from the command of God, and not from the concrete facts of situations where we find ourselves.

constant, and immutable, but it does not have direct ethical significance; it must be translated for the present conduct of the believer's life. But this eternal word is only the Word of God for man when it becomes present by the Holy Spirit. And the difficulty will be precisely that, as a living word, it cannot be integrated into an ethical system; but as a word given to our knowledge by God, it must give birth to an ethical demand. Thus, we have seen that this translation that we are bound to effectuate is limited in its validity and its applicability. But because the word of God must necessarily be made present, we must understand that this must happen not only in relation to its theological or spiritual content, but its ethical content as well. The problem is the same. But too often in these last fifty years or so we have forgotten this last element. Now, the Gospel of Grace is simultaneously the Gospel of the Demand of God, yes, the Gospel of his Jealousy.[22]

When we were saying above that the will of God can only be known and become fruitful *hic et nunc* (and consequently can neither be integrated in, nor give birth to a morality), at this point we must discuss an additional quality of morality that we have recognized for believers: it too is directly linked to present facts.[23] The opposition between the two terms Will of God and Ethics is completely legitimate if we claim, along with many moralists and Christians, that there is *One* permanent, eternal, natural morality—*one* definition of the Good in itself. But having recognized that ethics is essentially dynamic, at this convergence between the Word of the Lord and the fluidity of circumstances, social, political, and economic relations, having recognized that it can only be valuable for a certain (and perhaps very brief) time when things are stabilized, but that it must be modified according to events—we thus discern the possibility (not the necessity, and not the constant renewal, but only the possibility) of an encounter between the Word of God *hic et nunc* and the *hic et nunc* of a valid and true ethic for man. For the present of the Word of God, which all too often is interpreted only for

22. There can be no distinction in the Bible between what is law and what is gospel: everything is law, as Quervain says very exactly (225) (but everything is also gospel—cf. Karl Barth), so much so that ethics must be founded on the totality of Scripture, and not on this or that text that may seem more "moral"!

23. Hillerdal rightly assigns ethics a triple task (*ZEE* 1, 1957, 6): the description of the *ethos* of the New Testament; the method of interpretation of biblical ethics for present preaching; and the analysis of the present time where man who must live this faith is situated. In effect, the encounter of these three elements gives ethics its *truth* and its *reality*.

Niebuhr (*Interpretation of Christian Ethics*, 9) is perfectly correct to point out that the entire value of an ethic is linked to the quality of the tension that it establishes between the Transcendent and the historical. And he shows precisely (19) that this cannot result from anything but a transcendence, and that once the end is reintegrated into history, religious utopias and naturalisms end in moral laxity.

the soul of the believer who receives this particular revelation, is valid for the church too, and by this fact contains an element of duration, an inscription in the course of History, and is not only a flash of lightning in the dark night of a single heart. But, in conclusion, if all of this is correct, a series of prohibitions arise for Christian morality. It can no longer be a claim to objectively define the good in any way. It can no longer claim to possess or know this good at all.

Conceiving of the existence of this ethic is already an affirmation that "we do not know any free investigation of good and evil."[24] It can never be formulated as a way of being right with God, or of protecting us from him: "[Theological ethics] cannot cease to attest and interpret the reality of God, and therefore His Word . . . It cannot change either its direction or its theme . . . It cannot stealthily become an indicative or imperative representation of the Christian; an empirical or ideal depiction of Christian existence. It cannot turn its back on the Word of God in order, for a change, to see what has become of the man who hears the Word of God, or what will perhaps become of him."[25]

It never becomes imperative, for all that we have just said on the indispensable character of morality neither suppresses nor does away with the impossibility of this morality. We have not described two states that succeed each other, where the second would eliminate the first; the two continually confront each other, and neither can be done away with. If we accept these as two defining elements of our situation, right away we are obliged to observe that we cannot establish this ethic on the bases of orders of creation or of the kingdom of God. It belongs to this world (and to this Eon), between the fall and the return of Jesus Christ. Therefore it will not be founded on an alleged knowledge of God's will for Adam, as if there were no fall, nor on the reestablishment of all things in Christ, as if this had already taken place in its fullness. On the other hand, we have said that it can never be a question of a Christian ethic; all we can try is to describe an ethic for Christians, which will remain within all the limits indicated by its role as a servant, under the cross and in the hope of forgiveness.

What we have said of the impossibility of formulating a Christian ethic, and notwithstanding, of the necessity of constructing one, comes together at the level of the applicability and inapplicability of this ethic. Assuredly, as

---

24. Barth, *CD* II.2, 535.

25. On ethics as descriptive and not normative, see Piper, "Die Mittelbarkeit der christlichen Ethik," 125. Barth, *CD* II.2, 537.

Niebuhr notes, Christianity frightfully complicates the situation of the man who tries to respond to ethical problems by placing him in an ultimate situation. Certainly, the commandment of Jesus is inapplicable. His ethic has nothing to do with the immediate moral problems bearing on the relativity of the arrangements that must be arrived at in economics or politics, or the scales of power that must be balanced. Assuredly, the commandment of complete love is concretely unlivable, the kingdom of God cannot be lived as present in our midst, etc. But there can be no question of making a morality to render the truth applicable. That is not its role. It is not tasked with finding a middle way, nor establishing distinctions and compromises such that the "extraordinary" things required by Jesus become ordinary. Yet such is the temptation of almost all those who have developed an ethic, and even of Niebuhr when he makes love into a principle, and when he says that the commandment to love remains an impossibility *as well as* a possibility. All attempts to reduce this demand to the stature of man by way of principles and values reflect the quintessential betrayal of morality. And yet, it does not remain a pure impossibility; it is still included in Mary's "Fiat," and by this fact becomes a human reality—and not only in the unique and perfect accomplishment of the Son, who does not remain solitary in this accomplishment. Niebuhr's formula characterizing the ethical situation of the Christian as one of "impossible possibility"[26] is good, and present studies on finitude and the command are constructed along the same lines. This ethic is not ultimately applicable *or* inapplicable. It is both at the same time, since if it is considered by the measure of man alone, it is pointless, without foundation or signification; considered as life in Christ, the "either/or" is no longer even imaginable, since its applicability does not belong to us.

To conclude, we could say that even if all the analysis of the urgency for ethical development, if all the reasons advanced above count for nothing, we nevertheless cannot escape the necessity of risking the adventure of this ethic, for we cannot escape the necessity of responding to these questions: what does it mean to be liberated from the tyranny of things by Jesus Christ, and thus to recover the possibility of making use of them without being enslaved to them? What does it mean to be engaged by Jesus Christ in a true encounter with others, and thus to recover the possibility of serving them by loving them? What does it mean to be enlightened by Jesus Christ as to

---

26. Niebuhr, *Interpretation of Christian Ethics*, 202.

the destiny of the World, and thus to recover the possibility of serving God by loving him with all our heart, soul, and mind?[27]

---

27. Cf. Leenhardt, "Existe-t-il un 'système' chrétien?"

Bibliography

Ansart, Pierre. "Les cadres sociaux de la doctrine morale de Saint-Simon." *Cahiers internationaux de sociologie* 34 (1963) 27–46.
Arendt, Hannah. *Eichmann in Jerusalem: A Report on the Banality of Evil*. New York: Penguin, 2006.
Barth, Karl. *Church Dogmatics*. Edited by G. W. Bromiley and T. F. Torrance. Translated by G. T. Thomson et al. Edinburgh: T&T Clark, 1936–77.
Baruk, Henri. *Psychiatrie morale expérimentale, individuelle et sociale*. Paris: Presses universitaires de France, 1950.
Bastide, Georges. *Traité de l'action morale*. 2 vols. Paris: Presses universitaires de France, 1961.
Beauvoir, Simone de. *Pour une morale de l'ambiguïté*. Paris: Gallimard, 1947.
Berdyaev, Nicholas. *Christianisme et réalité sociale*. Paris: Editions "Je sers," 1934.
Bergson, Henri. *The Two Sources of Morality and Religion*. Translated by R. Ashley Audra and Cloudesley Brereton. Notre Dame: Notre Dame University Press, 1977.
Blanchard, Pierre. *Sainteté aujourd'hui*. Paris: Desclée de Brouwer, 1954.
Bois, Jacques. "La crise de la Morale et le Christianisme." In Jacques Bois, Jean Boisset, and Roger Mehl, *Le problème de la morale chrétienne*. Paris: Presses universitaires de France, 1948.
Bonhoeffer, Dietrich. *Ethics*. Edited by Clifford J. Green. Translated by Reinhard Krauss, Charles C. West, and Douglas W. Stott. Dietrich Bonhoeffer Works 6. Minneapolis: Fortress, 2005.
———. "A Theological Position Paper on the *Primus Usus Legis*." In *Conspiracy and Imprisonment: 1940–1945*, edited by Mark S. Brocker, 584–600. Translated by Lisa E. Dahill and Douglas W. Stott. Dietrich Bonhoeffer Works 16. Minneapolis: Fortress, 2006.
Cazaneuve, Jean. "Les cadres sociaux de la doctrine morale stoïcienne dans l'Empire romain." *Cahiers internationaux de sociologie* 34 (1963) 13–26.
Chambre, Henri. *Le marxisme en Union soviétique*. Paris: Seuil, 1955.
Chamson, André. *Le crime des justes*. Paris: Grasset, 1928.
Chesterton, G. K. *Orthodoxy*. 1908. Reprint, London: Global Grey, 2018.
Clendenin, Daniel. *Theological Method in Jacques Ellul*. Lanham, MD: University Press of America, 1987.
Crespy, Georges. *Le problème d'une anthropologie théologique*. Montpellier: Publications de la Faculté de théologie protestante, 1950.

———. "Une morale pour les Chrétiens." *Christianisme social* 65.9–10 (October 1957) 688–99.

———. "Une morale pour les Chrétiens II." *Christianisme social* 65.11–12 (November-December 1957) 827–40.

Cruvellier, Jean. *La Sanctification par la foi et le mouvement de Keswick*. Dieulefit: Editions Le Matin vient, 1930.

de Graaf, Johannes. "Marxismus und Moral in der sowjetrussischen Literatur." *Zeitschrift für Evangelische Ethik* 5 (1957) 219–27.

Delimars, E. *L'éthique marxiste et son enseignement en U.R.S.S.* Paris: Centre de recherche du bien politique, 1960.

Dippel, Cornelis Johannes. "Christliche Existenz in der modernen wissenschaftlichen und technischen Welt." *Zeitschrift für Evangelische Ethik* 2 (1958) 129–54.

Durkheim, Émile. *Moral Education*. Translated by Everett K. Wilson and Herman Schnurer. 1973. Reprint, Mineola, NY: Dover, 2002.

Ellul, Jacques. *Autopsy of Revolution*. Translated by Patricia Wolf. 1971. Reprint, Eugene, OR: Wipf & Stock, 2012.

———. *A Critique of the New Commonplaces*. Translated by Helen Weaver. 1968. Reprint, Eugene, OR: Wipf & Stock, 2012.

———. *Le défi et le nouveau: Œuvres théologiques, 1948–1991*. Paris: La Table Ronde, 2007.

———. *The Ethics of Freedom*. Translated by Geoffrey W. Bromiley. Grand Rapids: Eerdmans, 1976.

———. *Hope in Time of Abandonment*. Translated by C. Edward Hopkin. 1973. Reprint, Eugene, OR: Wipf & Stock, 2012.

———. *In Season, Out of Season: An Introduction to the Thought of Jacques Ellul*. Translated by Lani K. Niles. San Francisco: Harper & Row, 1982.

———. "Karl Barth and Us." *Sojourners* 7.12 (December 1978) 22–24.

———. *The New Demons*. Translated by C. Edward Hopkin. New York: Seabury, 1975.

———. *The Political Illusion*. Translated by Konrad Kellen. 1967. Reprint, Eugene, OR: Wipf & Stock, 2009.

———. *Prayer and Modern Man*. Translated by C. Edward Hopkin. New York: Seabury, 1970.

———. *Propaganda: The Formation of Men's Attitudes*. Translated by Konrad Kellen and Jean Lerner. New York: Vintage, 1973.

———. *Reason for Being: A Meditation on Ecclesiastes*. Translated by Joyce Main Hanks. Grand Rapids: Eerdmans, 1990.

———. *Sans feu ni lieu: Signification biblique de la grande ville*. Paris: Gallimard, 1975. Translated by Dennis Pardee as *The Meaning of the City*. 1970. Reprint, Eugene, OR: Wipf & Stock, 2011.

———. "Les structures de la liberté." In *Vivre et penser la liberté*, edited by Jean-Phillipe Qadri. Geneva: Labor et Fides, 2018.

———. *The Theological Foundation of Law*. Translated by Marguerite Wieser. New York: Seabury, 1969.

———. *Violence: Reflections from a Christian Perspective*. Translated by Cecelia Gaul Kings. 1969. Reprint, Eugene, OR: Wipf & Stock, 2012.

Garaudy, Roger. *Le communisme et la morale*. Paris: Éditions sociales, 1945.

Gollancz, Victor. *The Case of Adolf Eichmann*. London: V. Gollancz, 1961.

Gurvitch, Georges, ed. *Traité de sociologie*. 2 vols. Paris: Presses universitaires de France, 1962–63.

———. *Vocation actuelle de la sociologie*. 2 vols. Paris: Presses universitaires des France, 1963.

Gusdorf, Georges. *Traité de l'existence morale*. Paris: A. Colin, 1949.

Häring, Bernard. *La loi du Christ*. 3 vols. Tournai: Desclée, 1956–59. Translated by Edwin G. Kaiser as *The Law of Christ: Moral Theology for Priests and Laity*. Westminster, MD: Newman, 1961–66.

Hauerwas, Stanley. "Jacques Ellul, Courage and the Christian Imagination." *The Ellul Forum* 13 (1994) 4.

Hesnard, Angelo. *Morale sans péché*. Paris: Presses universitaires de France, 1954.

Hillerdal, Gunnar. "Unter welchen Bedingungen ist evangelische Ethik möglich?" *Zeitschrift für Evangelische Ethik* 1 (1957) 241–54.

Horney, Karen. *The Neurotic Personality of Our Time*. New York: Norton, 1937.

Kinsey, Alfred, et al. *Le comportement sexuel de l'homme (First Kinsey Report)*. Paris: Éditions du Pavois, 1948.

Kinsey, Alfred, et al. *Le comportement sexuel de la femme (Second Kinsey Report)*. Paris: Amiot-Dumont, 1954.

Le Senne, René. *Traité de morale générale*. Logos. Paris: Presses universitaires de France, 1961.

Leenhardt, Franz Jehan. "Existe-t-il un 'système' chrétien?" *Le Semeur* 18 (1950) 398–420.

Mehl, Roger. "Ethique et théologie." In Jacques Bois, Jean Boisset, and Roger Mehl, *Le problème de la morale chrétienne*, 25–75. Les Problèmes de la pensée chrétienne. Paris: Presses universitaires de France, 1948.

Michel, Andrée. "Les cadres sociaux de la doctrine morale de Frédéric Le Play." *Cahiers internationaux de sociologie* 34 (1963) 47–68.

Mounier, Emmanuel. "Pour une technique des moyens spirituels." *Esprit* 26 (1934) 182–98.

Müller, Denis, and Frédéric Rognon. "Introduction." In Jacques Ellul, *Le Vouloir et le Faire: Une critique théologique de la morale*. Geneva: Labor et Fides, 2013.

Murry, John Middleton. *The Free Society*. London: A. Dakers, 1948.

Nichols, James Hastings. *A Primer for Protestants*. New York: Association Press, 1947.

Niebuhr, Reinhold. *An Interpretation of Christian Ethics*. 1935. Reprint, New York: Seabury, 1979.

———. *Moral Man and Immoral Society: A Study in Ethics and Politics*. New York: Scribner's, 1960.

———. *The Nature and Destiny of Man: A Christian Interpretation*. New York: Scribner's, 1955.

Peabody, Francis Greenwood. *Jesus Christ and the Social Question*. New York: Macmillan, 1900.

Piper, Otto A. "Die Mitteilbarkeit der christlichen Ethik." *Zeitschrift für Evangelische Ethik* 1 (1957) 125–36.

Prunet, Olivier. *La morale chrétienne d'après les écrits johanniques*. Paris: Presses universitaires de France, 1957.

Quervain, Alfred de. *Ethik*. Vol. 1, *Die Heiligung*. Zollikon-Zurich: Evangelischer Verlag, 1946.

Ramsey, Paul. *Basic Christian Ethics*. New York: Scribner's, 1954.

Reiner, Hans. "Ethik und Menschenbild." *Zeitschrift für Evangelische Ethik* 5 (1958) 284–95.
Ricoeur, Paul. "Discerner pour agir." *Le Semeur* 48 (1950) 431–52.
———. *The Symbolism of Evil*. Translated by Emerson Buchanan. Boston: Beacon, 1969.
Rozental, Mark, and Pavel Judin, eds. *Petit dictionnaire philosophique*. Moscow: Editions en Langues Etrangères, 1955.
Roux, Hébert. *Les épîtres pastorals: Commentaire de I et II Timothée et Tite*. Geneva: Labor et Fides, 1959.
Sartre, Jean-Paul. *L'existentialisme est un humanisme*. Paris: Nagel, 1960. The English citation in the text comes from the 1956 translation by Philip Mairet, available at https://www.marxists.org/reference/archive/sartre/works/exist/sartre.htm.
Sertillanges, Antonin-Gilbert. *La philosophie morale de saint Thomas d'Aquin*. Paris: Aubier, 1946.
Søe, Niels H. *Christliche Ethik: Ein Lehrbuch*. Munich: C. Kaiser, 1957.
Van Peursen, Cornelis A. "Ethik und Ontologie in der heutigen Existenzphilosophie." *Zeitschrift für Evangelische Ethik* 2 (1958) 98–112.
von Rad, Gerhard. *Théologie de l'Ancien Testament*. Vol. 1, *Théologie des traditions historiques d'Israël*. Geneva: Labor et Fides, 1963.
Vos, H. de. "Zur Frage der natürlichen Sittlichkeit." *Zeitschrift für Evangelische Ethik* 6 (1958) 347–58.
Weil, Eric. "Raison, morale et politique." *Critique* 4 (1948) 540–51.

Name Index

Ambrose, 208, 215n7
Ansart, Pierre, 118n1
Aquinas, Thomas, 29–30, 126–7, 223n11
Arendt, Hannah, 87n12
Aristotle, 61, 74, 117, 126, 128
Augustine, 30, 122, 208

Barth, Karl, 1–2, 7–9, 13, 21n5, 27n11, 30, 31n22, 32n25, 35n1, 36, 37nn6–7, 38nn8–10, 41nn15–16, 42n19, 51n3, 54n6, 59, 65, 69n6, 79, 87n13, 89n15, 90–91, 92n20, 94n21, 96, 100nn29–30, 105, 107n36, 114n2, 123n9, 158n6, 182n7, 186n3, 188nn6–8, 189n10, 190n11, 193–94, 197n21, 198n23, 200nn25–26, 202n31, 204n34, 205, 208n1, 220n9, 227–28, 234, 235n14, 237n19, 238n21, 239n22, 240n24
Baruk, Henri, 30n18, 64n20
Bastide, Georges, 118n1
Bazin, Hervé, 169
Bazin, René, 169
Beauvoir, Simone de, 7, 123, 126, 131–32, 158n6, 193
Berdyaev, Nicholas, 118n2
Bergson, Henri, 7, 13, 71n8, 127n2, 128n4, 135n10, 138n1, 151n1, 152n2, 200
Beyle, Marie-Henri. *See* Stendahl
Blanchard, Pierre, 30n18

Bois, Jacques, 22n6, 36n3, 91n18, 118n2, 132n7
Boisset, Jean, 124n10
Bonhoeffer, Dietrich, 1, 7, 13, 20, 25n10, 27n12, 35n1, 37n6, 41, 49n1, 53n5, 66n22, 79n1, 85, 96n26, 102, 111, 125nn12–13, 139n2, 158n6, 189nn9–10, 194, 201n29, 202n30, 224n1, 228, 236, 238n20
Borne, Étienne, 140
Bosc, Jean, 8
Brunner, Emil, 30, 49n1
Buchman, Frank, 132
Bultmann, Rudolf, 187n5, 203, 205
Bussy-Rabutin, Roger de, 126

Caillois, Roger, 148
Calvin, John, 9, 22n6, 29n15, 57, 123, 200, 208, 224n2
Cazanueve, Jean, 118n1
Chambre, Henri, 172n1
Chamson, André, 165
Chauchard, Paul, 126, 130
Chesterton, Gilbert Keith, 1
Clement, 212
Clendenin, Daniel, 67
Comte, Auguste, 129n5
Confucius, 72, 90, 126, 133–35
Constantine, 213
Crespy, Georges, 23, 52n4, 185n1, 189n10, 203n32, 224n2, 232
Cruvellier, Jean, 196n21
Cullmann, Oscar, 7

247

Name Index

Delimars, E., 172n1
Dippel, Cornelis, 224n1
Dostoevsky, Fyodor, 166, 198
Durkheim, Émile, 7, 126, 129, 139, 153–54, 160

Eichmann, Adolf, 87n12
Ellul, Jacques, 1–14, 17n1
Erasmus, 126
Faulkner, William, 166
Freud, Sigmund, 169–70

Gandhi, Mohandas K., 81
Garaudy, Roger, 118n2
Gide, André, 168
Gollancz, Victor, 87n12
Graaf, Johannes de, 172n1
Gurvitch, Georges, 7, 113n1, 115, 118n1, 122n6, 123n7, 127n1, 129, 157
Gusdorf, Georges, 142, 160, 176

Häring, Bernard, 7, 20, 35n2, 61n13, 62nn14–15, 70n7, 86n11, 89n15, 95n23, 103n34, 122n5, 123n7, 193, 217n8, 229
Hauerwas, Stanley, 1, 10
Hegel, G. W. F., 126
Heraclitus, 119n3
Hesnard, Angelo, 126, 129–30, 163
Hillerdal, Gunner, 7, 91n19, 186n3, 187n4, 197n21, 203n33, 205n35, 226n4, 239n23
Hitler, Adolf, 11, 87n12, 161
Hopkin, C. Edward, 14, 88n14, 123n8
Horney, Karen, 73n10
Husserl, Edmund, 126, 128, 133

Jaspers, Karl, 133
Judin, Pavel, 118n2

Kant, Immanuel, 71n8, 74, 90, 117, 126–27, 133–34, 139, 156, 160, 189n10, 220
Kierkegaard, Søren, 8–9, 101, 190, 235

Lawrence, D. H., 168
Leenhardt, Franz-J., 242n27

Lenin, Vladimir I., 118n2, 121, 152
Lévy-Bruhl, Lucien, 121, 134
Liguori, Alphonse de, 217
Luther, Martin, 8–9, 42, 86n12, 96n26, 109n39, 110n41, 200, 208, 222, 224n2

Malraux, André, 146
Marcion, 212
Marx, Karl, 2, 8, 41, 118n2, 126, 133, 144, 153n4, 163n1, 169–70
McCarthy, Joseph, 165n3
Mehl, Roger, 79n1, 83n7, 128n4, 142, 156
Melanchthon, Philip, 219
Michel, Andrée, 118n1
Miller, Arthur, 164
Montanus, 212
Moses, 23, 126, 134–35, 191, 211
Mounier, Emmanuel, 152n2
Müller, Denis, 7, 13, 85n9
Murry, John Middleton, 114n3, 122n5
Mussolini, Benito, 11

Neher, André, 28
Nichols, James Hastings, 22n6
Niebuhr, Reinhold, 7, 9, 30n20, 51n3, 54n6, 55n7, 84n8, 86n11, 90n17, 94, 96n26, 102, 107n36, 109n39, 111, 118n2, 123n9, 127n3, 128n4, 173n2, 185n2, 186n3, 196n20, 204n34, 222n10, 228, 236, 239n23, 241
Nietzsche, Friedrich, 60, 74, 126, 133, 161

Oppenheimer, J. Robert, 181

Paul, 4, 6, 22, 36–37, 39, 42–43, 45, 48, 49n1, 56–59, 62–64, 82–83, 88, 93, 102n31, 135, 194, 198, 200–201, 204, 209–11, 220, 224n2, 230–31, 233–34
Peabody, Francis Greenwood, 22n6, 132n7
Peursen, Cornelis A. Van, 32n25
Piper, Otto A., 79n1, 224n1, 240n25
Plato, 54, 126

Name Index

Prunet, Olivier, 30n17, 37n6, 43n21, 49n1, 90n17, 190n11, 191n12, 197n21

Quervain, Alfred de, 30n21, 37n7, 41n14, 79n1, 196n21, 223n11, 237n19, 239n22

Rad, Gerhard von, 7, 200n27
Ramsey, Paul, 79n1
Reiner, Hans, 22n6, 30n19, 115n5, 133n9
Ricoeur, Paul, 7, 9, 13, 24n8, 26n11, 31, 49, 50n2, 50–51, 66n22, 68n3, 73, 83n7, 99, 109, 199n24, 209, 210n4
Ritschl, Albrecht, 189n10
Rognon, Frédéric, 7, 13, 84n9
Rostand, Jean, 182n6
Roux, Hébert, 63, 80n4, 91n19, 195n19, 220n9, 230n10
Rozental, Mark, 118n2

Sade, Marquis de, 126
Sartre, Jean-Paul, 7, 87, 114, 124n11, 126, 130–32, 159, 187

Scheler, Max, 126, 133
Senne, René Le, 142
Sertillanges, Antonin-Gilbert, 60n12
Socrates, 60, 62n14, 72, 90, 133
Søe, Niels, 7, 28n13, 30n17, 36, 42n18, 43n20, 62n14, 79n1, 91n18, 96n25, 108n38, 111, 193, 196n21, 226n4, 235
Sorel, Georges, 126, 128
Spencer, Herbert, 129n5
Spinoza, Benedict de, 126, 189n10
Stalin, Joseph, 11
Stendahl, 17

Teresa of Avila, 39n11
Tertullian, 213
Thielicke, Helmut, 111

Vos, H. de, 22n6, 55n7

Weber, Max, 99
Weil, Eric, 84n9, 114n4
Wesley, John, 207n36

Zedong, Mao, 170

Scripture Index

Genesis

	114
1–3	5
1:2	68n2
3:5	19, 23
3:7	25
3:8	26
3:11	26
3:22	25
4:6–7a	38
4:7	34, 38
4:12	62n15
44:4	46

Exodus

20:13	106

Leviticus

27:1, 28–29	191

Numbers

21:1–3	191
24:13	36

Deuteronomy

1:39	36
2:31–34	191
6:1	191
7:1–2	191
30:16	39
30:19	29n16

Joshua

6:21	191
7	192
11:12	191
11:20	191

1 Samuel

15:3	192

2 Samuel

24:10	62n15

1 & 2 Kings

	8

1 Kings

3:9	31
18:21	110
20:31–43	192
Job	8, 70

Psalms

14	39, 43
34:15	39
35:12	39

Psalms (continued)

36:4	43
37:4	39

Ecclesiastes

	8–9
5:2	54
7:20	43n22
12:14	28

Isaiah

1:15–17	35
5:20–21	45
41:2–24	44–45
41:23	28
55:8	188

Jeremiah

13:23	45
31:33	59

Lamentations

3:21, 24	233

Ezekiel

11:19	59

Hosea

8	36

Amos

5:4	39
5:14	39

Jonah

	8

Micah

6:8	20, 35–36, 39

Matthew

5:11	204
5:16	47
12:33	42
21:28	58
25:37	58

Mark

10:18	21

John

15:5	158

Acts

1	214
23:1	63
5:29	110
16:1–10	

Romans

	8
1:18–32	57
1:32	36
2	36, 55–61
2:13–16	56–58, 66
2:1	211
3:10–12	43
3:9	57
3:19	43n23, 57
7:14–25	45
7:24	194
9:1	62
11:13	59
11:24	56
12	224n2
12:2	3
12:17	46
13:3–4a	47
13:5	62
14:20–23	62n16
14:3–4	211
15:9	59

1 Corinthians

	210
1:23	93
2:14	56
4:3–4	64
4:5	211
5:9–12	102
8:7	62
10:29	62

2 Corinthians

	210
1:12	62
8:21	47, 82
9:21–22	83

Galatians

	210

Ephesians

2:3	55
4	220n9

Philippians

2:13	17
3:12	88

Colossians

	88
2:22	201

1 Timothy

	220n9
1:18–19	63

1:5	63
3:9	63

2 Timothy

	220n9

Titus

	220n9
1:15	65

Hebrews

	209–212
10:26–27	211
10:2	63

James

1	206
1:25	202
2	39–40
2:4	211
4:11–12	205
4:11	211

1 Peter

2:15	47
2:19	62
3:15	83

2 Peter

2:12	56

John 3

11	40

You may also be interested in:

Jacques Ellul and the Bible

Towards a Hermeneutic of Freedom

Edited by Jacob Marques Rollison

The hermeneutic contribution of the French theologian and sociologist Jacques Ellul is given new prominence in this striking collection of essays, revealing him to be one of the twentieth century's most creative and insightful interpreters of the Bible. With a breadth of contributors ranging from established biblical scholars and theologians to pastoral practitioners, from top Ellul scholars to emerging voices – and including six first-time English translations of Ellul's own articles – this volume not only provides a detailed overview of Ellul's biblical approach but also constitutes a crucial moment in Ellul's theological reception.

The essays gathered here represent a clear demonstration that the full potential of Ellul's theological interpretation of Scripture to rejuvenate and reconfigure contemporary biblical hermeneutics has yet to be seen.

> 'In order to understand his prophetic response to contemporary culture, one must consult Ellul's use and reading of the Bible. Rollinson et al. have provided an indispensable guide for all of us.' – **Michael Burdett**, University of Nottingham

Jacob Marques Rollison is an independent scholar living in Strasbourg, France. He holds a PhD in theological ethics from the University of Aberdeen. He is co-author of *Jacques Ellul* in the Cascade Companions series, and has recently translated Ellul's two-volume *To Will & to Do: An Introduction to Christian Ethics*. He is on the board of directors of the International Jacques Ellul Society.

Published 2022

Paperback ISBN: 978 0 227 17794 5
PDF ISBN: 978 0 227 17806 5

You may also be interested in:

Presence in the Modern World

A New Translation by Lisa Richmond

By Jacques Ellul

Presence in the Modern World is Jacques Ellul's most foundational book, combining his social analysis with his theological orientation. Appearing first in French in 1948, and later in English as *The Presence of the Kingdom*, it has reached the status of a classic that retains all of its relevance dealing with today's challenges.

How should we respond to such complex forces as technology or the state? How can we communicate with one another, despite the problems inner to modern forms of media? Do we have hope for the future of our civilisation? Ellul responds by describing how a Christian's unique presence in the world can make a difference. Instead of acting as 'sociological beings', we must commit ourselves to the kind of revolution that will occur only when we become radically aware of our present situation and undertake 'a ferocious and passionate destruction of myths'. In this way, states Ellul, we become the medium for God's action in the modern world.

This new edition presents a fresh translation along with new footnotes, an introduction to Ellul's life, and a complete bibliography in both English and French.

'*Read* Presence in the Modern World. *Not only is it the introduction to Ellul's entire body of work, but its emphasis on Christians' revolutionary situation in the world has never been more relevant.*'
– **Patrick Chastenet,** University of Bordeaux

Published 2017

Paperback ISBN: 978 0 227 17663 4
PDF ISBN: 978 0 227 90637 8